DEVELOPING COUNTRIES
IN BRITISH FICTION

DEVELOPING COUNTRIES IN BRITISH FICTION

D. C. R. A. Goonetilleke

Senior Lecturer in English
University of Sri Lanka (Ceylon)

ROWMAN AND LITTLEFIELD
Totowa, New Jersey

First published in the United States 1977
by ROWMAN AND LITTLEFIELD, Totowa, N.J.

© D. C. R. A. Goonetilleke 1977

Printed in Great Britain

Library of Congress Cataloging in Publication Data

Goonetilleke, D C R A
    Developing countries in British fiction.

    "Originally . . . a thesis accepted for the degree
of Ph.D. of the University of Lancaster".
    Bibliography; p.
    Includes index.
        1.   English fiction – History and criticism.
2.   Underdeveloped areas in literature.   I.   Title.
PR830.U48G6   1977   823'.009   76-40275
ISBN 0-87471-908-9

To
CHINCHI,
SURENDRA
and
DILHAN

Contents

		Page
	Foreword	ix
	Introduction	1
1	Antecedents	13
2	Challenges and problems of the Far East (i): Conrad's Tales	33
3	Challenges and problems of the Far East (ii): Conrad's Malayan novels	52
4	Conrad's Malayan novels: problems of authenticity	77
5	Conrad's African tales: ironies of progress	99
6	Conrad's *Nostromo*: the morality of 'material interests'	119
7	Difficulties of connection in India: Kipling and Forster	134
8	D. H. Lawrence: primitivism?	170
9	Joyce Cary: the clash of cultures in Nigeria	199
10	Between cultures	245
	Notes and references	253
	Select bibliography	271
	Index	277

Foreword

I explored the subject of this book because it was alive with significance for people in both developed and developing countries and because it was concerned with a central evolving tradition of English literature. My inquiry benefited from the suggestions and criticism of Dr David Craig, who was not merely the supervisor of my research but a fine friend. I was encouraged by the interest of Professor E. F. C. Ludowyk at every stage in my work, and I received useful advice from Mr M. I. Kuruvilla when I was preparing the book.

My work on this subject was originally done for a thesis accepted for the degree of Ph.D. of the University of Lancaster. My research in Britain was made possible when I was awarded a scholarship by the Commonwealth Scholarship Commission in the U.K. I must thank the Commission and the British Council for helping to make my stay in Britain both very enjoyable and most instructive. I must also thank the staffs of several libraries, notably those of the University of Lancaster and the British Museum.

Parts of this book originally appeared in *A Review of International English Literature* (*ARIEL*), *The Journal of Commonwealth Literature*, *The Kipling Journal*, *The Bulletin of the Association for Commonwealth Literature and Language Studies* and *The Ceylon Journal of the Humanities*. Joseph Conrad's unpublished letter to T. Fisher Unwin, dated 14 April 1897, is quoted with the permission of the Brotherton Collection, University of Leeds.

I would like to thank the following who have kindly given permission for the use of copyright material: Edward Arnold (Publishers) Ltd for the extracts from *A Passage to India* by E. M. Forster; Curtis Brown Ltd and Harper & Row Publishers Inc., on behalf of the Estate of Joyce Cary, for the extracts from *Aissa Saved*, *The African Witch* and *Mister Johnson*; Laurence Pollinger Ltd and the Estate of the late Mrs Frieda Lawrence and Alfred A. Knopf Ltd, for the extract from *The Plumed Serpent* by D. H. Lawrence, published by William Heinemann Ltd; and A. P. Watt & Son, on behalf of the late Mrs Elsie Bambridge and Eyre Methuen & Co. Ltd, for the poem 'Recessional' from *The Five Nations* by Rudyard Kipling.

D. C. R. A. G.

Introduction

This book is an attempt to discover how British writers reacted to developing countries and how they presented them in their writings. I have discussed mainly the fiction set in these countries after 1880 by Joseph Conrad, Rudyard Kipling, E. M. Forster, D. H. Lawrence and Joyce Cary. Their works seem to me the best of the fiction which embodies the major British reactions to and presentations of developing countries, which at the same time reflect their respective periods in important ways. Of course, the issues characteristically set in developing countries, such as imperialism, race relations and primitivism, were handled by British writers before 1880, though infrequently; my opening chapter is concerned with these antecedents.

The major writers in my field are so outstanding that their selection posed no problem; they select themselves, as it were. Joseph Conrad and Rudyard Kipling are the first to write important fiction about developing countries. Their works are composed during the same period, the heyday of imperialism, which can be roughly dated from 1880 to 1920; but they reflect different aspects of their age in their treatment of imperialism. Conrad belongs to the distinguished minority of radical contemporary critics of imperialism such as Mark Twain, Roger Casement and E. D. Morel. Kipling is not completely the crude champion of the British Empire, as it was commonly believed; it is only at times that his attitudes are very close to those of Joseph Chamberlain, Cecil Rhodes and the great majority of Englishmen of his day. Still, he does not usually get beyond the liberal imperialism of Sir Hugh Clifford and Sir Frank Swettenham, distinguished colonial administrators, who represent the most enlightened among the majority. In the 1920s, Forster's *A Passage to India* and Lawrence's Mexican fiction are the most valuable works set in developing countries; they mirror different facets of the decade. Forster confronts the Empire in India; his egalitarian liberalism is a development on the minority radical line of thinking about imperialism. His outlook is at one with the views of the leading Indian nationalists such as Gandhi, Motilal Nehru and Jawaharlal Nehru. Forster's and Kipling's visions are different partly because conditions in India had changed since Kipling's day. In his Mexican fiction, Lawrence is not concerned with imperialism, but his expression of primitivism reflects concerns of the 1920s as deep as imperialism: his primitivism springs mainly from an acute sense that

1

Western civilisation had declined and from a positive attempt to find a way of regeneration, two tendencies he shares with the majority of his distinguished contemporaries such as T. S. Eliot, W. B. Yeats, F. R. Leavis and Oswald Spengler. After 1930, the outstanding writer about developing countries is Joyce Cary. His non-racialist liberalism connects him with Conrad and Forster, but he betrays a paternalism, notably in his non-fiction. This relates him to Kipling and makes him, in a way, only slightly ahead of a Colonel Oliver Stanley, Secretary of State for the Colonies, and the mass of more enlightened opinion among the British in his time. Thus, Cary in the 1930s is not consistently as broadminded as Forster in the 1920s. Their visions are different partly because early twentieth-century conditions in India and in Nigeria were different.

 Naturally, fiction is the main field for my inquiry because British writers, both major and minor, have dealt with developing countries for the most part in terms of fiction. The only poetry about these countries worthy of notice is Kipling's poetry about the Empire and Lawrence's Mexican poetry. It is Kipling's fiction that is an indispensable part of my area of study, but I have examined his poetry, too, because this is necessary for an understanding of his total vision of India under the British. In the case of Lawrence, it is his fiction alone that is significant; the Mexican poetry is negligible. No important British drama about developing countries has appeared as yet, though there have been one or two recent plays such as Charles Wood's '*H*' and Conor Cruise O'Brien's *Murderous Angels*.

 I have examined mainly British literature set in developing countries after 1880 because most of this literature, and all the literature of merit, was written after this date. The tardiness is partly the consequence of a late development of serious anthropological interests in England and America. Sir Edward Burnett Tylor, 'the father of modern cultural anthropology',[1] says in his important work, *Primitive Culture*: 'already it seems not too much to say that the vague outlines of a philosophy of primeval history are beginning to come within our view'.[2] Tylor's book was first published in 1871 and, as late as that, he considers mere 'vague outlines of a philosophy of primeval history' significant. One has to wait till very late in the nineteenth century and the beginning of the twentieth for a considerable amount of anthropological activity to stimulate interest in, and spread knowledge about, non-European people on a large scale. Apart from the solid work of Edward Tylor himself, there were the researches of Sir James George Frazer whose *The Golden Bough, A Study in Magic and Religion* (first published in 1890) has overshadowed his other publications in the same field. W. H. Rivers and A. C. Haddon in England, and F. Boas in America, all important anthropologists, belong to the same period.

The more important cause for the late emergence of realistic literature about developing countries, however, is that the political and economic circumstances that made it possible, and at the same time acted as a potent stimulus to its creation, arose late; these circumstances were produced by imperialism. It was only after 1880 that European nations (notably, Britain, France and Germany) competed fiercely with one another to extend their colonial possessions because of a virtually simultaneous, increased awareness of the economic and political value of colonies; it was then that imperialism began to assume the proportions of one of the most important phenomena of world history. Developing countries began to matter seriously to British writers and the British reading public; there arose an enormous, growing body of British literature set in these countries. The connection between imperialism and the creation of the literature can be illustrated briefly by reference to the major writers. All of them write after 1880. All of them with the exception of Lawrence are concerned with imperial milieux in all their works in this field – Conrad with the Far East, the Congo and South America, Kipling and Forster with India, Cary with Nigeria. They had first-hand experience of these developing countries in the service of the imperial system – Conrad as an ordinary seaman and as an officer in the British Merchant Navy, Kipling as a journalist, Forster as private secretary to the Maharajah of Dewas State Senior, Cary as a member of the Nigerian Political Service.

In my inquiry, I have tried to see literature as art in the context of relevant historical, political and biographical facts. Such an approach, if it is to be profitable, has to be, in the first place, inspired and controlled by a literary-critical sense of the literature. At the same time, we must be aware of the complexities of the relation between the world of the imagination and the world of historical, political and biographical facts. For one thing, far from all the facts are relevant; we need a sense of what facts had most to do with fashioning the work of art. For another thing, facts as they strike the imagination and are organised by it, undergo decisive selection and shaping. Thus, to treat Kipling, Forster and Cary as 'chroniclers of British expansion', in the words of John Holloway,[3] is to overlook these complexities, to equate erroneously the world of the imagination with the world of facts, to confuse the ways of the artist with the methods of the historian.

I have found it necessary to deal with each selected major writer separately because the work of each is very different from that of the others. The differences are partly a matter of the differences in their personalities: economic imperialism is prominent both in South America and in Mexico in the late nineteenth and early twentieth centuries, but it is important only in Conrad's *Nostromo*, not in Lawrence's *The Plumed Serpent*. A chapter, at least, is needed to do justice to the distinctive achievement of each major writer, but I have made an exception in the case of Kipling and Forster. Their writings have been considered together because of common foci for discussion which derive from thematic similarity and a common setting. The countries with which the writers are concerned are important: each one has distinctively affected its presentation; the same writer, Conrad, writes differently about the Malay Archipelago, the Congo and South America, partly because conditions in each country at the same period were different and partly because he was then developing rapidly as an artist. Chronology, too, is important: the works reflect the different periods in which they were composed; Conrad's and Cary's views of negroes are different partly because Cary's views were expressed more than three decades after Conrad's, after negroes had come to be considered by distinguished European minds as people of interest in their own right. Thus, the quality of the fiction, the country and the period have guided the organisation of the book.

My own basis in Asian conditions has helped me to 'check up on' the authorial insights and material of all these works set in developing countries in a way no European could do. Asian nations have much in common with each other; with African countries, though the latter are generally at an earlier stage of development; with the developing countries of the Americas. Indeed, all such countries have much in common with each other, as suggested by their subjection to imperialism and their very state of being 'undeveloped'. For instance, when I read *Nostromo*, I am struck by the similarities between Costaguana and Sri Lanka not long ago – from the bullock-carts to the fluid national set-up, politically semi-patriotic, infiltrated economically and culturally by imperial interests.

The British literature set in developing countries throws light not only on life in these countries but also on Western civilisation and on life in general. The quality of life there could help the writer to achieve this remarkable multiple significance. For instance, Joyce Cary is concerned with the fundamental question, the root of all politics, all arts

... what do men live by,[4] and he sees a special advantage in the choice of Africa as a milieu for the examination of human values: 'Basic obsessions, which in Europe hide themselves under all sorts of decorous scientific or theological or political uniforms, are there seen naked in bold and dramatic action'.[5] Similarly, Wordsworth, dissatisfied with the sophistication of townsmen, had turned to 'low and rustic life': '... in that situation our elementary feelings exist in a state of greater simplicity and consequently may be more accurately contemplated and more forcibly communicated'.[6] Graham Greene, too, has expressed thoughts on these lines; during a television interview, in reply to a question, 'Do you think there is any one reason why you've gone so far from England in your books?' Greene said: 'It's a restlessness that I've always had to move around, and perhaps to see English characters in a setting which is not protective to them, where perhaps they speak a little differently, a little more openly'.[7] The views of Cary and Greene, with their clear relation to Wordsworth, are in the long minority tradition of scepticism about the Establishment.

The views of the writers are shared by major theorists of colonial experience. In 1853, Karl Marx wrote: 'The profound hypocrisy and inherent barbarism of bourgeois civilisation lies unveiled before our eyes, turning from its home, where it assumes respectable forms, to the colonies, where it goes naked'.[8] When imperialism was clearly making headway, Marx thus points to the notion that the essential truths of Western civilisation stand naked in developing countries, particularly colonies. This is complementary to the views, made explicit by Cary for one, that the essential truths of 'native' life and life in a universal sense as well stand exposed in such countries. All these are endorsed by Jean-Paul Sartre and Frantz Fanon in the 1960s when imperialism was in its last stage of collapse: 'First, we must face that unexpected revelation, the strip-tease of our humanism. There you can see it, quite naked, and it's not a pretty sight'. 'In the colonies the truth stood naked, ...'[9]

The notions of these writers and theorists do not seem to me fully correct because they tend to make an absolute distinction between life in developing countries and in the West. But I do think that features of life are more marked there than in the West. For instance, there the sense of racial superiority and acquisitiveness, common among Westerners, is released less guardedly; bribery is both more rampant and more open than in the West; race-friction and race-compartmentalisation are more obvious; class divisions within indigenous races are more prominent.

In examining literature set in developing countries one finds it necessary to use and be critical of terms such as 'imperialism', 'colonialism', 'race', 'primitive' and 'civilised'. These terms are so often used loosely and emotively that I propose to discuss and define them, and then use them myself in their defined factual meanings. First, 'imperialism' and 'colonialism'. The two classic accounts of imperialism were written during its heyday – by Hobson in 1902 (*Imperialism, A Study*) and Lenin in 1916 (*Imperialism, The Highest Stage of Capitalism*). Hobson distinguishes between colonialism and imperialism. He says: 'Colonialism, in its best sense, is a natural overflow of nationality; its test is the power of colonists to transplant the civilisation they represent to the new natural and social environment in which they find themselves'.[10] He endorses Professor Seeley's view of imperialism:

> When a State advances beyond the limits of nationality its power becomes precarious and artificial. This is the condition of most empires, and it is the condition of our own. When a nation extends itself into other territories the chances are that it cannot destroy or completely drive out, even if it succeeds in conquering, them. When this happens it has a great permanent difficulty to contend with, for the subject or rival nationalities cannot be properly assimilated, and remain as a permanent cause of weakness and danger.[11]

He goes on to deal with the core of imperialism of his period:

> The new Imperialism differs from the older, first in substituting for the ambition of a single growing empire the theory and practice of competing empires, each motivated by similar lusts of political aggrandisement and commercial gain; secondly, in the dominance of financial or investing over mercantile interests.[12]

Lenin develops Hobson's points. He sees essentially the same economic and political evils in imperialism as Hobson, but he gives the Englishman's economic analysis a new emphasis. His central thesis is that 'imperialism is the monopoly stage of capitalism'.[13]

D. K. Fieldhouse recently (1961) made an attempt to redefine imperialism (in '"Imperialism": An Historiographical Revision'). He concedes to Hobson and Lenin the important part played by 'vast capital exports' in the expansion of imperialism, but he considers Lenin's theory of monopoly an unjustified extreme step. He correctly points out that monopoly combines such as trusts or cartels in Britain and

Germany were very few during the most active period of imperial expansion (1885–1900) and become prominent only after about 1900.[14] Thus capitalism lies behind the crucial phase of imperial expansion; monopoly capitalism later consolidates and furthers this. What I wish to stress most now is a more general point, the economic drive behind imperialism. Hobson and Lenin, in fact, consider economic factors more important than any others in determining imperialism. Fieldhouse, however, speaks of 'the subordination of economic to political considerations, the preoccupation with national security, military power and prestige'[15] in the working of imperialism after the 1880s, though Hobson and he agree on the dominance of economic motives in the imperialism before that (Lenin does not take the early phase into account, but his view of it probably would have been much the same). Fieldhouse mentions two factors as the main arguments to support his view of the modern phase of imperialism. Firstly, he refers to 'the rise of this imperialist ideology, this belief that colonies were an essential attribute of any great nation'.[16] 'This imperialist ideology', held by millions from statesmen to 'the common people', did play a key role in the expansion of the empire, but it was less important than the economic motive, as will be shown below. Secondly, he says:

> It was already [by 1903–5] the common experience of all the countries that had taken part in the partition of Africa and the Pacific that, except for the few windfalls, such as gold in West Africa, diamonds in South West Africa, and copper in the Congo and Rhodesia, the new colonies were white elephants: and that only small sectional interests in any country had obtained real benefits from them.[17]

Here he is guilty of misleading half-truths and blindness to major relevant facts. He does not deny the self-interested economic motive of the imperialist countries, but he underestimates it. It is not sound to generalise about imperialism on the basis of Africa and the Pacific only, as he does, without considering Asia and Latin America, which were as important as Africa and far more important than the Pacific. It is true that from 1885 to 1905 'small sectional interests' (the capitalist interests) derived most of the 'benefits' from colonies. But this is not unexpected, given the class and property system in the metropolitan countries, and their 'benefits' were also 'benefits' to their respective states. 'The few windfalls' should be included in an estimate of the value of the colonies, and these 'windfalls' were so profitable that the colonies do not seem such 'white elephants'. Moreover Britain, for instance (and it is British imperialism that I am mainly concerned with), derived considerable revenue from numerous other sources – from tin and rubber in Malaya, from cotton and jute in India, from tea and rubber in Ceylon, from palm-oil, palm-kernels, groundnuts and cocoa in West Africa, from cotton in Uganda, from gold in South Africa and in Southern Rhodesia, from sugar in South Africa, from railway-building in Latin America. During the years 1885–1905, the cost of setting up systems of administration, of finding and making ready the sources of income, perhaps make the colonies seem unprofitable. But this is only a surface impression: as Michael Barratt Brown notes, 'not only the funds for investment in India itself but a large part of the total investment-income from overseas, that gave Britain her balance of payments surplus in the last quarter of the nineteenth century, was provided by India'.[18] Moreover, the initial cost was necessary and is of a kind incurred in any business enterprise. It was not long before the colonies became unquestionably paying propositions. Britain got back her investment, usually several times over, during the period of her administration and profited substantially from it even after these countries gained independence.

Thus self-interested economic motives form the primary factor in imperialism; self-interested political considerations are secondary. Altruism is clearly tertiary and a complex matter, though it was often proclaimed most loudly and simple-mindedly. The verbal altruism in Britain, like other aspects of British civilisation, rests on an economic foundation built partly out of 'exploitation': as Conor Cruise O'Brien notices,

> The age of Shakespeare was also the Age of Sir John Hawkins, whose slaving expeditions Shakespeare's Queen disapproved of but invested in. . . . Gladstone was the great voice of white liberalism. The family fortune, on which his career was founded, was in its time founded on the slave trade. The family crest, drawn by his father, was a Negro's head shedding drops of blood.[19]

Much of the altruism in action is inseparably mixed with self-interested economic and political aims. For instance, the European powers did develop roads, railways and harbours in their colonies but these developments were motivated mainly by the need for spheres of economic and political influence. The classic economic functions of the colonies were to supply food products and raw materials needed by their metropolitan countries and act as markets for metropolitan manufactures. Action in terms of these functions meant that colonial economies became highly specialised and very far from self-reliant; development was limited to the sectors which met the needs of the 'imperialists'. The failure of the European powers to meet the 'admitted obligation of education', in the words of Leonard Woolf,[20] is an index of their motives. The missionaries and the State furnished very little education for very few. They usually turned out a few indigenous people capable of manning the lowest rungs of the administration. This kind of education was provided partly because it was expensive to employ Europeans in these posts. Leonard Woolf throws light on imperialism with reference to education in Africa:

> It is no exaggeration to say that no European government in Africa had made a serious attempt to begin the education of the native so that eventually he might be capable of taking his place as a free man in the new economic and political society, which Europeans have introduced into Africa. Out of an estimated revenue of nearly two million pounds in 1924, the Kenya Government allotted £44,000 to be spent on prisons and £37,000 on education. I deny that any European government in the twentieth century can claim to be civilised if it spends 20 per cent more on providing penal servitude and hard labour for its subjects than it does on providing them with education. The population of Kenya includes nearly 2,500,000 Africans, 36,000 Asiatics and 10,000 Europeans. The Government spends £37,000 on the education of the 2,500,000 Africans and £25,000 on the education of 10,000 Europeans.[21]

All the imperial powers were actuated by essentially the same motives and they did not meet their obligations. The difference between the imperialism of one country and that of another is a difference of degree, not of kind.

Still, it is important to pay attention to Woolf's observation of 'the new economic and political society which Europeans have introduced into Africa'. Karl Marx made the same point with reference to India as early as 1853.[22] Whether it be in Africa, Asia or the Pacific, imperialism destroyed the old social system as well as provided the beginnings of a new modern order. It caused this desirable social revolution and brought these regions into the stream of modern international life though, as we have noticed, it was motivated by self-interest far more than altruism. After the Second World War, most of the colonies won independence, usually after a more or less militant struggle.

Thus 'imperialism' is a broad term, related to economic and political considerations, altruism and social change. 'Colonialism' and 'imperialism' are important in discussions about developing countries before or after independence. So is 'race'. Ruth Benedict defines race objectively and succinctly: 'race is a classification based on traits which are hereditary. Therefore, when we talk about race we are talking about heredity and traits transmitted by heredity which characterise all the members of a related group'.[23] The key hereditary traits in man are skin colour, quality and colour of hair, eye form, shape of nose and blood groups. Using them as criteria, one can distinguish between a Chinese with his yellowish skin and marked epicanthic fold and a Negro with his dark skin and wide, flat nose. Races can be distinguished, but one race is certainly not congenitally superior or inferior to another. Racism or racialism is the delusion that one ethnic group is innately superior or innately inferior to another. It was rampant particularly when imperialism was thriving and is still a commonly held belief. Cecil Rhodes and Enoch Powell are akin; the terms 'native' and 'coloured' have the same kind of racialist connotation. Racialism and imperialism often go together; racialist propositions such as the innate superiority of the English over all other races were often put forward – for instance, by Rhodes and Joseph Chamberlain – to justify imperialism. 'White' racialism does not relate only to 'white' men; there are 'coloured' people who believe in 'white' superiority because of their psychological backwardness and subordinate position. This tendency, too, was very common when 'imperialism' was prospering, and is not dead even today. On the other hand, 'coloured' people may be racialist and arrogant: Conrad, in *An Outcast of the Islands*, shows a Malayan, Omar el Badavi, looking down on a European, Willems, as 'an infidel and a dog'.[24] These qualities among 'coloured' people are not as common as they are among 'white' people no doubt partly because 'coloured' people have not been imperial powers on the scale of the Westerners.

Races and groups within the same race may be at different stages of development. When the European expansion overseas was reaching its peak period in the 1880s, the 'white' men and the people in developing countries were at different stages of development. The Europeans commonly felt that everything indigenous was 'primitive' and one of their declared aims was to 'civilise the natives'. Clearly, the terms 'primitive' and 'civilised' are important in discussions about developing countries. Primitive men live in small, homogeneous, rural, rather isolated communities; civilised men live in large aggregations of diverse people, designated 'cities', which are in touch with the rest of the world. Primitive societies are organised chiefly on the basis of kinship and personal status; in the organisation of civilised societies, residence is an additional important factor. Primitive men live in hut-like structures, made out of, say, reeds and palm branches; civilised men are capable of a monumental manner of building based, for instance, on mud-brick or stone. To the former, the universe is something personal and affects them in a personal way; to the latter, the cosmos is an indifferent system upon which they try to work their will. An important characteristic of a civilised economy, absent in a primitive economy, is 'the production of a social surplus', as Gordon Childe put it.[25] The population of a city would include a considerable number of full-time specialists such as craftsmen and artisans as well as rulers, officials and clerks. They were, as Childe observes, 'persons who did not themselves grow, catch, or collect their own food but were supported by the surplus above domestic needs produced by farmers, fishers, and huntsmen, who themselves became to that extent specialists'.[26] Citizens could obtain products not only from a large area around the city but from distant places through systematised trade. A system of tribute or taxation would be set up and, as a consequence, capital would accumulate at a central agency. Two key achievements of civilisation are the invention of writing systems and the evolution of exact sciences such as arithmetic, geometry and astronomy; primitive man is non-literate and unscientific. Thus, civilised life is a more complex and later stage of human development than primitive life. Each has its distinctive attributes which can be employed as criteria to judge the level of any society.

By these norms, when the Europeans came to Asia, the Asians were not primitive and were the inheritors of ancient civilisations. But their civilisations had entered a phase of decline and were at a lower stage of development than European civilisations. Thus the professed aim of Europeans to civilise them reveals, in a way, an uncomprehending sense of racial superiority; they could only claim to raise the Asians to a higher level of civilisation. The case of Africa is different. The common view among British experts on imperialism is that the Asians had ancient civilisations, but the Africans had none and consequently were very primitive.[27] I am inclined to disagree. It seems probable that the Africans, like the Asians, had civilisations in the past, as suggested by the impressive stone ruins of Zimbabwe in Rhodesia or the Benin bronzes. But Zimbabwe is still unexplained and the Benin bronzes have few counterparts. Generally it looks as though civilisation may have got much less far in Africa than it did in Asia. By the time the Europeans entered Africa, such civilisations as there had been had disintegrated and the Africans had regressed to a primitive stage. They were not as primitive as is usually believed: as Melville J. Herskovits has found out, the Akan-Ashanti folk of the Gold Coast, the Dahomeans, the Yoruba of western Nigeria and the Bini of eastern Nigeria were non-literate, but their economies did work to a certain extent in terms of 'the production of a social surplus'.[28] Still they were, on the whole, primitive and the Europeans could profess to civilise them. When European imperialism spread over Asia and Africa particularly after 1880, differences in human development coincided with differences in race, colour and nationality; the less civilised or primitive man was brown or yellow or black, Asian or African; the civilised man was 'white' and European. This kind of situation gives rise to racialism, colour prejudice, jingoism and like phenomena; to various tensions between and within people.

In my study of how British writers reacted to developing countries and how they presented them, there are problems which become central: What aspects of life in developing countries are the leading British writers concerned with and what significance do these aspects hold for them? How well do they portray their fellow Westerners in alien countries and alien people in alien countries? How do the level and pace of development of each country shape the kind of fiction written about it? What position does the outlook of each writer occupy in the context of his period? What problems of art do these writers face in common because they present these countries and how have they tried to solve them? In what ways can one account for the differences in their presentations? In what ways do they, as individuals and as a group, matter to us.

1 Antecedents

> People talked about the mysterious East, but London was much
> more mysterious than Cairo.
>   P. H. Newby, 'Something to Celebrate', in *The Guardian*, 23 April
> 1969.

It has been a common tendency for people of developing countries to
look at the West and for Europeans to look at developing countries, in
romantic fashion. This bent began to become general in Britain when
the developing world was brought prominently to the notice of the
British consciousness in the age of Elizabeth I – for this was the age
when the impact of the 'voyages of discovery' of Columbus, Vespucci,
Vasco da Gama and others was conspicuous; this was the age of
Drake, Frobisher and Hakluyt; the age when the trade in slaves, guns
and sugar between Western Europe, West Africa and the West Indies
was thriving; the age when the British East India Company was
founded. These pressures generated an exoticism partly because few
Englishmen at that time knew, or cared, much about the actualities.
But Shakespeare was not indifferent, though he shared something of
the contemporary ignorance.

Historical circumstances, then, make the Elizabethan age the
marked starting-point of the exotic as well as realistic traditions of
literature about developing countries. Let us consider these lines from
a soliloquy of Dido about her love for Aeneas in Christopher
Marlowe's *The Tragedy of Dido*:

> And thou, Aeneas, Dido's treasury,
> In whose fair bosom I will lock more wealth
> Than twenty thousand Indias can afford.
>   (Act III, sc. 1)

Here Marlowe is investing developing countries with the glamour and
fabled wealth of faraway places. This kind of conventional exoticism
commonly occurs in inferior writings about love. It branches off in
modern times to a kind of popular fiction typified at its worst by Edgar
Rice Burroughs' vulgarised version of 'the noble savage', Tarzan in

13

Africa. Still, it is not the fake exotic tradition, but the sustained serious writings about issues relevant to developing countries and those directly about such countries before 1880 that interest me most in this chapter.

The clash of European civilisation and primitive culture, which occurred in developing environments as a consequence of European activity overseas, is Shakespeare's theme in *The Tempest*. Prospero is the ruler of Caliban's developing island. He is educated and this fact indicates an advancement brought about by civilisation. But Shakespeare also shows an evil aspect to it: Sebastian and Antonio indulge in political trickery. These courtiers themselves are differentiated: the weaker, less guilty Sebastian needs the more ruthless Antonio to egg him on. Thus civilisation is presented in a carefully qualified way. The island itself is enchanting and pure; yet the life on it is extremely primitive as Caliban's role shows. Thus Shakespeare is presenting a place more real than a simple lotus-eating isle. He goes even further: these are the plans of the garrulous old courtier, Gonzalo, if he had the 'plantation of this isle':

> I' th' commonwealth I would by contraries
> Execute all things; for no kind of traffic
> Would I admit; no name of magistrate; . . .
> No occupation; all men idle, all;
> And women too, but innocent and pure;
> No sovereignty . . .
>
> (II. 1)

Shakespeare enhances the reality of the island by showing us how, in this instance, its ideal atmosphere could be given an absurd twist by a civilised person. Gonzalo's is a dream of an ideal of idleness and simplicity; virtually, of anarchism. Thus, there is no simple contrast, or simple interaction, between the civilised and the primitive.

This kind of complex vision lies behind Shakespeare's portrayal of Prospero and Caliban, his main characters and the chief representatives of the two stages of existence. Prospero is an equivalent in romance of one type of district officer. I have suggested that his education has a value, but it does not make him a good ruler. Magic gives him an arbitrary authority, and he often exercises it oppressively:

Caliban: As wicked dew as e'er my mother brush'd

> With raven's feather from unwholesome fen
> Drop on you both! A south-west blow on ye . . .
> Prospero: For this, be sure, to-night thou shalt have cramps,
> Side-stitches that shall pen thy breath up; . . .
>
> (ɪ. 2)

The play is most real at moments such as this one when the civilised
and the primitive clash openly. Both Prospero and Caliban resort to a
peculiarly venomous language. But whereas Caliban's speech is in the
vein of impotent folk imprecation, Prospero's language is educated
and linked to precise harsh punishments that would be inflicted on
Caliban. Thus by establishing a certain similarity, as well as by differ-
entiating, between their speech, Shakespeare 'places' both. Prospero's
attitude to Ariel goes with that towards Caliban; he reacts thus when
the spirit asks to be set free:

> If thou more murmur'st I will rend an oak
> And peg thee in his knotty entrails, till
> Thou hast howl'd away twelve winters.
>
> (ɪ. 2)

As Ariel never opposes his master even verbally, Prospero's severity
seems unwarranted. Thus, through Prospero's treatment of Caliban
and Ariel, Shakespeare shows how authority can become a rather
inhuman weapon of repression in civilised hands.

He depicts Caliban with even greater insight and complexity than
Prospero. Caliban is partly an embodiment of primitive nature itself;
there is truth when Prospero calls him, 'Thou earth, thou!' He is also
the typical aboriginal inhabitant whose impulses have not been
directed by civilisation. He instigates Trinculo and Stephano to sup-
plant Prospero and has grave misgivings:

> . . . We shall lose our time
> And all be turn'd to barnacles, or to apes
> With foreheads villainous low.
>
> (ɪᴠ. 1)

Caliban's fears are absurdly superstitious; it is a jester and a drunken
butler whom he sees as fit alternative rulers to Prospero; the change in
his position he wants to effect is from Prospero's slave to their 'foot-
licker'. Thus, Shakespeare ironically reveals the primitiveness of a

mind such as Caliban's and suggests that primitive human beings would remain in subjection whatever the changes of rule because they can do no better. Still, there are potentialities for development in Caliban. A part of his nature suggests destructive possibilities: he wishes to get rid of the civilised rule of Prospero and the murder of his master seems to him an unexceptionable method. He reveals an even worse tendency in his words to Prospero about his kind of desire to 'violate' Miranda:

> O ho, O ho! Wouldn't had been done.
> Thou didst prevent me; I had peopl'd else
> This isle with Calibans.
>
> (I. 2)

Caliban seems to revel idiot-like in unbridled natural power and gloat over the horrible. Thus, the positive side of Caliban can become definitely ugly, not merely destructive. But he also has potentialities which show that he could benefit by contact with civilisation. He can pick up civilised speech from Prospero. He responds to the atmosphere of the island:

> . . . Sometimes a thousand twangling instruments
> Will hum about mine ears; and sometimes voices,
> That, if I then had wak'd after long sleep,
> Will make me sleep again; and then, in dreaming,
> The clouds methought would open and show riches
> Ready to drop upon me, that, when I wak'd,
> I cried to dream again.
>
> (III. 2)

Shakespeare employs Caliban's words to help build the ideal spellbound atmosphere of the island and, at the same time, to reveal an aspect of his character. Caliban uses mellow tones exceptional for him, a sensuous auditory image, a climactic visual image in biblical language suggesting a miracle; and the pausing run of the poetry confirms our sense of his pathetic bewildred sensitivity to 'sounds and sweet airs that give delight'. His dreaming enhances our sense of his 'humanness' as this is a peculiarly human quality.

In *The Tempest*, then, Shakespeare perceptively presents the civilised and the primitive as having a mixed value. How does he contemplate people alien to him racially? Marlowe surrendered to

anti-semitism when he made Barabas in *The Jew of Malta* a caricature
of the conventional Jewish evil usurer. When Shakespeare wrote *The
Merchant of Venice*, anti-semitism was no less strong: a Portuguese
Jewish Doctor had been executed recently for an alleged attempt to
poison the Queen. Whether or not Shakespeare betrays 'the taint of
racism' can be discovered in the light of Claude Lanzmann's pregnant
words: 'A novel is a microcosm: if the only coward in it is a Jew, the
only Jew a coward, an inclusive if not a universal relation is established
between these two terms'.[1] Lanzmann's paradigm applies to all forms
of literature, not only to the novel, and to all the evils with which the
Jews are traditionally associated, not only cowardice. It has an even
wider relevance with which we are not concerned at the moment. In
Shakespeare's play, the only inhumanly acquisitive person is a Jew,
Shylock; the only important Jew is an inhumanly acquisitive person.
He is a contrast to Antonio who is Christian and unworldly, though a
fellow trader. Thus, in a way, Shakespeare follows the traditionally
prejudiced view of the Jew. Yet there is more to Shylock: here is a
scene in a street in Venice after his daughter's elopement:

Shylock: My own flesh and blood to rebel!
Solarino: Out upon it, old carrion! Rebels it at these years?
Shylock: I say my daughter is my flesh and my blood.
Salarino: There is more difference between thy flesh and hers than
between jet and ivory; more between your bloods than
there is between red wine and Rhenish. But tell us, do
you hear whether Antonio have had any loss at sea or
no?
Shylock: There I have another bad match: . . . He was wont to
lend money for a Christian courtesy; let him look to his
bond.
Solarino: Why I am sure, if he forfeit, thou wilt not take his flesh.
What's that good for?
Shylock: To bait fish withal. If it will feed nothing else, it will feed
my revenge. He hath disgrac'd me . . . If you tickle us, do
we not laugh? If you poison us, do we not die? And if
you wrong us, shall we not revenge? If we are like you in
the rest, we will resemble you in that. If a Jew wrong a
Christian, what is his humility? Revenge. . . .

(III. 1)

Shylock genuinely feels for his daughter and suffers because of her elopement. The prejudices against Jews which he experiences in the course of his life in society are real; they, quite credibly, anger him and make him hard. The concluding lines suggest that revenge is an understandable human tendency, common to both Christians and Jews. Shakespeare so presents Shylock that he has a convincingly human quality which rises above the convention which stereotyped the Jews as monsters of greed.

The complex of 'white'–'coloured' relations under imperialism began to make itself felt in Europe in Shakespeare's day. Eldred Jones notes that 'there were so many Negroes in London by 1601 that Elizabeth had cause to be "discontented at the great number of Negars and blackamoors which are crept into the realm since the troubles between her Highness and the King of Spain", and for her to appoint a certain Caspar Van Zenden, merchant of Lubeck, to transport them out of the country'.[2] In *Othello*, 'white'–'coloured' relations are an important part of the settings and the central drama. The eponymous hero is different from the other members of Venetian society in the play in physique and cultural background. They respect him as a successful general whom they cannot do without; at the same time, they look down on him as a social inferior because he is a 'coloured' alien belonging to a race with little power. Even before he enters the stage, he is referred to slightingly: Iago calls him his 'Moorship' and Roderigo mentions 'the thick-lips'. Roderigo's remark is particularly significant because, though Shakespeare calls Othello a Moor and he is constantly referred to as such, thick lips are a racial characteristic of negroes, not Moors. In medieval times and as late as the seventeenth century, 'white Moors' were known but it was commonly believed that most Moors were black or very swarthy; the word 'Moor' was often used for 'negro'. These contemporary tendencies work with the imprecision of the conventional cursory Westerner's view of 'coloured' people, an awareness of which made Conrad show Heyst telling Lena in *Victory*, 'One Chinaman looks very much like another';[3] obviously, realistically speaking, one 'coloured' man is no more like another than one Englishman is like another when regarded in the same way. Shakespeare has succumbed to the conventional influences so that he unconsciously portrays Othello, not in terms of a Moor, but in terms of a composite figure of a 'coloured' man.

The tragedy of Othello's marriage is Shakespeare's central preoccupation in the play. The marriage is inter-racial and this factor gives rise to problems which turn out to be important. Othello has to run away with Desdemona, a 'white' Venetian, because of her father's opposition to their marriage. Brabantio's rage, when he discovers the elopement, reveals both the causes of his anger and of his opposition:

> . . . If she in chains of magic were not bound,
> Whether a maid so tender, fair, and happy,
> So opposite to marriage that she shunn'd,
> The wealthy curled darlings of our nation,
> Would ever have, to incur a general mock,
> Run from her guardage to the sooty bosom
> Of such a thing as thou – to fear, not to delight.
>
> (I, 2)

Brabantio recoils from Othello's colour; he feels acutely the general's social inferiority and the social stigma of a mixed marriage. Clearly, he is a conservative 'white' Venetian. He puts his case to the Duke of Venice in these terms:

> She is abus'd, stol'n from me, and corrupted,
> By spells and medicines bought of mountebanks;
> For nature so preposterously to err, . . .
>
> (I.3)

He considers the relationship unnatural, refers to the supernatural and other peculiar means which were conventionally supposed to be open to 'coloured' people. Thus, racial elements in society, external to Othello, affect his status, the course and position of his relationship with Desdemona.

Othello is undone not so much by Iago's villainy as by certain weaknesses of his own. T. S. Eliot has observed Othello's 'attitude of self-dramatisation' and '*bovarysme*'. F. R. Leavis has perceived 'Othello's self-idealisation, his promptness to jealousy and his blindness'.[4] Othello is also too conscious of himself as a 'coloured' alien in Venice. Iago's insinuations are persuasive partly because he bases them explicitly on his position as a 'native' of Venice:

> I know our country disposition well:
> In Venice they do let God see the pranks
> They dare not show their husbands; their best conscience
> Is not to leave't undone, but keep't unknown.
>
> (III. 3)

Othello, as an alien, respects the words of a 'native', especially one whom he considers 'honest'. His kind of awareness of his race and colour makes him more vulnerable:

> Othello: I do not think but Desdemona honest.
> Iago: Long live she so! and long live you to think so!
> Othello: And yet, how nature erring from itself –
> Iago: Ay, there's the point: as – to be bold with you –
> Not to affect many proposed matches
> Of her own clime, complexion, and degree,
> Whereto we see in all things nature tends –
> Foh! one may smell in such a will most rank,
> Foul disproportion, thoughts unnatural.
>
> (III. 3)

Iago so plays upon the differences between Othello and Desdemona, in 'clime, complexion, and degree', that he grows far more conscious of them than of the feelings that brought them together. This mentality, in turn, reveals the inadequacies of those feelings, leads to a distorted view of them and to a greater credulity. He is no longer the masterful military captain:

> . . . Haply for I am black
> And have not those soft parts of conversation
> That chamberers have, . . .
>
> (III. 3)

His loss of confidence is thus related to his colour and inferior social position. The moment when Othello is almost convinced that his wife has been unfaithful is revealing:

> . . . Her name, that was as fresh
> As Dian's visage, is now begrim'd and black
> As mine own face.
>
> (III. 3)

He links his wife's supposed deterioration with his own colour. When Emilia opens his eyes, he has already strangled Desdemona.

The problems that arise because Othello is a 'coloured' alien in 'white' Venetian society to which Desdemona belongs, play an important secondary role in Othello's tragedy. Leavis underestimates their importance when he says that Othello's colour is to be taken merely as 'emphasising the disparity of the match'.[5] But G. M. Matthews topples over on the other side when he elaborates a thesis that 'the racial contrast between Othello and his associates' is 'the core of the play'.[6]

What inferences can we draw from, say, *The Tempest* and *Othello*, as to Shakespeare's views on problems relevant both to developing countries and life in general? The answer is, none at all. His characters enact in *The Tempest* the mixed value of civilisation and primitive life; in *Othello*, the problems of a 'coloured' alien in 'white' society. Typically, he not only treats his characters with an all-sided sympathy, but also identifies himself with all of them.

When we leave the Elizabethans and Jacobeans, and come to the Augustans, we find that British activities overseas have increased. In 1657, Cromwell granted the East India Company monopoly rights and Charles II gave it even more power. By 1688, among other things, the Company had established the presidencies of Madras, Bengal and Bombay. There is now more contact between Britain and developing countries; for the most part, she is 'exploiting' them to a greater extent and more systematically. Dryden, in *Annus Mirabilis*, reacts to this situation:

> Thus to the Eastern wealth through storms we go;
> But now, the Cape once doubled, fear no more:
> A constant Trade-wind will securely blow,
> And gently lay us on the Spicy shore.

The Augustan poetic idiom lends itself easily to this stereotyped puff to British trade. Dryden sees the 'wealth' from the East as the product of brave legitimate commerce, not of 'exploitation'. Addison, in *The Spectator*, piously rhapsodises over British prosperity in the same vein:

> Our Ships laden with the Harvest of every Climate: Our Tables are stored with Spices, and Oils, and Wines: Our Rooms are filled with Pyramids of *China*, and adorned with the Workmanship of *Japan*: Our Morning's-Draught comes to us from the remotest Corners of the Earth: . . .[7]

But Pope is ironical:

> . . . The various off'rings of the world appear;
> From each she nicely culls with curious toil,

And decks the Goddess with glitt'ring spoil. . . .[8]

These lines are a part of his mock-epic presentation of Belinda at her toilet, as a goddess, in *The Rape of the Lock*. 'Off'rings' is ironical; he calls the products from developing countries 'spoil', and the use of this term reveals a critical-realistic view of them as the unearned profit of conquest and plunder. Still, in Britain, it is Addisonian thinking that predominates. The foundations of the tradition to which Joseph Chamberlain, Cecil Rhodes, Kipling (in part) and Enoch Powell belong, are being laid.

Developing countries enter Augustan literature in a piecemeal way. Writers notice the products from these countries and the profit from them that contributed to prosperity in Britain. They more or less complacently enjoy their vague glamourised vision of British activities overseas. Yet there were elements in their society that suggested some of the realities behind this kind of vision. It was a noticeable trend in fashionable society to have 'coloured' boys as pages for picturesque purposes as Hogarth records in 'The Harlot's Progress – in Affluence', 'Marriage à la Mode – The Toilette' and 'Taste in High Life, in the year 1742'. There were handcuffs, shackles and thumbscrews in ship chandlers' shops in Liverpool. Doctors visited the slave ships to inspect the stock as it were, and James Currie, the first editor of Burns, helped to set up in 1789 the Liverpool Board which examined these doctors before granting them licences. As Benjamin Kidd has noted, slave 'operations were conducted on so great a scale that in the 20 years before the opening of the eighteenth century, 300,000 slaves were exported from Africa by the English, and in the 80 years which followed, over 600,000 slaves were landed in the Island of Jamaica alone'.[9] But factors such as these did not influence the Augustans to think deeply of British interests abroad. They viewed English life in terms of life in Britain alone; they did not see that these concerns of Englishmen were organically linked to it and formed an important support. It is only a tiny minority who break through the insularity, and among them are a few writers – Defoe and less interesting writers such as William Roscoe and Mrs Aphra Behn.

Roscoe's humanity is aroused against the slave trade in particular partly because he spent a great deal of his life in Liverpool, the British headquarters for 'this traffic in the human species' (Roscoe's own words),[10] whereas the noteworthy Augustans (Addison, Swift, Pope, Fielding, Richardson, Dr Johnson, for instance) were in effect Londoners and their work was London-oriented. Roscoe's *The Wrongs of*

Africa is a small-scale epic on the subject of slavery. It opens thus:

> Offspring of love divine, Humanity!
> Come Thou! and weep with me substantial ills,
> And execrate the wrongs, that Africa's sons,
> Torn from their natal shore, and doomed to bear
> The yoke of servitude in Western climes,
> Sustain.

This formal apostrophe to Humanity is part of the epic style and suggests that the poem is going to be a didactic public one. The latinised and conventional idiom is unpromising. When Roscoe is most passionate, he writes:

> Can it be,
> That he, the foulest fiend that ever stalked
> Across the confines of this suffering world;
> He, the dread spirit of commercial gain, . . .

Characteristically for the poem, he uses blank verse which moves in long periods. But this declamation is couched in nerveless conventional rhetoric. Roscoe belonged to a Liverpool cultural group which included James Currie and Edward Rushton. They formed a wing of the anti-slavery agitation, but they were not artists enough to create significant poetry out of their genuine humane convictions.

Defoe was a Londoner; but, as Angus Ross observes, 'as a writer he is not "Augustan"'.[11] This is partly why he could be seriously interested in the quality of life of Alexander Selkirk in Juan Fernandez, and Robert Knox in Ceylon. It is likely that he set *Robinson Crusoe* in an island, not like the rather commonplace, temperate Juan Fernandez, but tropical like Ceylon and markedly 'undeveloped' to help present the same universal theme as *The Tempest* – the interaction of the civilised and the primitive. It is Crusoe's relationship with Man Friday that is most relevant to my concerns. Crusoe takes the attitude of a well-meaning, domineering patron towards Friday. He does not realise that Friday, though primitive, has an individuality. When he rescues Friday from his enemies, he does not bother to find out his name; he gives him a new one. He wants to transform him from a 'savage' to a civilised *European*. He makes him wear clothes in a European way. He cures his cannibal tendency. He teaches him civilised speech, and after a while Friday is able to express his thoughts in English though he does not quite succeed in mastering it. As Friday's patron, Crusoe is, above all, a Christian:

> From hence, I sometimes was led too far to invade the soverainty of Providence, and as it were arraign the justice of so arbitrary a disposition of things, that should hide that light from some, and reveal it to others, and yet expect a like duty from both. But I shut it up, and checked my thoughts with this conclusion, . . . as we are all the clay in the hand of the potter, no vessel could say to Him, Why hast Thou formed me thus?[12]

The problems posed by Friday call in question Crusoe's beliefs, but he suppresses his doubts quickly by coming down heavily on the side of orthodoxy. He tries to wean Friday away from his primitive beliefs: '. . . He listened with great attention, and received with pleasure the notion of Jesus Christ being sent to redeem us, and of the manner of making our prayers to God, and His being able to hear us, even into Heaven'.[13] And it is not Friday alone who benefits from Crusoe's sermons: '. . . by his serious enquiries and questionings, made me, as I said before, a much better scholar in the scripture knowledge that I should ever have been by my own private mere reading'.[14] The loosely-flowing moral language, evident in these extracts, perfectly suits the character of Crusoe, the earnest trader, and helps to make real the first-person narrator convention; it has the immediacy of an artless recounting of experiences. Crusoe and Friday become increasingly attached to each other as benevolent master and loyal servant. When Crusoe is able to leave the island for Europe, Friday accompanies him as his servant.

Whereas Shakespeare dramatises the mixed value of both the civilised and the primitive, Defoe implicitly endorses Crusoe's attitudes and actions. He assumes that the 'benighted savage' must be civilised – this meant, made European – in a domineering way by forcing on him Christianity, English and the like. He intends Crusoe to be the average civilised man, but Crusoe carries the stamp of his period. His Christian zeal anticipates the religious mask of imperialism and, to put it at its highest, the genuine missionary spirit which got its chance under the British Empire. These aspects are expressed prominently and consciously later, say, in Cary's *Aissa Saved*.

Mrs Aphra Behn is one of the first among the British to have actually lived in a developing country, the West Indies, and to have drawn on her experiences to write literature set there. The hero of her novel, *Oroonoko or the Royal Slave* (1678), is an African, a prince:

> He was pretty tall, but of shape the most exact that can be fancied:
> the most famous statuary could not form the figure of a man more
> admirably turned from head to foot. . . . His nose was rising and
> Roman, instead of African and flat: his mouth the finest shaped that
> could be seen: far from those great turned lips which are so natural
> to the rest of the Negroes. . . .
>
> Nor did the perfections of his mind come short of those of his
> person: . . .[15]

Mrs Behn tries to praise the African, but she piles extravagant terms
and makes him markedly European even to his nose and lips. Apart
from her feebleness as a writer, this kind of description discloses a kind
of racialism in her. She is unable to appreciate the Africans for what
they are and for whatever levels of development they, as Africans, are
capable of rising to. Oroonoko is a wooden, false portrayal of an
African. Indeed, Mrs Behn's is a grosser and less restrained version of
Marlowe's view of Dain Waris in Conrad's *Lord Jim*. Yet this kind of
description also reveals a regard for the African and an anxiety to get it
across to a reading public which was extremely prejudiced. Mrs Behn's
is a pioneering, rather humane view of the 'native'.

In the Augustan age, then, developing countries play a more prominent part in the consciousness of the British than earlier. After Pitt's
India Bill (1784), the Government began to control the activities of the
United Company of Merchants (the enlarged East India Company)
and by 1833 was virtually in charge. The Empire was being run on an
even larger scale and much more systematically. The Government
employed people different from those engaged in the slave trade, and
among them were individuals with creative or intellectual powers. In
mid-Victorian times, it was two colonial officials, William Arnold and
William Knighton, who wrote *Oakfield* and *Forest Life in Ceylon*, respectively. These works were not artistically noteworthy; but they have
a value because, at that time, no Englishman thought and felt as creatively about developing countries in their own right as they did.

It is profitless to discuss the pedestrian language, loose organisation
or moralising stretches of Arnold's novel. Its art is uninspired. What
matters is the notable qualities of mind it reveals. Arnold shares a
characteristic habit of the Victorian liberal: he approaches social problems in terms too purely moral. His chief character, Edward Oakfield,

is a moral hero, like George Eliot's Felix Holt who is meant to be a
Radical but elevates the purely moral above the social. Still, the more
intelligent among the liberals are able to see the problems themselves,
though not the 'solutions', with unusual penetration. Of course, Arnold
is far more of a moral reformer than George Eliot. All his important
characters are highly moral themselves and overt moralists, as in the
case of Oakfield, Hugh Stanton and Mr Middleton, or they soon
develop into such people, as do Arthur Vernon and Fred Wykham.
Oakfield, in fact, is religious-minded and comes to India to find
fulfilment:

> In the colonies, – in a new, fresh, and vigorous society, he thought
> form would, at any rate, weigh less heavily upon truth; society if it
> did not help, would surely not hinder him. In this direction he was
> met by practical difficulties at all hands; till at last, transferring his
> notions of colonial to Anglo-Indian society, with an ignorance mar-
> vellous indeed, but common to all Englishman not connected by
> family ties with India, he fancied he had solved the problem, – that
> by obtaining an Indian appointment a maintenance would be
> secured to him, while he, under utterly new circumstances, might
> begin life anew, try once more to realise his theory of bringing
> religion into daily life, without the necessity of denying it at every
> turn in obedience to some fashion or dogma of society; and then, as
> to his work in life, was not every European in India engaged in the
> grand work of civilising Asia?[16]

Arnold attributes Oakfield's notions of Anglo-Indian society to a
common 'ignorance'. He thus virtually states their falsity and suggests
that his objective view of his hero and a part of his own stance are
knowledgeable realism. He proceeds to expose diverse aspects of
Anglo-Indian society mainly in terms of Oakfield's awakening to them.
'The overbearing coarse animal worldly existence'[17] of the Anglo-
Indians, as he sees it, is bodied forth concretely during Oakfield's
assignments in two regiments – the 81st regiment at Hajeepoor whose
evils at their worst are represented by Lieutenant Cade, and a less
reprehensible, different kind of regiment, the 90th, whose weaknesses
at their worst are represented by Stafford. Oakfield finds army society
less uncongenial during the war with the Sikhs because of its 'physical
earnestness, although he still sought in vain, and still regretted the
absence of that moral earnestness which should give its character to
war as to everything else.'[18] As a reward for courageous military

service, he is appointed to the civil service in Punjab and thus Arnold opens up another side of Anglo-India. This is Oakfield's reaction to it:

I like it better than I expected, or rather dislike it less.[19]

Take the majority of officials in this country: their vigour, their strong sense, their prompt and business-like dexterity, have earned for them as a class, a justly honourable distinction. These are what may be called the commercial virtues. But except good men of business what are they?[20]

As E. M. Forster thinks, the novel 'has the Arnold integrity'.[21] Its brave and knowledgeable exposure of Anglo-India in mid-Victorian times has a value. William Arnold's view of it is sombre, as revealed by the fates of his worthy central characters: at the end of the novel, Stanton and Middleton are inclined to quit India, Wykham goes to England on furlough and decides against return, Vernon and Oakfield himself are unable to come to terms with Anglo-India and contract fatal illnesses. In the face of Anglo-India which they regarded as more or less unsatisfactory, these characters had become friends and this helped to keep alive 'the chords of their finer nature'. 'Fellowship', as the sub-title has it, is important to Arnold as it is to Forster, but Arnold is concerned only with the Europeans.

This preoccupation suggests the boundaries of his view of India. He pays most attention to life in the army. And, indeed, the army does bulk large in literature set in places subject to imperialism; apart from Kipling, military contributions were prominent in *Blackwood's Edinburgh Magazine*, which became staple reading for army officers, planters, administrative officials and other members of the imperial service and was the usual magazine to which they wrote. This interest reflects the importance of the army in gaining empires, extending and maintaining them; when Fanon says that colonialism 'is violence in its natural state',[22] he is stating a part of the truth.

To turn now to the role of the Indians in Arnold's novel: on the social relations of British soldiers, Edward Oakfield says in conversation with Miss Middleton:

'Beyond our official connexion with the sepoys, and our domestic relations with our servants, we see really nothing of the people, have nothing to do with them, no influence, nor any opportunity of gaining influence with them.'

'I dare say,' said Miss Middleton, 'that that is quite true; intercourse with the natives is just one of those vague sweeping expressions which the people in England are so fond of with regard to India.'[23]

When Oakfield serves in the army, he is very friendly with a British civil servant, Middleton, but he is not even acquainted with a single Indian inside or outside the army. Even when he himself becomes a civil servant, he remains aloof from the Indians. The Indians themselves appear only briefly in the novel, as servants and bearers of palkis; none of them is individualised; none of them speak a word. Because of the prevailing apartheid, they do not matter in the area of European social life which Arnold has chosen to depict. His presentation is true to his selected area, but it is narrow.

Yet Arnold is not wholly unconcerned with the kind of relations between the races which was to preoccupy Forster in *A Passage to India*. There is this conversation of Oakfield's with Wykham at Simla:

'Well, I do detest the natives, they are a mean, lying, fawning, sordid race; and after ten years experience, I say that to call a native "a man and a brother" is a lie. He is not a man; and I repudiate the fraternity of a scoundrel who lies at every other word.'

'My experience is much less than yours, and I grant you their lying is most awful; but then this is just one of the evils which I say weigh upon us in this country. It is grievous to live among men, and feel the idea of fraternity thwarted by facts; and yet the idea must not be abandoned as false or hopeless. We must not resign ourselves, without a struggle, to calling them brutes.'[24]

Wykham is an utter racialist, but it is the less superior Oakfield who has Arnold behind him. Oakfield goes on to say: 'We esteem them the better, the more we know them. Why? because we learn to look at things from their view, instead of assuming our own as the true one, and condemning them for not coming up to it'.[25] He wishes to remove the distinctions of colour and language, and to achieve 'a growing sense of unity'.[26] But the 'unity' he advocates is between a superior 'white' race and an inferior race which has somehow got rid of its inferiority: 'But after all, I grant freely that they are a deplorably inferior race, but I do not see why they should be considered hopelessly so'.[27] Thus Arnold rises above the characteristically imperial attitudes of Wykham, but he makes the traditional Western mistake of confusing a less developed state of culture with an alleged inferiority of race. But Arnold and Oakfield are not 'the same person', as Forster takes them to be.[28] Arnold does endorse his hero's views to a considerable extent, but he also differs from him at times. Apart from explicit criticism, Arnold also uses a less obvious method of implicit criticism, which is evident when Middleton sketches his idea of India's progress to Oakfield and Mr Wallace:

> To preach Christianity to the natives of India, is to begin at the end. Physical improvement first, then intellectual, then spiritual, that seems the natural order of things; and if it is the natural order, that is to say the true one, fixed by the laws of the universe, then whole universities of missionaries will not alter it.[29]

It is the practical, experienced Middleton whose attitudes Arnold shows up as always sound. He is Arnold's mouthpiece rather than Oakfield. By playing off their characters, he implicitly 'places' Oakfield as an over-moral idealist. 'The natural order of things', to which Arnold subscribes, is sensible. But he cannot escape the limitations of traditional attitudes: he tends to equate the 'spiritual' with the religious, considers Christianity necessary for India and sees all improvement as work of the British. This exchange between Oakfield and Middleton is also important:

> 'But do you not contemplate a time when this government shall pass into the people's own hands?'
> 'Surely; I do contemplate it, but I confess, as an infinitely remote event, of which, at present, it is I think impossible to detect any, the faintest symptom. The grand fault in our government has been and is, that it does not contemplate this, and does not therefore try to find out the causes which at present make it so utterly unfeasible.'[30]

As early as 1853, Arnold can look upon self-rule as a worthy and neglected goal in India; at that time it would naturally appear 'an infinitely remote event' even to him. But Middleton sees the two key problems in these terms: 'What is the point at which the European and the Native mind begin to diverge?' 'Why is English society in this country so woefully behind all European society elsewhere?'[31] Then he gives his own 'solution':

The solution of a problem like that can hardly be stated

categorically; it is the work of our lives, of yours and mine, to solve it; or rather to make some approach to it, for he who really does solve it will be the great man of India. The solution of it will be a revelation made to us by some man of genius; the great business for ordinary honest workers is pioneering, trying to clear away some of the jungle of falsehood and absurdity which might stop the hero, or impede him, when he does come.[32]

This positive 'approach' is absurdly visionary.

Arnold reveals the strength of an exceptional mid-Victorian liberal: he is courageously honest, sees problems realistically and can transcend common prejudices. But he is limited by conventional thought and by his period to a certain extent. The wishful and over-moral side of his mind belongs to the weak side of the liberal tradition: his brother, Matthew, keenly grasped the problems of contemporary England but adumbrated inadequate solutions.[33] Of George Eliot, David Craig has written: 'all George Eliot can offer, through Felix, is high-mindedness, unrooted in any particular activity or movement'.[34]

Both *Oakfield* and Knighton's *Forest Life in Ceylon* are rooted in actual experience and information. But in the latter the dividing line between fact and art is thin, and it is not organised into a unified novel. I think it is best approached in terms of the author's own conception of his work, 'a collection of light sketches professing to describe life.'[35] What strikes me as valuable in it is his exceptionally intelligent contemplation of colonial situations in Ceylon in mid-Victorian times:

> 'There is much in an Asiatic life generally,' observed Hofer, 'that tends to unfit a man for active duties in England afterwards; here, and more especially on the continent of India, a man begins naturally to regard himself as one of the aristocracy, however humble his lot at home. He sees the great mass of the population beneath him, . . .'[36]

On the other hand, there is little of this intelligence in his pondered comments on the 'rebellion' soon after the British conquest of Kandy, the last stronghold of the Sinhalese:

> United the Kandians might possibly at this juncture have succeeded in again achieving independence, although I cannot agree with Marandhan in thinking that such a consummation would have ultimately been for the good of the country, but, distracted by dissen-

sion, and divided by clashing interests and pretensions, all hope of ultimate success was foolish.

The second was that invariable good fortune, which makes the British advance in the East the march of destiny, which no accident can arrest, no temporary losses retard.[37]

His confident views are conventional, especially the notion of 'the British advance' as a matter of 'destiny'.[38] He is not as far-seeing as William Arnold.

Nevertheless, when he sets himself the straightforward task of describing his journey by pilot-boat after his ship entered the Galle harbour, he is capable of remarkable honesty:

To my unsophisticated eyes, the crew of this boat appeared to be tame monkeys. . . . My feelings were shared by my companions, and, as we muttered to each other, 'These are the natives', we could not help wondering how humanity could degenerate into such figures; forgetting that the want of dress and difference of colour were the only real points of contrast between them and similar specimens of our own countrymen.[39]

Knighton's candour, though naive, is valuable. On later reflection, he is sensible enough to realise 'that the want of dress and difference of colour were the only real points of contrast between them (the Sinhalese crew) and similar specimens of our own countrymen', to self-critically diagnose racialism. It happens again in his account of dinner at an hotel ashore: 'Nor was it without a feeling of unpleasantness that I saw my plate handed about by the dark fingers – a transient feeling, which I distinctly remember having once felt, but which must very soon have passed away with use'.[40] Observe the characteristic frankness and the living detail of the incident. Though Knighton is not as far-seeing as Arnold, his writing has more verve and immediacy; it is more closely and specifically rooted in his colonial context. Whereas Arnold's moral view was formed before his Indian experience, and was applied to it as it would be to any other, Knighton's broadening outlook arises out of his Ceylon experience and is being shaped by it. He is more alive in his alien setting, and this is one reason why he can bring into his 'sketches' a 'native', Marandhan, as an important and respectworthy person.

Understandably, there is no notable British literature set in Africa before 1880; Conrad's African tales appear only at the very end of the

nineteenth century, and a Cary does not appear till the 1930s. Mungo
Park's travels in the Western Sudan were undertaken as late as 1795
and even after them the exploration of Africa was intermittent. The
'scramble for Africa' started only in the 1880s and it was then that
colonial officials and others began to go there in substantial numbers.
Moreover, it was India that was considered, in Churchill's words, 'that
most truly bright and precious jewel in the crown of the King, which
more than all our other Dominions and Dependencies constitutes
the glory and strength of the British Empire'.[41] Thus the British
Government usually sent its best officials to India and, in imperial
times, India did attract capable people more than Africa. Percival
Spear says of the Indian Civil Service: 'It threw up many able and some
remarkable figures and collectively was one of the ablest groups of men
to be found anywhere. It was almost entirely British. Since 1853 it had
been recruited by competition and took the cream of the more adven-
turous talent from the universities'.[42] Furthermore, the pressure to
write about Africa was less because the Africans were primitive and
made their presence felt long after the Asians: as early as 1854, Knighton presented Marandhan, an educated Sinhalese planter, who mixed
with Europeans on terms of friendship.

 William Arnold and Knighton are immediate forerunners of
Conrad, Kipling, Forster, Cary and Graham Greene, on the one hand,
and of Mulk Raj Anand, R. K. Narayan, Chinua Achebe, James Ngugi
and V. S. Naipaul, on the other. It is colonial officials such as they who
contribute most to setting up the tradition which leads to these writers
of literature in English about situations in the Third World. But is it
surprising that the most significant literature before 1880 about issues
pertinent to both developing and developed countries is by
Shakespeare?

2 Challenges and problems of the Far East (i): Conrad's tales

> I do wish that all those ships of mine were given a rest, . . .
> Joseph Conrad, letter to Richard Curle, 14 July 1923.

One cannot consider Conrad a British writer in the same way one would Kipling, Forster, Lawrence and Cary, though his work is an important, integral part of the tradition of British fiction. It is true that he used English as the medium for his creative work though he knew French from childhood and learnt English only when an adult. He found that fiction in English had established itself as a serious art form. His period in the British Merchant Service was to him a spiritual experience and lies behind his art. He became a British citizen and settled down in Britain to become a full-time writer. He was attached to the country of his adoption. But he achieved only a temporary working-comradeship in the Merchant Navy. He could not root himself in British society and did not find much joy among English literary men. His Continental affiliations are as important as his English ones; it is this fact that makes F. R. Leavis's attempt to place him in 'the great tradition', coming down from Jane Austen and George Eliot through to D. H. Lawrence, not quite convincing.[1] Even as a British merchant seaman, he was in part the Continental nobleman; he was known as an extremely stand-offish captain. His literary methods, such as his strict objectivity, his rigorously economical and highly wrought style, his tight and complex construction, have their antecedents in Flaubert and Maupassant rather than in Jane Austen and George Eliot. Still, Conrad was adrift from Poland and found no resting-place in France or Belgium. Indeed, he found no community anywhere. He was part-British and part-Continental, an aristocratic European *deraciné*.[2] Thus, his reaction to and presentation of developing countries (as well as developed countries) are European rather than British. He is a peculiarly individual figure among the major writers of fiction in English.

His experience of developing countries played a major role in his career as writer. Though he had experience of several European countries such as Poland, Russia, France, Spain and Britain by 1888, it was his experience of a developing country in the Far East, Borneo, that first stimulated him to creativity. Indeed, were it not for this experience, he may not have become a writer at all; he himself put the point more decidedly: 'If I had not got to know Almayer pretty well it is almost certain there would never have been a line of mine in print'.[3] He had completed the first seven chapters of *Almayer's Folly* when he went to the Congo in 1890. His experience of another developing country, this time in Africa, had crucial consequences. It was largely the breakdown of his health because of his Congo journey that made him give up his career as a seaman, as a naval officer (by this time); it confirmed him in another newly-discovered vocation, that of a writer. Moreover, he told Edward Garnett, one of his best friends: 'Before the Congo I was only a simple animal'.[4] His Congo experience jolted him into a deep awareness of life. Still, he brought this awareness to a contemplation of Africa itself in only two tales – *An Outpost of Progress* (1898) and *Heart of Darkness* (1902). It was to the Far East that he turned during most of the first phase of his literary career, the phase before *Nostromo* (1904); it provided most of the material necessary for him to establish himself as a professional writer. When his powers began to falter after *Under Western Eyes* (1911), it was to the Far East he turned again, this time to renew his powers. In *The Secret Sharer* (1912) and *The Shadow-Line* (1917), he wrote superbly as in *Typhoon* (1903) or the *Patna* section of *Lord Jim* (1900). But *Victory* (1915) and *The Rescue* (1920) show that, unlike life on board ships in Far Eastern seas, Far Eastern countries did not save Conrad from marked decline, though they continued to provide material of interest.

It is an error of judgement to lump together all Conrad's work set in the Far East as V. S. Pritchett does.[5] One must discriminate between, say, *Almayer's Folly, An Outcast of the Islands, Karain, The Lagoon*, the Patusan phase of *Lord Jim, Victory, The Rescue*, on the one hand, and *The Nigger of the 'Narcissus'*, the *Patna* side of *Lord Jim, Youth, The End of the Tether, Typhoon, The Secret Sharer, The Shadow-Line*, on the other. The fiction in the former category is set almost wholly in Far Eastern countries, whereas the stories in the latter group are set for the most part on board ships in Far Eastern seas; each class has its respective thematic concerns and artistic attributes. Still, certain aspects of the stories in the latter category are pertinent to my study of how

Conrad reacted to and presented developing countries in the Far East.

These countries enter tales such as *Youth, The Secret Sharer* and *The Shadow-Line*, and their role is not negligible. In *Youth*, an integral part of Conrad's presentation (through a first-person narrator, Marlow) of the phase of youth in the life of a 'white' man is his response to the East. Marlow recreates an episode of his youth (he was twenty years old then) from the standpoint of his youth and also comments upon it from his present stage of self-aware middle age (he is now forty-two). In London he had joined a barque which was to take a cargo of coal to Bangkok: 'To Bankok! Magic name, blessed name. Mesopotamia wasn't a patch on it. Remember I was twenty, and it was my first second-mate's billet, and the East was waiting for me'. He reacts to the East in a way common to Western people for ages, generally people without first-hand knowledge and little second-hand information. He conceives it vaguely as an exotic, mysterious place and is greatly attracted to it. The narrating Marlow explicitly ascribes this kind of response to his youthfulness and Conrad seems to agree with his narrator because he implies nothing to the contrary. Marlow and his fellow seamen have to abandon their ship near Indonesia because of a fire on board; they reach Java in boats: 'The mysterious East faced me, perfumed like a flower, silent like death, dark like a grave. And I sat weary beyond expression, exulting like a conqueror, sleepless and entranced as if before a profound, a fateful enigma'. He responds to the East in reality in the same conventional way he did in his imaginative fantasy. By using the same kind of language, Conrad implies that Marlow is too young to profit from his experience of the East just as from his experiences on board the barque. He continues to be drawn towards the East: 'I have known its fascination since; I have seen the mysterious shores, the still water, the lands of brown nations, where a stealthy Nemesis lies in wait, pursues, overtakes so many of the conquering race, who are proud of their wisdom, of their knowledge, of their strength'. When Marlow grows older, he thus acquires a realistic, ironic sense of the inability of some 'superior' members of the 'ruling race' to cope with living in the conquered, developing East, but, as Conrad reveals through implications in the language which lie beyond Marlow's consciousness, this sense is swamped by a persisting romanticism; not only are the 'shores' still 'mysterious', this sense itself is conceived half-romantically as 'a stealthy Nemesis' which overwhelms an exaggerated number ('so many') of 'white' people. Marlow seems too conventional to achieve a sufficiently realistic view of the East even at maturity. When he becomes more middle-aged, his view alters again: 'But for me all the East is contained in that vision of my youth. . . . a moment of strength, of romance, of glamour – of youth!' He regards the East as in his youth, but the difference is that he is now aware that his youthful view is romantic. Still, he refuses to be realistic even to the extent possible to him at this stage, and his deep-seated conventionality is accurately reflected in his speech. Thus, Conrad presents through Marlow, in terms of drama, narrator's comment and authorial implication, a changing view of the East as a part of important stages in the life of a frank, conservative European. The East itself enters the tale as the setting of its closing phase; but Conrad only presents Marlow's romantic general impression of the landscape and the people, and briefly too; what matters is Marlow's reaction. The East is not important in its own right and is treated as a testing-ground for the mind of the European foreigner.

In *The Secret Sharer* and *The Shadow-Line*, too, the East has a psychological–moral significance but in different and deeper ways. The action of *The Secret Sharer* begins in an unnamed Thai port: 'On my right hand there were lines of fishing-stakes resembling a mysterious system of half-submerged bamboo fences, . . . To the left a group of barren islets, suggesting ruins of stone walls, towers, and blockhouses, . . .'. Whereas Marlow in *Youth* had mainly recounted his experience as a callow youth, appointed second mate for the first time, the narrator of this tale appears older and less immature, though young; he has just been promoted to the rank of captain; he is 'the youngest man on board' with the exception of the second mate (Marlow's position). Conrad 'places' his character more subtly than that of Marlow; there is nothing like middle-aged Marlow's constant exclamation, 'O! Youth!'. At this point, Conrad briefly renders the narrator–captain's impression of the East from his anchored ship. It contains an element of Marlow's superficial, conventional view of the East as 'mysterious', but most of it is quite realistic. Still, he does not look beneath the surface and does not see any serious threat to a peaceful voyage:

> I descended the poop and paced the waist, my mind picturing to myself the coming passage through the Malay Archipelago, down the Indian Ocean, and up the Atlantic. All its phases were familiar enough to me, every characteristic, . . . except the novel responsibility of command. But I took heart from the reasonable thought that the ship was like other ships. . . .

He does not have the naive expectations and eagerness of the extremely young Marlow, but Conrad implies a certain excess and shallowness in his confidence which show that he, too, lacks experience though to a lesser degree. The deficiencies in his understanding of life are ironically underlined by Conrad when he juxtaposes this scene with the appearance of Leggatt. Leggatt becomes a serious psychological–moral problem to the captain. He has killed a fellow seaman, but the captain affords him refuge partly because he is unable to judge the extent of his guilt; this is part of the captain's moral difficulty. The reader shares it: Leggatt's account of his deed contains extenuating circumstances and rings true, but we are given only his point of view. Moreover, the captain, with a part of himself hitherto unknown to him, feels a strong affinity with Leggatt; this is an important part of his psychological embarrassment. He suffers from a tension between his moral–psychological attachment to a suspect figure, on the one hand, and his sense of responsibility to society and his sailors, on the other.

The East increases in importance at the climax of the tale which brilliantly makes for both a *dénouement* and a resolution of the themes. The captain takes his ship close to land:

> The wind fanned my cheek, the sails slept, the world was silent. The strain of watching the dark loom of the land grow bigger and denser was too much for me. I had shut my eyes – because the ship must go closer. She must! . . .
>
> When I opened my eyes the second view started my heart with a thump. The black southern hill of Koh-ring seemed to hang right over the ship like a towering fragment of the everlasting night. . . .

The Eastern setting is actively related to the human drama; indeed, the realistic description of the setting is inside the presentation of the drama. Up to a point, the East appears as a testing-ground for the mind of the European foreigner as in *Youth*: the calmness of the sea and the menace of the hilly island add to the responsibilities of the captain. As the ship draws closer to land, the significance of the East deepens. Leggatt wants to reach the remote islands off Cambodia partly to escape the predictable condemnation of conventional justice. More importantly, he wishes to be marooned there as a self-imposed expiation for his dubious crime. The captain wants to help Leggatt by bringing his ship close to land; he seriously endangers the lives of his crew and his ship. He puts his loyalty to a person, Leggatt, above his professional and social responsibilities; he breaks through his conventionality to perform a deed like Leggatt's own offence. But he goes further; he wants to take his ship even closer to land than is necessary for Leggatt to swim ashore; he wants 'to shave the land as close as possible' as a self-imposed expiation for violating social values and the seamen's code in harbouring Leggatt. Thus, the East becomes for the captain what it is going to be for Leggatt – a kind of purgatory. On the level of plot, when Leggatt swims away as the ship draws near land, the action reaches its climax; the captain has gained in maturity as a captain and as a man as a consequence of his experiences.

In *The Shadow-Line*, the East is as important as in *The Secret Sharer* and in a similar way, as helping in the maturation of a newly appointed captain. The tale begins and ends in an unnamed Eastern port; but unlike in *The Secret Sharer*, Conrad takes us ashore. Shore life is presented from the characteristic point of view of a 'white' seaman, but with a solidity and realism absent in *Youth*. Conrad needs to deal with the European contacts of a European naval officer; two Malayans (a peon and a policeman) are briefly referred to. The Harbour Office and the Officers' Sailors' Home are the places in the port important to Conrad and he renders them as memorably as any of Forster's little-Europe-in-India milieux; this scene at the Sailors' Home is typical:

A loud whispering from the steward succeeded and then again Hamilton was heard with even intenser scorn.

'What? That young ass who fancies himself for having been chief mate with Kent so long? . . . Preposterous.'

Giles and I looked at each other. Kent being the name of my late commander, Captain Giles' whisper, 'He's talking of you', seemed to me sheer waste of breath. The Chief Steward must have stuck to his point whatever it was, because Hamilton was heard again more supercilious, if possible, and also very emphatic:

'Rubbish, my good man! One doesn't *compete* with a rank outsider like that. There's plenty of time.'

'That's a very insulting sort of man,' remarked Captain Giles – superfluously, I thought. 'Very insulting. You haven't offended him in some way, have you?'

'Never spoke to him in my life,' I said grumpily. 'Can't imagine what he means by competing. He has been trying for my job after I left – and didn't get it. But that isn't exactly competition.'

Conrad dramatises finely, the narrator's conceited brusqueness which betrays his inexperience, the 'commonplace wisdom' of the old captain, the slyness of the abject steward, the false confidence of the inept Hamilton, and the treachery which the narrator is too immature to suspect. Captain Giles, who is able to sense the treachery, helps the narrator to discover it. Thus, the Eastern milieu at the beginning of the tale provides him with a 'lesson' in life.

When he puts out to sea, a captain on his first voyage, the East again tests his character: 'The island of Koh-ring, a great, black upheaved ridge amongst a lot of tiny islets, lying upon the glassy water like a triton amongst minnows, seemed to be the centre of the fatal circle. It seemed impossible to get away from it. Day after day it remained in sight. . . .'. Conrad sensitively conveys the captain's reactions to this daunting tropical seascape as his ship lies becalmed; the vivid presentation of the seascape merges into the rendering of his reactions. Apart from difficulties created by nature, he is beset with human problems. His crew is stricken with tropical fever. He had neglected to inspect the ship's medicine chest before setting sail and it lacks quinine, the medicine which he needs to combat the disease. Ransome is the only member of his crew to escape the fever, but he has a weak heart. Still, the captain copes with all the problems which he faces on the seas.

The tale ends in the Eastern port from which it led out; this symmetry rounds off the tale plot-wise and thematically. Conrad confirms the captain's growth:

'And there's another thing; a man should stand up to his bad luck, to his mistakes, to his conscience, and all that sort of thing. Why – what else would you have to fight against?'

I kept silent. I don't know what he saw in my face, but he asked abruptly:

'Why – you aren't faint-hearted?'

'God only knows, Captain Giles', was my sincere answer. . . .

'I am going on board directly', I said. 'I shall pick up one of my anchors and heave in to half-cable on the other as soon as my new crew comes on board and I shall be off at daylight to-morrow'.

'You will?' grunted Captain Giles approvingly. 'That's the way. You'll do'.

'What did you expect? That I would want to take a week ashore for a rest?' I said, irritated by his tone. 'There's no rest for me till she's out in the Indian Ocean and not much of it even then'.

Conrad is as close to the captain as Lawrence is to Birkin in *Women in*

Love when he suggests that the captain's view of life is mature – a seasoned and flexible acceptance of the continual demands of living. Thus, in *The Shadow-Line*, Conrad approaches the East positively as a fit testing-ground for the young captain's manhood.

Indeed, in all the tales such as *Youth*, *The Secret Sharer* and *The Shadow-Line*, Conrad treats the East more or less skilfully in a variety of ways but from one angle, as an area having a psycho-moral significance for the European foreigner from the standpoint of an intelligent European – an environment testing and changing character or a kind of purgatory.

In these tales, the Far Eastern seas are more important than the countries; they are important as distinctively Eastern agencies having a psycho-moral significance for the European foreigner. The storms of *The Nigger of the 'Narcissus'* and *Typhoon*, the calms of *The Secret Sharer* and *The Shadow-Line*, bring out, among other things, the courage, resourcefulness and discipline of the European seamen (especially the officers), the virtue of collaborative endeavour; with great skill, commonly acknowledged by critics, Conrad affirms these positive values as relevant not only to the Merchant Service but to life in general. Still, the more searching tests for the European at sea are provided by human difficulties. Problems such as those created by Leggatt in *The Secret Sharer* and those created by the fever-stricken crew in *The Shadow-Line*, are associated distinctively with sailing in the Far East. But it is the negro in *The Nigger of the 'Narcissus'* and the Chinese coolies in *Typhoon* who raise issues intimately related to developing countries.

The Nigger of the 'Narcissus' (1897) is Conrad's first work in which his talent appears unmistakably extraordinary. Let us begin our discussion of his attitudes to and treatment of the 'nigger' by looking at a part of the scene when he first appears:

The nigger was calm, cool, towering, superb. The men had approached and stood behind him in a body. He overtopped the tallest by half a head. He said: 'I belong to the ship.' He enunciated distinctly, with soft precision. The deep, rolling tones of his voice filled the deck without effort. He was naturally scornful, unaffectedly condescending, as if from his height of six foot three he had surveyed all the vastness of human folly and had made up his mind not to be too hard on it. . . . The disdainful tones had ceased, and breathing heavily, he stood still, surrounded by all these white men. He held his head up in the glare of the lamp – a head vigorously modelled into deep shadows and shining lights – a head powerful and misshapen with a tormented and flattened face – a face pathetic and brutal: the tragic, the mysterious, the repulsive mask of a nigger's soul.

In this instance Conrad is unable to come to terms sufficiently with the 'coloured' alien. He strains to express Wait's unusual and powerful personality; his prose deteriorates into redundancy and exaggeration. At times Wait is referred to patronisingly as 'Jimmy', but the constant use of a term such as 'nigger', like 'native', reveals a worse tendency of Conrad and conventional 'white' people – a tendency to reduce 'coloured' people to an anonymous inferior mass, to be blind to or to refuse to see the individuality of each 'coloured' person. This generalised tendency includes less generalised fallacies which are revealed when Conrad wishes to bring out certain specific qualities of Wait: '. . . – a face pathetic and brutal: the tragic, the mysterious, the repulsive mask of a nigger's soul'. He considers Wait and all negroes as alike and as destined to have a common unsatisfactory character and a common hard fate. He thinks all of them have one kind of soul and a soul of a peculiar unsatisfactory kind. He shows a condescending sympathy ('pathetic', 'tragic') as if all negroes were in difficulties and these difficulties were in the nature of things. He recoils from and fears them ('brutal', repulsive'). He betrays an exotic interest in them and an incomprehension ('mysterious'). He speaks as if he is voicing proved points accepted by all mankind. This complex of feelings and reasoning reveals a limited understanding of and sympathy for Wait and his whole race that horrify me. Yet Conrad was extraordinarily intelligent and knowledgeable in many respects. He knew that there were widespread prejudices against the negroes: when this tale was first published in America (30 November 1897), he changed its title *The Nigger of the 'Narcissus'*, adopted in editions in Britain since the first (1897), to *The Children of the Sea* 'in deference to American prejudices'. But the conventional views were so influential and insidious that even people such as he succumbed unwittingly to certain prejudices especially when they knew little about negroes. He was no worse than, say, Thackeray. From New York, Thackeray wrote: 'Sambo is not my man and my brother; the very aspect of his face is grotesque and inferior'.[6]

Conrad's view of the negro, then, has an element of conventionality and these artistic deficiencies recur in a minor way. Yet the very choice of a negro for an important role during this extremely prejudice-ridden period indicates that his view has room for exceptional liberalism, too. Here is a scene representative of the action before the storm:

> He [James Wait] looked powerful as ever, but showed a strange and affected unsteadiness in his gait; his face was perhaps a trifle thinner, and his eyes appeared rather startlingly prominent. . . .
> He made a longer pause, during which he worked his ribs in an exaggerated labour of breathing. It was intolerable. . . .
> 'I tried to get a wink of sleep. You know I can't sleep o'nights. And you come jabbering near the door here like a blooming lot of old women. . . . You think yourselves good shipmates. Do you? . . . Much you care for a dying man!'
> . . . . .
> Men stood around very still and with exasperated eyes. It was just what they had expected, and hated to hear, that idea of a stalking death, thrust at them many times a day like a boast and like a menace by this obnoxious nigger. . . .

The tale is dramatised for the most part as this scene is – from the point of view of one of the European sailors aboard the 'Narcissus'. To him (and to Conrad), the reactions of the European seamen to Wait are evidently more important than the negro himself. The ordinary seamen are shown as disturbed by Wait partly because of an impercipience and irresolution in them and partly because Wait's appearance and behaviour make it extremely difficult for them to distinguish between the 'reality' and the 'sham'. The prose conveys the predicament of the seamen with precision and Wait's situation with an effective ambiguity. It suggests that Wait's illness is partly pretence ('affected unsteadiness in his gait', 'an exaggerated labour of breathing') and partly truth ('his face was perhaps a trifle thinner, and his eyes appeared rather startlingly prominent'). Conrad himself does not disclose the exact degree of dissimulation and genuineness and, partly as a consequence of this, the reader himself is drawn in to grapple with the problem posed by Wait (as in the case of Leggatt's guilt in *The Secret Sharer*).

A. J. Guerard argues that 'in certain early pages Wait is A Death, and a test of responses to death'. Similarly, Cecil Scrimgeour thinks that 'death, nature in one of her most impenetrable mysteries, is one of the ultimate realities [the sea is the other] against which the crew of the "Narcissus" have to measure themselves'.[7] It seems to me that the problem raised by Wait is, rather, one of equivocalness and that the question of his death is part of and intensifies it. Conrad's selection of a negro for such a role does not betray 'the taint of racism': if one applies Lanzmann's paradigm about Jews (quoted above) to negroes and to this tale, it turns out that the only negro in it is a shirker, but the negro is not the only shirker (Donkin, a European seaman, is another); the only negro is an unscrupulous self-seeker, but Donkin is no better. Donkin is contemptuous and crafty like Wait; and when he comes on board, he exploits the seamen as Wait does. They react to him as to the negro – with a complexity and tension of attitudes which include doubt, disdain, pity and 'the latent egoism of tenderness'. Their response to him prepares us for their reaction to Wait who appears later; the similarity of reaction is convincingly logical, given the similarity of the problem. But it also has a deep import: it suggests that their response to Wait is not something queer, elicited purely because he is a negro, but an expression of their basic nature.

Yet, in some ways, Wait is different from Donkin and his racial affiliations do matter. Donkin is a shirker, but he is not a malingerer like Wait who uses even death as a pretext; he is not as subtle and strong in personality. Indeed, as such, Wait is different from all the other seamen of the 'Narcissus'. In one way, his position is like that of Mrs Verloc in *The Secret Agent*, an ordinary incurious woman mixing with a double-dealing husband and a nest of revolutionists, or like that of Razumov in *Under Western Eyes*, a 'reasonable' follower of autocracy forced to become a slave of extreme absolutism, a law-abiding anti-revolutionary compelled to pose in Geneva as a revolutionary for the purposes of spying. Thus in this tale, Conrad is employing a method which became typical of him – placing a character in a context in which he or she is highly exceptional. Moreover, Wait is the only 'coloured' seaman aboard the 'Narcissus'; his colour accents his exceptionality. His role matters more than Donkin's, but it is not as important as Razumov's or even Mrs Verloc's. He is important, not in himself, but as the agent of a serious psycho-moral test for the European sailors. As an individual, he is the most prominent of the characters in the tale, and this is commensurate with his kind of secondary role; he is the agent of the most serious of the tests for the seamen and this applies to *all* of them, none of whom is a 'hero'. The title of the tale is, certainly, appropriate.

Its core is Conrad's balanced examination of the values of the Merchant Service. 'The courage, the endurance, the unexpressed faith, the unspoken loyalty that knits together a ship's company', their 'decencies' (to quote Conrad's words in the tale) enable the European seamen to deal with grave but straightforward and not unfamiliar problems such as those caused by the storm, by nature. But in this tale, these values do not equip them to cope with serious, unfamiliar, subtle problems such as those posed by Donkin and, above all, by Wait. Wait matters even during the storm: 'We had so far saved him; and it had become a personal matter between us and the sea'. The two major problems, Wait and the storm, interpenetrate. Thereby Conrad makes the problems of the seamen as acute as possible in the given context and tests the very essentials of their character, of their values. Wait continues his kind of dissembling, the ordinary seamen continue to be caught in their complex of feelings, Old Singleton and the officers continue to be unaffected by the negro. Conrad's comparative immaturity as an artist shows in his tendency to render these insights rather too much through description and analysis, at the expense of drama, yet the analytic descriptions are themselves acutely penetrating in their use of physical detail to embody moral qualities:

> Jimmy's steadfastness to his untruthful attitude in the face of the inevitable truth had the proportions of a colossal enigma – of a manifestation grand and incomprehensible that at times inspired a wandering awe; and there was also, to many, something exquisitely droll in fooling him thus to the top of his bent. The latent egoism of tenderness to suffering appeared in the developing anxiety not to see him die. . . . He was becoming immaterial like an apparition; his cheekbones rose, the forehead slanted more; the face was all hollows, . . .

Conrad focuses at times on the reactions to Wait of a few seamen (for instance, Donkin, Belfast and Podmore) as individuals. Here he analyses mass psychology. The portrayal of Wait here also demands attention. Earlier Conrad had suggested that he was ill but less so than he pretended to be; he knew this fact, but not the others. And the author did not indicate the exact degree of sickness. The situation is the same during the storm. But after it dies down, he clearly shows, as in this instance, that Wait is wasting away. He offers himself for duty when he is 'near enough to the pay table and smells the shore'. At this very time, he is more sick than he think he is, and the crew observe this; his imminent death, formerly a pretext, becomes a reality. The seamen 'wanted to keep him alive till the end of the voyage', even though they regard him as a blight. Only Singleton and Donkin do not wish him to live. Singleton considers him a blight which it would be an advantage to be rid of; Donkin wants to steal his belongings after his death. Wait is most friendly with the seaman who bears most malice towards him and is the only one to act in this way. Thus, Conrad is not dealing with a simple case of dishonesty. He is contemplating the complex ironies of a case where pretence is hard to distinguish from the objectively true.

The abstractions and touches of vague, pseudo-elevated rhetoric in Wait's presentation above are part of a minor strain of immature art in the tale. As such, it is a poor justification for Guerard's views which presumably rest partly on it: Wait is 'the mysterious Negro', 'the very convention of the novel is that Wait must remain shadowy, vast, provocative of large speculation, in a word symbolic', 'he comes in some sense to represent our human "blackness"',[8] and so on. Guerard's 'symbolic' view of Wait is also connected with an interpretation of him (made by Guerard himself and Cecil Scrimgeour) *as something the ship and the men must be rid of before they can complete their voyage*'.[9] This probably arises from a confusion of Conrad with his characters (the narrator included). After the storm Singleton voices this view and the rest of the ordinary seamen, including the narrator, think that 'the old man's ideas might be true'. But these 'ideas' are not endorsed by Conrad. At this stage in the tale, he is showing how the rationality of these men with 'average' minds has been weakened by psychological and physical strain so as to make them susceptible to false supernatural explanations and consolations. At a later stage, the crew quarrel over the question whether 'the glass started down' before or after Wait's death; it is soon after Wait's burial at sea that a 'fair wind' blows. In these instances, Conrad shows how coincidences are liable to take a false meaning for these men under strain, with their already-aroused superstitions. He does not invest the negro with the kind of symbolic extension of meaning, postulated by Guerard and Scrimgeour.

Wait, then, is a fully realistic character, and exceptionally important for a secondary one. He is far more important than the Congolese in *Heart of Darkness*, who appear mainly as the anonymous victims of imperialism, or Makola in An *Outpost of Progress*, who is the sardonic witness of what is presented as the typical 'white' man's doom on the fringes of a rapacious empire. Conrad never selected a negro to be a chief character. He is not, in this respect, a Cary. Wait stands as his fullest and most significant attempt to portray a negro, and my case is that the element of conventionality in his attitudes and the degree of artistic immaturity detract only slightly from the originality – as manifest in the choice of subject as in the rendering – which makes Wait the first outstanding negro character in British fiction.

The coolies in *Typhoon* (1903) play the same kind of role as James Wait, but they are presented differently. The core of *Typhoon* is the same as that of *The Nigger of the 'Narcissus'* and, indeed, of all Conrad's stories set chiefly in Far Eastern seas – an examination of the values of the Merchant Service. Naturally, it is the European sailors who matter most among the characters. The chief interest of *Typhoon* for Conrad and for us is the same as the interest felt by the author and his fellow seamen when they heard of the actual episode which inspired this tale: 'the extraordinary complication brought into the ship's life at a moment of exceptional stress by the human element below her deck' (the words are Conrad's).[10] The 'moment of exceptional stress' refers to the typhoon and 'the human element below her deck' to the coolies.

The Chinese pose a psycho-moral test to the seamen as did Wait, but they really matter as a group. None of them is important as an individual. The only Chinese who is presented as an individual at all is the clerk of the Bun Hin Company. At the beginning of the tale, Captain MacWhirr instructs Jukes to show him the arrangements aboard the Nan-Shan for the coolies:

> He was gruff, as became his racial superiority, but not unfriendly. The Chinaman, gazing sad and speechless into the darkness of the hatchway, seemed to stand at the head of a yawning grave.
>
> 'No catchee rain down there – savee?' pointed out Jukes. 'Suppose all'ee same fine weather, one piecie coolie-man come topside,' he pursued, warming up imaginatively. 'Make so – Phooooo!' He expanded his chest and blew out his cheeks. 'Savee, John? Breathe fresh air. Good. Eh? Washee him piecie pants, chow-chow top side – see, John?'
>
> With his mouth and hands he made exuberant motions of eating rice and washing clothes; and the Chinaman, who concealed his distrust of this pantomime under a collected demeanour tinged by a gentle and refined melancholy, glanced out of his almond eyes from Jukes to the hatch and back again. 'Velly good', he murmured, in a disconsolate undertone, and hastened smoothly along the decks, dodging obstacles in his course.

Here, and throughout the tale, Conrad is the omniscient narrator. Jukes appears a conventional amiable Englishman. He sees the clerk as 'John Chinaman' in the same way the 'English clerk in a Dutch House' in Sourabaya looks upon Schomberg's 'boy' in *Victory*. This term and notion are applied by conventional Westerners to the Chinese, as 'nigger' to the negroes. Jukes' speech and manner dramatise qualities which the author puts down explicitly in the ironical comment: 'He was gruff, as became his racial superiority, but not unfriendly'. Conrad does not follow the conventional image of the inscrutable or wily 'Chink': the clerk is presented as a critical but helpless member of a subject race ('gazing sad and speechless', 'disconsolate undertone'); in fact, he has more dignity and a keener consciousness than Jukes. He is not important enough in the tale even to be given a name and he makes only this brief appearance; but he is sketched as an individual. The image of 'a yawning grave' powerfully suggests the inhuman conditions under which the coolies are going to live. Thus Conrad can creatively present a balanced view of Jukes, a fellow 'white' man and a fellow seaman too, as well as of the clerk, an alien 'coloured' man of a subject race in an alien profession. He is free of the conventional Western misconceptions about and attitudes to Chinese; he can contemplate them critically when they appear in Westerners such as Jukes.

Just as the Indians were taken to Malaya, Ceylon and Africa, the Chinese were transported to the West Indies, Peru and Malaya by the British to provide labour for their profit-bringing ventures. When the Nan-Shan with the coolies on board is on the seas, the threat of a typhoon impels Jukes to speak to his captain:

'Rolling like old boots', he said sheepishly.
'Aye! Very heavy – very heavy. What do you want?'
At this Jukes lost his footing and began to flounder.
'I was thinking of our passengers', he said, in the manner of a man clutching at a straw.
'Passengers?' wondered the Captain, gravely. 'What passengers?'
'Why, the Chinamen, sir,' explained Jukes, very sick of this conservation.
'The Chinamen! Why don't you speak plainly? Couldn't tell what you meant. Never heard a lot of coolies spoken of as passengers before. Passengers, indeed! What's come to you?'
. . . . .
He [MacWhirr] raised his eyes, saw Jukes gazing at him dubiously, and tried to illustrate his meaning.
'About as queer as your extraordinary notion of dodging the ship

head to sea, for I don't know how long, to make the Chinamen comfortable; whereas all we've got to do is to take them to Fu-chau, being timed to get there before noon on Friday. If the weather delays me – very well. There's your log-book to talk straight about the weather. But suppose I went swinging off my course and came in two days late and they asked me: "Where have you been all that time, Captain?" What could I say to that? "Went around to dodge the bad weather", I would say. "It must've been damn bad", they would say. "Don't know", I would have to say; "I've dodged clear of it". See that, Jukes? I have been thinking it all out this afternoon'.

This scene is great sustained comedy. Jukes desperately refers to the Chinese to cover his concern for the ship and his fellow seamen; Mac-Whirr takes his words at their face value; Conrad's irony shows up Jukes' prevarication and MacWhirr's misunderstanding. Several ironies centre on the term 'passengers': the reader is aware that the term is absurd in the light of the already-exposed, living conditions of the Chinese, that Jukes does not use the term seriously because of his (already exposed) racialism, that MacWhirr has mistakenly taken it seriously. MacWhirr's reactions are perfectly in character. His literal-mindedness has already been established as one of his key traits. When he says, 'Never heard a lot of coolies spoken of as passengers before', it seems to me perfectly acceptable as the literal truth. V. G. Kiernan notes that the 'coolie trade' was called the 'pig trade' by dealers.[11] As Conrad suggests through these words of MacWhirr and in the earlier scene with the clerk, the attitudes of the Captain and his chief mate reflect general facts in the imperial world: 'white' men usually treated coolies as slaves, shipped them off as cargo, and were blind to their wrongs. These facts were based partly on the 'habit of the "higher" races', in Kiernan's words, 'to take comfort from supposing that the "lower races" did not feel things as sensitively as they did'.[12] Mac-Whirr shares in this habit, and to people such as he the comfort of the Chinese coolies would seem a ridiculous consideration. The scene contains other points of interest: MacWhirr is literal-minded about storms as about Jukes' words to him and the ironic humour exposes this as a limitation of his mind and as having a kind of courage; the unusual rolling of the ship does not disturb the phlegmatic MacWhirr, but it ironically suggests the validity of Jukes' advice and the 'rules' in books which the Captain does not believe in. British–Chinese relations are superbly integrated with the other aspects and the whole scene is presented through a unified ironic vision.

When the typhoon strikes the ship, more light is thrown on British–Chinese relations and their significance for the tale increases. The problems created by 'the wrath and fury of the passionate sea' (to use Conrad's words in the tale) draw forth the deeper qualities of Mac-Whirr and Jukes. As the seamen try to impose some order on the struggling mass of Chinese below deck, the speech of one of them 'penetrated Jukes with a strange emotion as if a brute had tried to be eloquent'. Jukes looks upon the Chinese as virtually animals. He is 'not unfriendly' towards them in normal circumstances, but under stress he thinks, 'What the devil did the coolies matter to anybody?' Thus the crisis serves to expose the full extent of the sense of superiority and the inhumanity in Jukes' racialism. On the other hand, at the same time it calls forth the best in MacWhirr:

'You left them pretty safe?' began the Captain abruptly, as though the silence were unbearable.

'Are you thinking of the coolies, sir? I rigged lifelines all ways across that 'tween-deck'.

'Did you? Good idea, Mr Jukes'.

'I didn't . . . think you cared to . . . know', said Jukes – the lurching of the ship cut his speech as though somebody had been jerking him around while he talked – 'how I got on with . . . that infernal job. We did it. And it may not matter in the end'.

'Had to do what's fair, for all – they are only Chinamen. Give them the same chance with ourselves – hang it all. She isn't lost yet. Bad enough to be shut up below in a gale –'.

The enormous difficulties and hazards involving the typhoon and (to a greater extent) the Chinese, particularly for a character such as Mac-Whirr whose career has been uneventful, have brought out remarkable reserves of courage, responsible competence and more. His racialism ('they are only Chinamen') and general unimaginativeness do not permit him to realise adequately the plight of the Chinese, but his humanity and sense of fairness extend to them, unwaveringly till the very end of a period of severe strain, the distribution of cash. Jukes himself, though more racial-minded, can be considered a good officer of the Merchant Service: he obeys his captain's orders even when they go against the grain; he carries them out bravely and efficiently. Conrad reveals more sympathy and approval for MacWhirr than for Jukes, and by playing them off against each other he implicitly 'places' both.

With the exception of the clerk, the Chinese are presented literally *en masse*. They begin to matter in the life of the ship when the typhoon strikes. The storm heightens the condition of the coolies as cargo; and Conrad creates an impression of 'an inextricable confusion' of commodities. The coolies are dehumanised because they are victims of the imperial economy which was run partly on the lines of slavery. The imperial economy is, of course, not Conrad's subject in this tale, but he gets to grips with its coolie aspect in so far as it enters his tale." He sympathises with the Chinese and, at the same time, he is never less than realistic. Here MacWhirr explains to Jukes why he distributed all the cash, collected by the seamen, equally among the coolies:

> You couldn't tell one man's dollars from another's, he said, and if you asked each man how much money he brought on board he was afraid they would lie, and he would find himself a long way short. I think he was right there. As to giving up the money to any Chinese official he could scare up in Fu-chau, he said he might just as well put the lot in his own pocket at once for all the good it would be to them.

Conrad presents MacWhirr's surmises as fair and he seems to me right. He could present a Chinese thus:

> Suddenly one of the coolies began to speak. The light came and went on his lean, straining face; he threw his head up like a baying hound. From the bunker came the sounds of knocking and the tinkle of some dollars rolling loose; he stretched out his arm, his mouth yawned black, and the incomprehensible guttural hooting sounds, that did not seem to belong to a human language, . . .

The extended animal analogy expresses exactly and powerfully the dehumanised, helpless state of the coolie and the impression he creates on a Westerner such as Conrad. The image is chilly, but it does not suggest a latent racialist prejudice. He employs an image of the same kind to present a European seaman during the same critical period: 'The second mate was lying low, like a malignant little animal under a hedge'. The animal analogy conveys the contemptible malice and cowardice of the European with the same sort of effectiveness. The question of racialism on the part of Conrad does not arise. Thus, he is remarkably impartial in his treatment of both races. This chilly side of his mind is a permanent characteristic and emerges most prominently in *The Secret Agent*. It is, probably, partly the consequence of an aristocratic aloofness, an aspect of the lasting influence of his origins. Both his father, Apollo Korzeniowski, and his mother, Eva Bobrowska, were from landowning families going back for centuries; in Poland the gentry formed a section of the nobility and was, indeed, as Zdzislaw Najder observes, 'the most important part of Polish society'.[13] Here is one instance of Conrad's persisting aristocratic tendencies in ordinary life, as recorded by Jerry Allen: 'To the French owners of his first ships, Delastang et Fils, he was "Conrad de Korzeniowski", the implied title and mannered airs earning him the nickname of "The Count" on the *Saint-Antoine*'.[14]

Conrad presents admirably the coolie system and all its ramifications in their secondary but not unimportant role in *Typhoon*, the interaction of the British, the coolies and Chinese officials in a whole range of situations. No doubt Conrad knew less about Chinese than about negroes: Bun Hin's clerk is a very minor character and speaks two words ('Velly good'), while the others are presented *en masse* and their speech is not rendered. But in presenting the Chinese, unlike in the case of James Wait, Conrad shows no sign of conventional Western prejudice and works perfectly within his capacity. Prejudice against the Chinese was less strong than against the negro. Westerners knew of great Chinese civilisations in the past but not of African civilisations; Chinese civilisation at that time, though in a state of decline, was not primitive, whereas such African civilisations as there had been had regressed into a primitive state. Conrad himself saw primitive conditions in the Congo without any knowledge of ancient African achievements and was thereby all the more conscious of the backwardness of the black cultures. Secondly, Westerners suffered more from guilt about the treatment of negroes than of Chinese, as the trade in negro slaves was conducted on a far larger scale and much more brutally than the trade in Chinese coolies. Moreover, *The Nigger of the 'Narcissus'* is a transitional work from Conrad's first two prentice novels to the artistic maturity which begins with *Typhoon*.[15]

3 Challenges and problems of the Far East (ii): Conrad's Malayan novels

> Greater Britain furnishes a convenient limbo for damaged characters and careers.
>
> J. A. Hobson, *Imperialism: A Study.*

The tasks which we have seen Conrad undertake in the tales set mainly in Far Eastern seas are tackled on a larger, more complex scale in his Malayan novels. In them he portrays fellow Europeans and alien peoples, not on board ships, but in environments completely alien to him. The novels are written during two distinct phases in his literary career – *Almayer's Folly* (1895), *An Outcast of the Islands* (1896) and *Lord Jim* during his maturation, *Victory* and *The Rescue* during his artistic decline. They reflect their respective phases of composition and can therefore be discussed in chronological order. But it is also necessary to keep in mind what they have in common.

The most important figures in Conrad's Malayan works are usually Europeans – Almayer in *Almayer's Folly*, Willems in *An Outcast of the Islands*, Jim in *Lord Jim*, Heyst in *Victory* and Lingard in *The Rescue*. The only Malayan chief characters are Arsat in *The Lagoon* (1898) and Karain in *Karain, A Memory* (1898), but these stories are very short and, to use Conrad's comment on *Karain*, 'magazine'ish'.[1] In the case of the prominent European characters, Conrad employs his characteristic method of placing major characters in contexts in which they are highly exceptional. All of them are at a stage of civilisation different from the Malayans and have markedly different motives. Just as the dark complexion of the 'nigger' accents his exceptionality among the 'white' sailors of the *Narcissus*, the 'whiteness' of the Europeans accents their exceptionality among the brown Malayans.

Conrad's settings are markedly isolated and remote – Sambir in his

52

first two novels, Arsat's clearing in *The Lagoon*, the 'corner of Mindanao' in *Karain*, Patusan in *Lord Jim*, Sourabaya and Samburan in *Victory*, Carimata, the Shore of Refuge and the Land of Refuge in *The Rescue*. The social position of the Europeans in such places is different from that of those in Chandrapore in Forster's *A Passage to India* or in Rimi in Cary's *The African Witch*. The latter are generally cut off from indigenous society, but form exclusive societies of their own. In Conrad's kind of milieux, however, there are only one or two Europeans. They may live with a 'native' woman with whom they have more or less insufficient *rapport*, and are cut off from indigenous society. Their link with their own civilisation is tenuous: their only usual contact with it is through a steamer which may call once a month or more infrequently. Thus they are placed in very isolated and extreme situations which make for Conrad's kind of concentrated contemplation of life. These make the human drama 'stand out with a particular force and colouring', test and disclose the essentials of human character and values. These are situations analogous to those on the ships in 'complete isolation from all land entanglements',[2] caught in a storm or a 'calm'. Moreover, as in the tales with sea settings, the more searching tests for the Europeans here are posed by human complications rather than by nature. Almayer finds himself in difficulties, not because of the menace of his Malayan surroundings, but because the promise of riches held out by Lingard is always too tempting for him to resist. Jim dies because he cannot cope with Gentleman Brown. Heyst's life ends disastrously, not because of the inhospitableness and extreme isolation of his island, but because he is unable to tackle the desperadoes. Thus Conrad's characteristic sources of strength are found in his Malayan fiction. But have they been used well?

Let us examine the human drama. In the first three novels, the most important characters are Europeans, but the Malayans are not insignificant. Almayer and Willems are driven by a ruling passion to 'make their pile'. They represent the category of Europeans who are prepared to go to even remote imperial outposts to do this and those among them who deteriorate physically and morally in these places.[3] Almayer wishes to realise his ambitions in an easy way by 'inheriting' Lingard's wealth, but Lingard imposes a condition:

> He wanted Almayer to marry his adopted daughter. 'And don't you kick because you're white!' he shouted, suddenly, not giving the

surprised young man the time to say a word. 'None of that with me! Nobody will see the colour of your wife's skin. The dollars are too thick for that, I tell you! . . .'

Startled by the unexpected proposal, Almayer hestitated, and remained silent for a minute. He was gifted with a strong and active imagination, and in that short space of time he saw, as in a flash of dazzling light, great piles of shining guilders, and realised all the possibilities of an opulent existence. . . . As to the other side of the picture – the companionship for life of a Malay girl, that legacy of a boatful of pirates – there was only within him a confused consciousness of shame that he a white man – . . . He had a vague idea of shutting her up somewhere, anywhere, out of his gorgeous future. Easy enough to dispose of a Malay woman, a slave, after all, to his Eastern mind, convent or no convent, ceremony or no ceremony.

He lifted his head and confronted the anxious yet irate seaman.

'I – of course – anything you wish, Captain Lingard'.

Conrad's criticism of Lingard's sense of 'white' racial superiority is implicit in the excess in Lingard's consciousness of his 'adopted daughter's' colour and in his defensiveness. Almayer shares Lingard's sense of superiority and is callous in addition. Conrad's criticism of Almayer is implicit in the way he shows how Almayer suppresses his racial prejudice and cruelty in order to express a reluctant compliance with Lingard, in his detached description of Almayer's mind as 'eastern' though he is Dutch. One looks forward eagerly to complications in Almayer's 'mixed' marriage and fortunes partly because Conrad has a sense of the equality among races and a balanced critical sense; these are qualities likely to help him to see deep into the fate of a European in a Malayan context. Almayer's marriage is the cue for the novel to shift to its main setting, Sambir, and for Malayans to enter the narrative.

In Sambir, Almayer suffers reversals of his expectations:

Almayer went on struggling desperately, but with a feebleness of purpose depriving him of all chance of success against men so unscrupulous and resolute as his rivals the Arabs. The trade fell away from the large godowns, and the godowns themselves rotted piecemeal. The old man's banker, Hudig of Macassar, failed, and with this went the whole available capital. The profits of the past years had been swallowed up in Lingard's exploring craze. Lingard was in the interior – perhaps dead – at all events giving no sign of life. Almayer stood alone in the midst of those adverse circumstances, deriving only a little comfort from the companionship of his little daughter, born two years after his marriage, and at the time some six years old. His wife had soon commenced to treat him with a savage contempt expressed by sulky silence, only occasionally varied by outbursts of savage invective.

The blows to Almayer's financial prospects are put in bald, cursory fashion. Even more damaging is the fact that key points in personal relations and character-change are put in the same way – Almayer's loss of morale, his marital problems and the regression of his wife into a primitive state. The general overbalance of reportage at the expense of drama affects all sides of the action.

But Conrad does not disappoint us completely. Almayer's fate does evoke an interest. The frictions of his 'mixed' marriage and also his reversals of fortune are dramatised significantly at times, as in the scene when the Dutch officers arrive in Sambir to arrest Dain:

'You have had enough, Almayer,' said the lieutenant, as he lighted a cigar. 'Is it not time to deliver to us your prisoner? I take it you have that Dain Maroola stowed away safely somewhere. Still we had better get that business over, and then we shall have more drink. Come! don't look at me like this.'

Almayer was staring with stony eyes, his trembling fingers fumbling about his throat.

'Gold,' he said with difficulty. 'Hem! A hand on the windpipe, you know. Sure you will excuse. I wanted to say – a little gold for a little powder. What's that?'

'I know, I know', said the lieutenant soothingly.

'No! You don't know. Not one of you knows!' shouted Almayer. 'The government is a fool, I tell you. Heaps of gold. I am the man that knows; I and another one. But he won't speak. He is –'.

The interaction of the officers and Almayer is rich in ironies. Almayer mistakenly thinks that Dain is dead and feels that his prospects have been ruined; he tries to momentarily lose his bitter sense of failure by getting drunk and by pulling their leg. But not only is Dain not dead, his being alive is not going to help Almayer. The officers are mistaken both in their belief that he has Dain 'stowed away' as a live prisoner and in their later belief that Dain is dead. Conrad conveys both the pathos and humour of this scene at the same time. Almayer's failure and the ironies at his expense make him a pathetic figure. There is humour in his joke at the expense of the officers, in their credulity and in their various efforts to cope with an intoxicated shattered European. One can sense here the power with which the mature Conrad drama- tises major preoccupations of his such as failure in isolation, human frailty and the evils in life in European settings as in the presentation of the Verlocs or Razumov.

Almayer's fate is tied up with the role of the Malayans. Indeed, the love relationship of Dain and Nina is the other equally important centre of interest in the novel, and it is integrated with the Almayer theme: Almayer seeks to get hold of gold with Dain's help; it is with his daughter that Dain falls in love. Finally, the Almayer theme hinges on the love theme: when Dain and Nina decide to escape from Sambir, leaving Almayer to his own devices, Dain's departure implies the end of his hopes of riches and Nina's departure implies the end of half his 'dream of wealth and power' in Europe which would be 'witnessing her triumphs'. The complexities of Nina's side of the love relationship are clear in the scene when she is about to flee with Dain:

'You speak like a fool of a white woman', she [Mrs Almayer] ex- claimed. 'What do you know of men's anger and of men's love? Have you watched the sleep of men weary of dealing death? Have you felt about you the strong arm that could drive a kriss deep into a beating heart? Yah! you are a white woman, and ought to pray to a woman god!'

'Why do you say this? I have listened to your words so long that I have forgotten my old life. If I was white would I stand here, ready to go? Mother I shall return to the house and look once more at my father's face'. [Nina]

'No!' said Mrs Almayer, violently. 'No, he sleeps now the sleep of gin; and if you went back he might awake and see you. No, he shall never see you. When the terrible old man took you away from me when you were little, you remember –'

. . . . .

Between those two beings so dissimilar, so antagonistic, she stood with mute heart wondering and angry at the fact of her own exist- ence. . . . With the coming of Dain she found the road to freedom by obeying the voice of the new-born impulses, and with surprised joy she thought she could read in his eyes the answer to all questionings of her heart.

Nina's vacillations between Almayer and his wife, 'between those two beings so dissimilar, so antagonistic', is usually put in the cursory rhetorical reportage of the latter half of the passage above. In fact, whatever Conrad probes directly in the Malayan novels, whether it be Nina's tensions, the changes within Almayer and his marital problems in *Almayer's Folly* or the conflicts within Lingard in *The Rescue*, the result is often much the same. Edward Crankshaw was sweeping but on the right track when he said of Conrad: 'He was aware intellectually of the other man's state of mind, just as he could be aware intellectually of concrete phenomena unseen by him, but he was unable to transform an intellectual concept into a sensuous image, to dramatise a state of mind. . . . we find that he was an analytical psychologist of a most distinguished order, but not a creative psychologist at all'.[4] I think Conrad can be a fine 'creative psychologist': in parts of *Under Western Eyes*, he does dramatise in a sustained, sensuous way the mind of Razumov, say, when he is suffering from the agonies of leading a double life. But Conrad usually needs an indirect vehicle for his analytical powers like, say, Marlow or the teacher of languages. It is partly because he did not find one in *Almayer's Folly*, *An Outcast of the Islands*, in *Victory* for the most part and *The Rescue* that his exploratory hand in these novels is weak. Still, at times he has insights into the minds of both the Europeans and the Malayans, and these create an impact on the reader when dramatised: in the first part of the passage above, the actions and speech (in simple English with a Malayan flavour) of the two convent-educated Malayans convey how Mrs Almayer's balance has been undermined by her experiences at the hands of certain Europeans, her hatred of and contempt for her husband and Europeans in general, her dominating influence over Nina and Nina's wavering. As the last part of the passage above shows, the release of a conventionally romantic kind of love in Nina for Dain is plausible in the given circumstances, but it is not rendered convincingly.

Dain's love for Nina, like her love for him, is of a conventionally romantic kind. Here is Conrad's presentation of their first impressions of each other:

From the very first moment when his eyes beheld this – to him – perfection of loveliness he felt in his inmost heart the conviction that she would be his; he felt the subtle breath of mutual understanding passing between their two savage natures, and he did not want Mrs Almayer's encouraging smiles to take every opportunity of approaching the girl; and every time he spoke to her, every time he looked into her eyes, Nina although averting her face, felt as if this

bold-looking being who spoke burning words into her willing ear
was the embodiment of her fate, the creature of her dreams –
reckless, ferocious, ready with flashing kriss for his enemies, and
with passionate embrace for his beloved – the ideal Malay chief of
her mother's tradition. . . .

Theirs is love at first sight; but this is not justified by circumstance and
is presented more perfunctorily in Dain's case than in Nina's. Still,
Conrad's awareness of their 'Malayanness', their 'savageness', the
mixed and contending influences in Nina's life, his critical view of
romantic love implicit in the parenthetic qualification ('. . . this – to
him – perfection of loveliness . . .'), all hold out interesting developments. But the promise is not fulfilled. The touches of realistic complications in the Dain–Nina relationship are buried under an exotic
sentimentality.

An Outcast of the Islands has only one major centre of interest, the
affairs of Willems, and two non-European women play a central role in
them. Like Almayer, he marries an alien, Joanna, for the sake of ambition, feels that he has lowered himself, and does not strike a reciprocal
relationship with her. His rapid professional success ends abruptly
when he is dismissed by Hudig for embezzling; he is spurned by his
wife and her family. Lingard rescues him and sends him to Sambir. The
phase in Macassar is sketched quite interestingly at points – for example, the rejection of Willems. It is a necessary prelude to and remains
connected to the main drama in Sambir; Willems's relationships
with Lingard and Joanna play an important part in his 'tragedy' in
Sambir.

In this novel Conrad's interests in personal relationships are rather
different from those in his first novel. The relationship of Almayer and
his wife hardly matters. We noticed a similarity between Almayer's and
Willems's marriages. But Joanna is different from Mrs Almayer;
she is a town 'half-caste'. Willems's relationship with her takes place in
Macassar and, towards the close of the novel, in Sambir. The relationship of Willems and Aissa is one between a European and a Malayan
without experience of Western civilisation. It takes place entirely in
Malayan-occupied areas in Sambir and dominates the action. Willems
is, in part, a figure from exotic romance, the European enslaved by the
seductive 'native' woman. But does their relationship develop on much
the same lines as that of Dain and Nina? Here are some of their first
reactions to each other:

To her he was something new, unknown and strange. He was bigger, stronger than any man she had seen before, and altogether different from all those she knew. He was of the victorious race. . . . He had all the attractiveness of the vague and the unknown – of the unforeseen and of the sudden; of a being strong, dangerous, alive, and human, ready to be enslaved.

She felt that he was ready. She felt it with the unerring intuition of a primitive woman confronted by a simple impulse. . . .

Every day she came a little nearer. He watched her slow progress – the gradual taming of that woman by the words of his love. . . .

This prose is the repetitive rhetorical reportage, familiar to us from the first novel. Yet it contains suggestions of realistic complexities of feeling. These lead to 'the richly ironic scene after Willems virtually promises Abdulla that he would betray Lingard, the scene when Willems's pretences assuage Aissa's sense of insecurity. There follows the scene when Willems's racial prejudices well over soon after Aissa saves him from being murdered by her father, the scene when he continues to want her but recoils from her whole race. Later, his feelings towards her change significantly, as revealed in this scene which he shares with Lingard and Aissa:

'She begged me for your life – if you want to know – as if the thing was worth giving or taking!'

'And for three days she begged me to take yours', said Willems quickly. . . .

'Ah! She is a ferocious creature', he went on. 'You don't know . . . I wanted to pass the time – to do something – to have something to think about – to forget my troubles till you came back. . . . She, a savage. I, a civilised European, and clever! She that knew no more than a wild animal! Well, she found out something in me. She found it out, and I was lost. I knew it. She tormented me. . . .'

Lingard listened, fascinated and amazed like a child listening to a fairy tale, and, when Willems stopped for breath, he shuffled his feet a little.

'What does he say?' cried out Aissa suddenly.

The two men looked at her quickly, and then looked at one another.

. . . . .

'I don't want to die here'.

'Don't you?' said Lingard, thoughtfully.

Willems turned towards Aissa and pointed at her with a bony forefinger.

'Look at her! Always there. Always near. Always watching . . . for something. Look at her eyes. Ain't they big? Don't they stare? You wouldn't think she can shut them like human beings do. . . . The eyes of a savage; of a damned mongrel, half-Arab, half-Malay. They hurt me! I am white! I swear to you I can't stand this! Take me away. I am white! All white!'

He shouted towards the sombre heaven, proclaiming desperately under the frown of thickening clouds the fact of his pure and superior descent. He shouted, . . . a being absurd, repulsive, pathetic and droll. . . .

The interaction of Willems, Lingard and Aissa is competently dramatised. Conrad sees deep into the mind of Willems, a prejudiced, self-seeking European who has 'gone native'. The crumbling of his morale is conveyed in his unbalanced speeches – in his recoil from Aissa, his hallucinatory fear of her, and his acute sense of his 'degradation'. A wise authorial irony operates beyond his consciousness. He has already betrayed Lingard, and now he tries to win his favour by another betrayal, by betraying Aissa; all his betrayals work against his expectations. Aissa's devotion, especially as it emerges obliquely in the opening words of Lingard and Willems and in the last words of Willems, is a kind of implicit indictment of Willems. Her inability to understand the conversation of the Europeans, underlined by her single question, points up Willems's cruelty and her pathetic position. Lingard appears a dignified figure of justice. Conrad's racial objectivity is virtually explicit in his remarks on Willems as 'a being absurd, repulsive, pathetic, and droll'. It helps him and is indeed necessary for him to present the kind of relationship between Willems and Aissa, realistically and in depth at times.

Conrad does not share the commonly accepted views of 'going native' which were held by eminent contemporaries in various fields. Sir Hugh Clifford, one of the most distinguished British colonial administrators in Malaya, said of Maurice Curzon, the hero of his novel, *A Freelance of Today*:

The air of latent energy which inspired the whole man, even in repose, marked him for a white man of the white men – a masterful son of the dominant race; yet circumstance and inclination had combined to well-nigh denationalise him, to make him turn from his own kind, herd with natives, and conceive for them such an affection and sympathy that he was accustomed to contrast his countrymen unfavourably with his Malayan friends. This, be it said, is not a wholesome attitude of mind for any European, but it is curiously common among such white men as chance has thrown for long periods of time into close contact with Oriental races, and whom Nature has endowed with imaginations sufficiently keen to enable them to live into the life of the strange folk around them.[5]

Clifford considers Curzon a representative 'denationalised' European and dissociates himself from such men. He explicitly comments on Curzon's 'attitude of mind' as 'not wholesome for any European'. He is sympathetic to the Malayans but, at the same time, feels that Europeans should maintain their own identity. This conviction derives partly from his conventional assumption of 'white' racial superiority which is evident in the fulsome description of Curzon as 'a white man of white men – a masterful son of the dominant race' and in the expression 'herd with natives'. Benjamin Kidd, the sociologist, argued:

in climatic conditions which are a burden to him; in the midst of races in a different and lower stage of development; divorced from the influences which have produced him, from the moral and political environment from which he sprang, the white man does not in the end, in such circumstances, tend so much to raise the level of the races amongst whom he has made his unnatural home, as he tends himself to sink slowly to the level around him.[6]

Kidd's thesis betrays the same assumptions and feelings as Clifford's notion of 'denationalisation'.

Conrad's racial objectivity is more important in *Lord Jim* as Jim, unlike Almayer and Willems, is closely involved with the whole indigenous society. The circumstances and motives which take him to Patusan are very different from those that took Almayer and Willems to Sambir. He is an adolescent romantic idealist who feels neurotically 'the lost honour' (in Conrad's words)[7] of having 'jumped' off the *Patna* in an emergency. He faces the *Patna* inquiry, but after that he is able to work in a place only as long as he feels the episode is not known there. So he moves on from one place to another till Marlow accurately perceived: 'He wanted a refuge, and a refuge at the cost of danger should be offered him – nothing more'. Thus, Patusan offers Jim 'a refuge' and a romantic opportunity to redeem his honour. Indeed, the first movement of the Patusan phase of *Lord Jim* renders how it became a refuge for Jim and how he rehabilitates himself. There are weaknesses in Conrad's presentation – for instance, the touch of popular melodrama in Jim's escape from Tunku Allang and in the rout of Sherif Ali; the romantic element in Jewel's portrayal as a sort of guardian angel at the beginning of her relationship with Jim. But the predominant impression is one of critical realism. It emerges in Marlow's narration of a part of his visit to Jim after he had established himself as the 'white lord' of Patusan:

> He had to give in to my arguments, because all his conquests, the trust, the fame, the friendships, the love, – all these things that made him master had made him a captive, too. He looked with an owner's eye at the peace of the evening, at the river, at the houses, ... but it was they that possessed him and made him their own to the innermost thought, to the slightest stir of blood, to his last breath. ...
> Now and then, though, a word, a sentence would escape him that showed how deeply how solemnly, he felt about that work which had given the certitude of rehabilitation. That is why he seemed to love the land and the people with a sort of fierce egoism, with a contemptuous tenderness.

Jim has turned his trading area in a remote developing country into a State. He reaches this position after siding with the rightful Malayan chief, Doramin, against the pretender, Tunku Allang, as James Brooke had set himself up as the 'Rajah of Sarawak (known in the East as the White Rajah)' after joining 'the Sultan of Brunei Proper – Omar Ali' against the rebel Makota.[8] Patusan has given Jim an opportunity to develop from a romantic in dream to a romantic in action. It holds him in the paradoxical position of both 'master' and 'captive'. Though his stay there has been already long, eventful and deeply affecting, his sense of racial superiority shows itself to be too deep-seated to be eradicated; it is betrayed by his 'contemptuous tenderness'. Marlow sensitively records these feelings and also Jim's 'fierce egoism', but he is too conservative to see anything wrong with them. Still, the terms given Marlow by Conrad are instinct with criticism and through them the author implies his criticism of Jim which is beyond Marlow's mind.

In fact, Marlow is even prepared to accept these opinions of the anonymous person whom Conrad neatly calls 'the privileged man', the person to whom Marlow addresses his written account of the final phase of the action:

> You said also – I call to mind – that 'giving your life up to them'
> (*them* meaning all of mankind with skins brown, yellow, or black in
> colour) 'was like selling your soul to a brute'. . . . In other words,
> you maintained that we must fight in the ranks or our lives don't
> count. Possibly! You ought to know – . . .

These opinions are part of the privileged man's view of Jim's kind of
life in Patusan. Conrad's critical approach to 'the privileged man' is
implied in his appellation itself. Jim's attitudes to the Malayans belong
to the category of people such as Hugh Clifford and Benjamin Kidd.
The opinions of 'the privileged man' belong to the much larger class of
people who held the same attitudes in a more callous, self-righteous
form; one of them was Charles Kingsley who, in a letter to J. M.
Ludlow, justified Rajah Brooke's extermination of the Dyaks:
'Sacrifice of human life?' Prove that it is *human* life. It is beast-life.
These Dyaks have put on the image of the beast, and they must take
the consequence. . . .[9]
The careers of Jim and Lingard, who becomes a 'hero' in *The
Rescue* after his secondary roles in *Almayer's Folly* and *An Outcast of
the Islands*, are justified by imperial realities. Jocelyn Baines notes that
'there were, at the time of Conrad's service on the *Vidar* and earlier, a
number of white men, traders or adventurers, who had established
themselves is out-of-the-way places and gained influence over the local
native rulers'. He instances the actual Lingard, Wyndham and James
Brooke.[10] But if we glance at the whole history of European activities
in Asia, we notice as early as the seventeenth century such figures as
Samuel White, the most notable of the 'Interlopers', and Constant
Phaulkon in the kingdom of Siam; we see a very long tradition of
'British Free Merchants'. Conrad's Jim and Lingard belong to this
tradition. For their portraits he turns to, at least, the careers of the real
Lingard and James Brooke, as Baines and Norman Sherry have
shown.[11] Thus Conrad is trying to present a conspicuous aspect of
imperial social realities, not a melodramatic figment, and is basing
himself on some of them. Given these facts, one has to examine further
the value of his presentation.
Jim's role as 'white lord' is presented solidly in terms of both everyday social life and activity in times of crisis. His ordinary tasks such as
settling the problem of the 'old fool's' divorce or the problem of the
'rotten turtles eggs', body forth dramatically his 'contemptuous ten-

derness'. When the narrative moves to a crisis, his place in Patusan society is spotlighted; it is brought out clearly in his actions after his parley with Gentleman Brown:

> Jim went into one of the houses, where old Doramin had retired, and remained alone for a long time with the head of the Bugis settlers. . . .
> 'Tamb' Itam behind his chair was thunderstruck. The declaration produced an immense sensation. 'Let them go because this is the best in my knowledge which has never deceived you', Jim insisted. . . . most of them simply said that they 'believed Tuan Jim'.
> . . . . .
> But if Jim did not mistrust Brown, he was evidently anxious that some misunderstanding should not occur, ending perhaps in collision and bloodshed. . . . 'I am responsible for every life in the land', he said. . . . 'There's no sleep for us, old girl', he said, 'while our people are in danger'.

Jim is conscious of his achieved position. He exercises the powers of a revered ruler and shoulders the responsibilities of one. The other side of the relationship, how his 'subjects' treat him, is clearer when they try to tackle the problem of Brown in his temporary absence:

> All the events of the night have a great importance, since they brought about a situation which remained unchanged till Jim's return. . . . Beloved, trusted and admired as he [Dain Waris] was, he was still one of *them*, while Jim was one of *us*. Moreover, the white man, a tower of strength in himself, was invulnerable, while Dain Waris could be killed. Those unexpressed thoughts guided the opinions of the chief men of the town, . . .

Jim, being a person from a developed country, has shown himself to be so much more efficient than the Malayans that they have begun to consider his efficiency as something miraculous. He adds to his prestige because he belongs to the 'ruling race' in these colonies and because of his very complexion which is different from that of the Malayans and associated with efficiency and power. Conrad dramatises convincingly how they, because of their backwardness, accept themselves to be racially inferior, the inverse of 'white' people who believe in their racial superiority. Indeed, they regard Jim virtually as a deity and one of their own able leaders, Dain Waris, as a mere mortal, in much the same way (as Alfred Russel Wallace records) the Malayans of Sarawak had looked up to James Brooke when he established his sway: 'They naturally concluded that he was a superior being, come down upon earth to confer blessings on the afflicted. In many villages where he had not been seen, I was asked strange questions about him. Was he not as old as the mountains? Could he not bring the dead to life?'[12]

Conrad's presentation of the general texture of social life rings true. He highlights certain particular, personal relationships. The most important of them is Jim's association with Jewel. I noted the touch of the guardian angel in Jewel's portrayal at the beginning of their relationship; she watches over him and saves him from death. But the course of their love is often rendered with sufficient realism and depth to be convincing. Jim feels indebted to Jewel for saving him from death, sympathises with her because of her sufferings under Cornelius, and is constantly in her company. These factors help him to realise, though late, that she loves him and that his own feelings have developed into love for her. His love is romantic, and this is perfectly in character: Jewel is the name he chooses for her. She has a mixed Malayan–European parentage and her experience is limited to Patusan. Conrad employs Marlow as a narrator and as a participant in the action to help present their relationship. His dramatisation of the tensions of the relationship is particularly interesting; take the scene when Jewel waylays Marlow, during his visit to Patusan, to seek an assurance that Jim would not desert her:

... 'They always leave ·us,' she murmured. The breath of sad wisdom from the grave which her piety wreathed with flowers seemed to pass in a faint sigh. . . . Nothing, I said, could separate Jim from her.
. . . . .
She knew him to be strong, true, wise, brave. He was all that. Certainly. He was more. He was great – invincible – and the world did not want him, it had forgotten him, it would not even know him.
. . . . .
'Why' she murmured. I felt that sort of rage one feels during a hard tussel. The spectre was trying to slip out of my grasp. 'Why?' she repeated louder; 'tell me!' And as I remained confounded, she stamped with her foot like a spoilt child. 'Why? Speak'. 'You want to know?' I asked in a fury. 'Yes!' she cried. 'Because he is not good enough', I said brutally. . . .

'This is the very thing he said . . . You lie!'
The last two words she cried at me in the native dialect. . . .

Conrad reveals sustained dramatic power in presenting this long delicate interaction of a European and a Malayan, which conveys among
other things the attachment of Jewel and Jim, her fatalistic insecurity,
their failure to achieve mutual understanding, the inability of both Jim
and Marlow to make her grasp Jim's weakness and true position in the
outer world. The dialogue and actions render precisely a shifting complex of thoughts and feelings. Conrad has that insight into an alien
mind necessary to show Jewel using her 'native dialect' when she
speaks from her deepest emotional springs. For her English is an acquired foreign tongue which has not become part of her essential
personality and is not commonly spoken in Patusan; soon after
Marlow comes to know her, he reports: 'Her mother had taught her to
read and write; she had learned a good bit of English from Jim, and she
spoke it most amusingly, with his own clipping, boyish intonation'.
Thus Conrad carefully justifies the kind of speech he gives her. Her
inability to understand Jim had made her over-value him. After he has
gone to his romantic death, the same inability makes her under-value
him with fatalistic prejudice of a member of a subject race against a
member of the 'ruling race':

'What have I done?' she asked with her lips only.
'You always mistrusted him', I [Marlow] said.
'He was like the others', she pronounced slowly.
'Not like the others', I protested, but she continued evenly,
without any feelings:
'He was false'.

The extended development of this relationship – between two people
different in racial origins, character and cultural experience who are
not able to bridge the gulfs between them – is often presented
movingly.

Jim's role in Patusan society in general and his relationship with
certain individuals do matter, but these words of Marlow deserve
attention: '. . . In other words, you ["the privileged man"] maintained
that we must fight in the ranks or our lives don't count. Possibly! You
ought to know – . . . The point, however, is that of all mankind Jim had
no dealings but with himself, . . .'. Marlow's point is an overstatement
partly because he is pushed to an extreme by the need to resist pron-

ouncements of a person such as 'the privileged man', but it goes to the core of Jim's case. Jim came to Patusan for romantic personal, not social, reasons. His successes in Patusan are undercut by ironies. He becomes its 'white lord'; but he is cut off from its society and is aware that this society does not understand him. He finds a companion in Jewel, but his hope that she will come to understand him is not fulfilled. Thus he suffers from 'the loneliness of his soul'. It is to the outer European world that he feels finally answerable for all his actions. He feels that his place is there and that he has not yet won it back. He has not built up sufficient confidence to re-enter that world. Thus he has found 'refuge' in Patusan and 'honour' in Malayan eyes, but his deepest needs remain unalterably European-oriented and are not sufficiently satisfied by them. That is why he is vulnerable to Gentleman Brown: 'He asked Jim whether he had nothing fishy in his life to remember . . .'. Brown and his men present Jim with another emergency and test, though different in circumstances from those on board the *Patna*. These men are 'emissaries' of the European world. Because of his neurotic sense of his past disgrace and of his unfitness for that world, he is unable to deal effectively with them; his first failure is one fundamental cause for the second. The prose at this point in the novel is rich in irony because Brown plays upon Jim's 'weakest spot' more deeply than he knows. Jim's deficiencies prompt him to propose that Brown and his men should be granted 'safe-conduct'; the Malayan chiefs agree. When the ruffians break their word, he shoulders his responsibility and faces certain death despite Jewel's passionate attempts to make him change course:

> . . . They say that the white man sent right and left at all those faces a proud and unflinching glance. Then with his hand over his lips he fell forward, dead. . . . For it may very well be that in the short moment of his last proud and unflinching glance, he had beheld the face of that opportunity which, like an Eastern bride, had come veiled to his side.

Jim's fate is poignant in its tragic ironies. It is only in death that he finds contentment, that he is able to seize an 'opportunity' to live up to his incurable, egoistic–romantic ideals. His death does not win him a place and 'honour' in the European world he esteems. At the same time, he loses his position and 'honour' in the only world which revered him but which he did not value sufficiently. He sticks to his 'Europeanness' in a developing Malayan milieu without adjusting himself sufficiently to make for contentment.

The main significance of Jim's drama is psycho-moral, but its social import is not negligible. Jim's position as 'white lord', the fate of Jewel and Dain Waris, the fortunes of Patusan do matter. The workings of Malayan society and the roles of individual Malayans contribute to the total meaning in their own right. In this novel the texture of social life is denser and the drama more consistently realistic than in Conrad's first two novels. The fiction derives distinctive strength and significance from the interaction of individuals, both the Europeans and the Malayans, and the interaction of these individuals with Patusan society.

Victory and *The Rescue* are markedly different from Conrad's early Malayan novels. Let us first consider *Victory*. Axel Heyst, like Willems and Jim, is virtually a protagonist. But all those who play a decisive role in his drama are Europeans – his father, Morrison, Lena and the desperadoes. The Malayans are referred to as part of the background, but they never come on stage. Indeed, *Victory* is unique among the Malayan novels in this respect. The only 'coloured' characters who appear as *dramatis personae* are the three Chinese immigrants, and they are very minor figures.

Heyst's character is strikingly dissimilar to all Conrad's earlier Europeans in the Malay Archipelago. He scorns mankind.

> Heyst was not conscious of either friends or of enemies. It was the very essence of his life to be a solitary achievement, accomplished not by hermit-like withdrawal with its silence and immobility, but by a system of restless wandering, by the detachment of an impermanent dweller amongst changing scenes. In this scheme he had perceived the means of passing through life without suffering and almost without a single care in the world – invulnerable because elusive.

Thus when he goes to Samburan, he is not running away from life but coping with it in a peculiar way. His extreme scepticism, like that of Decoud in *Nostromo*, goes with rootlessness; and in this way, both of them bear affinities to Conrad's own sensibility. Moreover, in the case of Heyst, to these is added isolation, another condition familiar to Conrad. Thus, Heyst is particularly close to the author. True insight makes Conrad place Heyst in a developing region; as Hobson puts it in his words which form a part of the epigraph to this chapter, 'Greater

Britain furnishes a convenient limbo for damaged characters'. Heyst does not recover from the damage caused to his mind when young by the influence of his deeply unhappy cynical father.

A convincing impression of 'white' colonial society in the tropics is created by the accumulation of a wealth of authentic features: there are the white suits, cork helmets and pipe-clayed white shoes of the Europeans; there is the apartheid in Schomberg's hotel. But Heyst lives, not in this exclusive society of Sourabaya, but on a distant island without any company until he takes Lena there. A part of his drama takes place in Sourabaya, but most of it in Samburan. Conrad's central concern in *Victory* is with Heyst's affairs. Thus the success of the novel depends on his presentation of Heyst's drama, not on his evocation of European society in Sourabaya.

The key to Heyst's plight lies in these words of the anonymous narrator of the early phases of *Victory*: '. . . his detachment from the world was not complete. And incompleteness of any sort leads to trouble'. What essentially makes Heyst vulnerable is an humanity which has not been killed by his scepticism. It goes out to decent people in distress and makes him appreciate worthiness; it leads to ties with certain people. His first relationship is with Morrison. He pities the unbusinesslike trader and helps him financially. He is unable to resist participation in Morrison's activities and even becomes 'the manager on the spot of the Tropical Belt Coal Company, with offices in London and Amsterdam'. As the opening of the novel suggests, his humanity extends to developing countries:

> We doubted whether he had any visions of wealth – for himself, at any rate. What he seemed mostly concerned for was the 'stride forward', as he expressed it, in the general organisation of the universe, apparently. He was heard by more than a hundred persons in the islands talking of a 'great stride forward for these regions'.

He is idealistic in a conventionally Victorian optimistic way, but his motives win our respect; they are the reverse of Almayer's and Willems's. His involvements meet with disaster: Morrison dies, before long, on a visit to England and the Tropical Belt Coal Company soon goes into liquidation. Heyst detaches himself from 'facts' again, but these setbacks leave their mark: he feels 'a sort of shame before his own betrayed nature'; he suffers absurdly from 'remorse' over Morrison's death and from a new 'sense of loneliness'. His appreciative kindness remains: he confessed to Davidson, 'I am touched by your humanity', because he 'understood in a proper sense the little *Sissie's* periodical appearance in sight of his hermitage' after his reversals.

These episodes, indeed all episodes of the first part of the novel, are rendered efficiently. Heyst comes alive dramatically as a complex and developing character. But our interest flickers when his relationship with Lena occupies the centre of the stage. This is the first time that Conrad presents a relationship between a 'white' man and a 'white' woman in a developing country. It brings about the more important developments in Heyst and, indeed, forms the body of the drama. His humanity makes him pity Lena, and she is glad to be rescued from Zangiacomo's orchestra. Their feelings for each other at the beginning are very romantic, and this is plausible given their respective circumstances: though thirty-five years old, Heyst has not as yet become friendly with any woman and Lena appeals to him; Lena has suffered from miseries since childhood; Heyst is her rescuer and he is a distinguished person. But Conrad's very presentation of their relationship as it develops, is vitiated by a conventional romanticism. The final developments in their relationship and in Conrad's themes take place when the three desperadoes, Jones, Ricardo and Pedro, enter the drama. And Conrad lapses into melodrama when he portrays them. But now let us ponder the *dénouement* to which all the trends in the novel lead. To break through the 'sense of incompleteness' in their love, Lena wishes to prove her feelings for Heyst by undertaking the dangerous task of getting hold of Ricardo's weapon. She dies in the attempt, and her death scenes form the climax of the novel. Her death brings out ironically the novel's positive significance. It is useless as far as her relationship with Heyst or their lives as individuals are concerned (Heyst commits suicide soon afterwards). At the same time, on her side, it is a victorious assertion of love – victorious because Heyst finally recognises the full value of her love for him and of love as a valuable human quality in a general sense. On his side, it leads to this recognition of love and complementary qualities, to a final triumph over lifelong deep scepticism: these are 'practically the last words he said to' Davidson: 'Ah, Davidson, woe to the man whose heart has not learned while young to hope, to love, – and to put its trust in life!' Here Conrad, however, is putting the novel's positiveness in terms which are explicit, sentimental and unnecessary. The prominence of sentimentality and melodrama in the presentation of Heyst and Lena and their affairs reduce their lifelikeness, and make Lena especially a simplified character. The positive values are unexceptionably humane; but these artistic weaknesses and the moral tag enfeeble their affirmation. In fact,

Conrad's method of affirmation suggests that he is seeking ethical consolation rather than facing life whole and steadily; this tendency forms a marked contrast to, say, the naked and unflinching disillusion of *The Secret Agent*.

In *The Rescue*, the two major characters are, as in *Victory*, a European man, Lingard, and a European woman, Mrs Travers. But its themes are different and the Malayans are not unimportant. Like Lord Jim, Lingard is treated as an overlord by the Malayans in his trading area and he desires honour. But he is closer to the known 'British Merchant Adventurers': one of his main motives is to 'make his pile'. As a wandering and independent trader, his area is enormous, not one small place like Patusan; the Rajah Laut is far more powerful than the Tuan. His concern is to win and maintain honour, not to redeem it. Thus he is like Jim in certain ways and, at the same time, so different in others that he is a personality in his own right.

Lingard is saved from death at the hands of Papuans by Hassim, a Malayan prince.

... 'Will you burn the village for vengeance?' asked the Malay with a quick glance down at the dead Lascar who, on his face and with stretched arms, seemed to cling desperately to that earth of which he had known so little.

Lingard hesitated.

'No', he said, at last. 'It would do good to no one'.

'True', said Hassim, gently, 'but was this man your debtor – a slave?'

'Slave?' cried Lingard. 'This is an English brig. Slave? No. A free man like myself'.

'*Hai*. He is indeed free now', muttered the Malay with another glance downward. 'But who will pay the bereaved for his life?'

'If there is anywhere a woman or child belonging to him, I – my *serang* would know – I shall seek them out', cried Lingard remorsefully.

'You speak like a chief', said Hassim, 'only our great men do not go to battle with naked hands. O you white men! O the valour of you white men!'

. . . . .

'Your country is very powerful – we know', began again Hassim after a pause, 'but is it stronger than the country of the Dutch who steal our land?'

'Stronger?' cried Lingard. He opened, a broad palm. 'Stronger? We could take them in our hand like this –' and he closed his fingers triumphantly.

'And do you make them pay tribute for their land?' enquired Hassim with eagerness.

'No', answered Lingard in a sobered tone; 'this, Tuan Hassim, you see, is not the custom of white men. We could, of course – but it is not the custom'.

'Is it not?' said the other with a sceptical smile. 'They are stronger than we are and they want tribute from us. And sometimes they get it – even from Wajo where every man is free and wears a *kris*'.

There was a period of dead silence while Lingard looked thoughtful and the Malays gazed stonily at nothing.

'But we burn our powder amongst ourselves', went on Hassim, gently, 'and blunt our weapons upon one another'.

Conrad has noted precisely both Lingard's and Hassim's behaviour. That is why he can present so convincingly the interaction between the 'white rajah' who is humane but rather conservative and the Malayan rajah who is sensible but not quite 'emancipated'. Conrad has responded sensitively and critically to both sides of a colonial situation. On the European side, he suggests Lingard's civilised humanity as well as his national pride, the operation of 'double standards' when 'white' men deal with people of their own colour and when they deal with 'coloured' people. On the Malayan side, he suggests Hassim's primitive idea of revenge, his naive sense of racial inferiority to the 'white' men as well as his quick understanding of the discriminatory use of power by 'white' men and his ironic sense of the weakening of Malayan opposition to this kind of militarism because of internal strife.

When Hassim is forced by an usurper to flee from his kingdom, Lingard promises to restore him, his sister Immada and their followers to their rightful place in Wajo. But when Lingard is about to begin the final stage of his self-imposed task of honour, he has to decide whether, before this, he should rescue the Europeans in a yacht stranded on the Shore of Refuge. His decision is made difficult because he finds himself being attracted to the only woman on board and, to make matters more complicated, she is the wife of the owner of the yacht:

'I expect you to be generous', she said.
'To you?'
'Well – to me. Yes – if you like to me alone'.

'To you alone! And you know everything!' His voice dropped.
'You want your happiness'.

She made an impatient movement and he saw her clench the
hand that was lying on the table.

'I want my husband back', she said sharply.

'Yes. Yes. It's what I was saying. Same thing', he muttered with
strange placidity. She looked at him searchingly. He had a large
simplicity that filled one's vision. . . . The glamour of a lawless life
stretched over him like the sky over the sea down on all sides to an
unbroken horizon. Within, he moved very lonely, dangerous and
romantic.

. . . . .

He seemed to be tasting the delight of some profound and amazing
sensation. And suddenly in the midst of her appeal to his generosity,
in the middle of a phrase, Mrs Travers faltered, becoming aware
that she was the object of his contemplation.

'Do not! Do not look at that woman!' cried Immada. 'O! Master
– look away. . . .' Hassim threw one arm round the girl's neck. Her
voice sank. 'O! Master – look at us'. Hassim, drawing her to himself,
covered her lips with his hand.

Mrs Travers represents love and the Malayans represent honour. The
clash of love and honour, the novel's central theme, is put in terms of a
psychological exploration of the tensions within the characters. It is
externalised, too. Conrad's critical sense of Lingard, virtually the protagonist, is almost explicit, say, when he describes him as 'very lonely,
dangerous and romantic'. More interesting is Conrad's critical–ironic
exposure of all the characters as he presents them movingly in dramatic interaction – Lingard's 'simplicity' in his failure to suspect the
lovelessness of Mrs Travers's marriage; his love for the married
woman which dominates his mind; she imposing her will for the sake
of the Europeans of the yacht, regardless of the Malayans; the naive
impulsiveness of Immada's appeals to Lingard over which Hassim
exercises a mature restraint. Conrad presents his central theme rather
diagrammatically. This kind of arrangement is acceptable when competently dramatised as here – even though the clash of honour and love
within Lingard is not very intense because his love is far more powerful
than his sense of honour. Yet the organisation often looks crude because his language often is in his poor vein. This kind of style appears
briefly here: 'He seemed to be tasting the delight of some profound and
amazing sensation'.

The overall vision of life created by the Malayan novels is sombre. The challenges of living in remote Eastern places are too difficult for any of the leading European characters to realise his ambitions and hopes; the consolations these places offer people such as Lord Jim and Heyst are equivocal and short-lived. *Karain* is Conrad's only work set in the Malay Archipelago in which (as he said) 'the ending is cheerful',[13] and it is a 'magazine'ish' piece which cannot alter our impression of Conrad's pessimism.

Conrad, then, had approached the East as a place testing human character or as a kind of purgatory in his tales set chiefly in Eastern seas and race relations under imperialism entered *The Nigger of the 'Narcissus'* and *Typhoon*. The central approaches to the East in the novels are more varied. Sambir is a place where the Europeans, Almayer and Willems, go to 'make their pile'; Patusan is a place where a humiliated European goes for refuge and rehabilitation; Samburan is for Heyst a retreat from life; the Archipelago in *The Rescue* is a suitable environment for the career of a 'merchant-adventurer' who finds he is torn between loyalties to his own race and the subject race. Inside this range certain characters and situations are repeated without sufficient change and this indicates limitations in Conrad's vision: Lingard as a 'merchant-adventurer' appears in three novels, *Almayer's Folly*, *An Outcast of the Islands* and *The Rescue;* Almayer appears unchanged in both Conrad's earliest novels; Almayer and Willems are alike in their greed; Lingard offers Willems a refuge in Sambir, while Marlow and Stein offer one to Jim in Patusan; Gentleman Brown and his men in *Lord Jim* are in character and function like the desperadoes in *Victory*: they are criminals from the outer world who undo the 'protagonists'.

Victory apart, the Malayans are not unimportant in these novels; but all except Dain and Nina play secondary roles. Their fates are not developed to a conclusive point. Malayan life is seen under fewer aspects than European life: it has mainly to do with the politics of intrigue involving foreigners, and with the struggles for power within the tribes. Moreover, Conrad's presentation of these aspects has a certain sameness. The politics of intrigue played by Tunku Allang and Kassim in *Lord Jim* and by Daman and Tengga in *The Rescue* are different; but it is the same in both *Almayer's Folly* and *An Outcast of the Islands* with the same chief participants, Babalatchi and Lakamba. The struggles for power between the Doramin–Dain group and the Allang–Kassim group in *Lord Jim* and the Belarab group and the Tengga–Daman group in *The Rescue* are not identical in form, but essentially not very different.

By contrast Sir Hugh Clifford places a wide range of Malayans at the centre of numerous stories. The eponymous heroine of *Wan Beh, The Princess of the Blood* falls into difficulties because of her passion for a commoner, the Panglima. The chief in *The Weeding of the Tares* abuses his power to gratify his lust, and kills brave Daman to force his wife, Minah, to join his household. The hero of *The Fate of Leh, the Strolling Player* is a kind of minstrel whose ability to captivate the interest of the women in Kelantan incurs the fatal displeasure of certain men. Unlike Conrad, Clifford penetrates very deeply into Malayan culture, ranging from the marital conventions of royalty in *Wan Beh, Princess of the Blood* to the special habits of commoners during pregnancy in *Umat*; he even brings in closed ceremonies such as the *bângun* in *The Quest of the Golden Fleece*:

> Then for the first time, O'Hara understood what was happening to him. He had often heard of the ceremony known to the wild Mûruts as a *bângun*, which has for its object the maintenance of communication between the living and the dead. He had even seen a pig hung up, as he was now hanging, while the tamer Mûruts prodded it to death very carefully and slowly, charging it the while with messages for the spirits of the departed, and he remembered how the abominable cruelty of the proceeding had turned him sick . . .[14]

Clifford sees this ceremony only from the viewpoint of a European as an 'abominable cruelty'; he cannot show it from the Malayan point of view too. Evidently it takes a Cary to present so alien an event as a witch-trial (the trial of Osi in *The African Witch*) from both European and African viewpoints. Clifford's presentation is awkward, 'literary' reportage. This want of success in presenting Malayan culture, for all the range that he attempts, cannot be because writers are unable to present centrally and well a culture alien to them. Graham Greene in *The Quiet American* can render a love affair between an Englishman and a Vietnamese in a way that does justice to the individuality of both. Joyce Cary selects Africans to be the most important characters in three out of his four Nigerian novels, and renders centrally various situations of people alien to him with powers beyond even Conrad in his Malayan fiction. Clifford's fiction suffers basically from his lack of talent. Yet its content suggests the richness and variety of experience in Malayan regions. Conrad had the talent but not the experience, yet great talent can make a few glimpses of an environment go a long way. *Victory* and the Patusan phase of *Lord Jim* are clearly above the conventionally exotic. We-can endorse Clifford's judgement, especially authoritative coming from such a man, that in English literature Conrad was 'the supreme interpreter of Malaya'.[15]

4 Conrad's Malayan novels: problems of authenticity

> And, behold, here was a writer, of whose very existence I had not previously heard, at work in the same field and displaying withal a degree of finish, a maturity and originality of style, a sureness of touch and a magical power of conveying to his readers the very atmosphere of the Malayan environments, which to me was so familiar, yet whose knowledge of the people, about whom he wrote with such extraordinary skill, was superficial and inaccurate in an infuriating degree.
>
> Hugh Clifford, 'Concerning Conrad and his work'.

Conrad was in the Far East between 1883 and 1888, but the actual time he spent there was no more than a year. Moreover, his Eastern experiences were gained as second mate of the *Palestine*, first mate of the *Vidar*, and master of the *Otago*. As an active seaman, he spent little time ashore.[1] Thus, his first-hand experience of Eastern countries and peoples was slight. Indeed, Norman Sherry estimates that Conrad spent altogether only about twelve days (three days each during the four times the *Vidar* called) at Tandjong Redeb,[2] which he transmutes into Sambir and Patusan in his fiction. Given his extremely slight experience of the Malay Archipelago, it is in a way a logical consequence that the authenticity of his Eastern fictive world should be called in question. But is it as false as it has been often made out (by writers like Hugh Clifford and F. R. Leavis)?[3]

Let us first examine Conrad's presentation of the Malayan setting. Its quality in his first two novels is much the same as in *The Rescue*. One can put one's finger on it by comparing a typical passage from Conrad with a typical and similar passage from an average contemporary writer about Malaya such as Clifford. Here is Conrad (in *Almayer's Folly*):

> As he skirted in his weary march the edge of the forest he glanced now and then into its dark shade, so enticing in its deceptive appea-

rance of coolness, so repellent with its unrelieved gloom, where lay, entombed and rotting, countless generations of trees, and where their successors stood as if mourning, in dark green foliage, immense and helpless, awaiting their turn. Only the parasites seemed to live there in a sinuous rush upwards into the air and sunshine, feeding on the dead and the dying alike, and crowning their victims with pink and blue flowers that gleamed amongst the boughs, incongruous and cruel, like a strident and mocking note in the solemn harmony of the doomed trees.[4]

Here is Clifford (in 'The East Coast'):

These forests are among the wonderful things of the Earth. They are immense in extent, and the trees which form them grow so close together that they tread on one another's toes. All are lashed, and bound, and relashed, into one huge magnificent tangled net, by the thickest underwood, and the most marvellous parasitic growths that nature has ever devised. No human being can force his way through this maze of trees, and shrubs, and thorns, and plants, and creepers; and even the great beasts which dwell in the jungle find their strength unequal to the task, and have to follow game paths, beaten out by the passage of innumerable animals, through the thickest and deepest parts of the forest.[5]

The emphasis in the first passage is on nature dead or dying and, in the second, on nature alive; but both are alike in their concern with nature in its raw plenitude. They are not purely factitious descriptions of 'the Malayan exotic' (in Leavis's phrase).[6] Both writers are trying to render genuinely Malayan settings, and their observations are accurate. But the touches of striking, human metaphor for inanimate nature in the Clifford, unlike in the Conrad, are lost in the obtrusively literary rhetoric. Descriptive epithets such as 'countless', 'immense', 'most marvellous' can be considered, at best, only vaguely impressive; the impressiveness is soon lost in the woolliness and exaggeration. This kind of description occurs in both passages. Conrad's prose is less repetitive and less artificial than Clifford's. But the laboured effects in both appear to arise from an identical source – the struggle of European writers who are trying to come to terms with environments alien to them and render them in terms suited to Western readers for whom they would generally be even more unfamiliar. Still, when Conrad comes to *Lord Jim*, he develops 'that special power of conjuring up for the reader an alien environment'[7] and retains it to much the same degree in *Victory*:

> Patusan is a remote district of a native-ruled state, and the chief settlement bears the same name. At a point on the river about forty miles from the sea, where the first houses come into view, there can be seen rising above the level of the forests the summits of two steep hills very close together, and separated by what looks like a deep fissure, the cleavage of some mighty stroke. . . .[8]

The spoken idiom is rather plain; but it is clear and has a living naturalness. The locale here is presented as it strikes a sensitive observer (Marlow, when he first sees it); it thereby gains immediacy and verisimilitude. Yet, Conrad's main settings, whether in *Almayer's Folly* or *Lord Jim*, are rendered with sufficient precision to make them identifiably Malayan, but without a high degree of specification which would locate them in particular places in Malaya. London in *The Secret Agent* is nothing but London, whereas Sambir or Patusan is not Tandjong Redeb in Eastern Borneo and nothing else besides. Of course, some regions within the same country, whether it is tropical or temperate, usually resemble one another. But Conrad's descriptions themselves possess a general quality which works with this likeness, to make it possible for them to be taken as relating to a number of regions in the Malay Archipelago. This factor contributes to the general significance of the novels, which is that they reflect life in the Archipelago as a whole and life in a universal sense.

Let us consider the role of the Malayan environment in Conrad's novels. J. I. M. Stewart argues that 'external nature as a sinister and alarming mystery constitutes – it is perhaps not too much to say – the central emotional focus of the novel' [*Almayer's Folly*].[9] But his reasoning appears unconvincing to me. It is true that Conrad at times refers to 'external nature as a sinister and alarming mystery'; but this manner of description, as in the extract analysed above, is usually part of Conrad's failure to present well the alien surroundings and is not 'central'. It is also true, for instance, that Almayer calls Sambir 'this infernal place' when he feels that his hopes are shattered after Dain Maroola's supposed death; it is true that Dain imagines that Nina and he 'would be together on the great blue sea that was like life – away from the forests that were like death'. But such references by the characters are infrequent and are evoked by particular occasions. They do not contribute to build the kind of central symbolism Stewart posits –

the jungle which 'speaks mysteriously of deeply buried dreads' and is set over against the ocean, the way out to happy civilised living.[10]

There are two characteristic ways by which the setting becomes more than surroundings. One way is evident in the scene in *Victory* when Heyst and Lena are contemplating the threat to their lives posed by the arrival of desperadoes, a threat particularly serious as Wang has stolen their revolver and left them:

> Beyond the headland of Diamond Bay, lying black on a purple sea, great masses of cloud stood piled up and bathed in a mist of blood. A crimson crack like an open wound zigzagged between them, with a piece of dark red sun showing at the bottom. Heyst cast an indifferent glance at the ill-omened chaos of the sky.

Conrad is using nature to charge the atmosphere in a simple theatrical 'pathetic-fallacy' manner. At other times he attempts to link the natural scene with the human situation more closely, as when Willems first sees Aissa in *An Outcast of the Islands*: 'She seemed to him at once enticing and brilliant – sombre and repelling: the very spirit of that land of mysterious forests, . . .'. Willems views the 'native' woman as a symbol of her tropical environment in a way typical of exotic romances.

In Conrad's Malayan fiction, then, the alien surroundings whether their presentation is undistinguished as in *Almayer's Folly*, *An Outcast of the Islands* and *The Rescue* or competent as in *Lord Jim* and *Victory*, appear clearly authentic. They seem rather conventionally exotic only during his infrequent attempts to relate them actively to the human drama. He has the good sense to see all his characters, European and Malayan, in true relation to both the imperial system and the Malayan social system. We noticed that Europeans are usually at the centre of his Malayan novels and that, except in *Victory*, the Malayans are not unimportant. His kind of emphasis suggests that his perspective is European, but it is not distorted: the Europeans enjoyed an importance in the colonies enormously out of proportion to their numbers because they belonged to the 'ruling race' if not to the ruling nation; indeed, the Europeans in Conrad's Archipelago were in a more powerful position than those in Kipling's India, during the same period too, because the country was more 'undeveloped'.

The world of his Eastern novels was ruled by the Dutch and, to a very small extent, by the Portuguese and Spanish. In *Lord Jim*, Gentleman Brown had travelled among Spanish settlements and had been

arrested by a Spanish patrol. In *Victory*, the crookedness of Portuguese officials in Timor is illustrated by the way they tried to cheat
Morrison. The novels, however, are set almost wholly in Dutch terri-
tory. Among his milieux, only Macassar in *An Outcast of the Islands*
and Sourabaya in *Victory* are important enough to have a number of
Europeans who form exclusive societies. We noticed that his chief
settings are all remote. The characters afford insights into Dutch rule
in the course of their actions and conversations. Lingard is a powerful
'British Free Merchant'; it is he who appoints Almayer and Willems,
the two Dutchmen, to Sambir. Stein, a Bavarian, traded in dangerous
areas such as Patusan 'by special permit from the Dutch authorities';
Cornelius, a Portuguese, and Jim, an Englishman, are his nominees.
Moreover, both the large-scale traders and their agents enjoy a considerable measure of independence. Thus, Conrad shows how the
Dutch allowed other Europeans to trade rather freely on the outskirts
of their empire and even set up pockets of influence. But the overall
sway of the Dutch is felt even in these spots: Babalatchi intrigues with
the Arabs to oust them; Hassim speaks of 'tributes' paid by the Malayans to them; Jewel and Hassim are openly defeatist. The Dutch as
colonial masters enter the outposts directly only once – when certain
officers come to Sambir to arrest Dain Maroola. We have seen how
effectively Conrad dramatises their encounter with Almayer.

Conrad, then, conveys an accurate impression of Dutch rule in so
far as it affects his milieux. It is interesting to find that he strives to
depict life in these places as it actually moves in its complex way. But
his presentation of the interaction of Dutch rule, other European col-
onialists, the Arabs and Malayan society is not wholly successful.
Intrigue and villainy play a prominent part and they have a real social
basis in his kind of developing milieux. Yet they set him delicate
artistic problems: with the same material, Conrad could write *The
Secret Agent* and Alfred Hitchcock make *Sabotage*. Let us first examine the European side: take Cornelius and Gentleman Brown in *Lord
Jim*, Jones, Ricardo and Pedro in *Victory*. Cornelius is a trading agent
who tries to oust and even kill another, Jim, to save his position by
scheming with Brown and his men, as well as with Malayans (Kassim,
Tunku Allang and their men). When he guides Brown and his men
through a secret tributary to attack Dain Waris, the episode appears
melodramatic. But his treachery often takes the form of convincingly
human drama. Conrad skilfully presents his overwrought attempt to
persuade Jim to accept his 'little plan wherein for one hundred dollars
– or even for eighty – he, Cornelius, would procure a trustworthy man

to smuggle Jim out of the river, all safe'; with equal skill, Conrad dramatises Cornelius' behaviour soon after:

> Then Cornelius appeared from somewhere, and, perceiving Jim, ducked sideways, as though he had been shot at, and afterwards stood very still in the dusk. At last he came forward prudently, like a suspicious cat. 'There were some fishermen there – with fish', he said in a shaky voice. 'To sell fish – you understand'. . . . It must have been then two o'clock in the morning – a likely time for anybody to hawk fish about!
>
> Jim, however, let the statement pass, and did not give it a single thought. . . .

Cornelius's absurdly defensive actions and speech betray his guilt and cowardice. Jim's nonchalance reveals his courage and happy unawareness of Cornelius' viciousness. Gentleman Brown is different from the Portuguese. He belongs to the category of European ruffians who prowl around developing countries, cruder versions of the 'Interlopers'. As Conrad puts it in the novel,' What distinguished him from the ordinary buccaneers like Bully Hayes or Pease was the arrogant temper of his misdeeds and a vehement scorn for mankind at large and for his victims in particular'. Conrad's account of how Brown captured his schooner is cursorily melodramatic, but Brown is usually a credibly human villain as in his key scene with Jim which was discussed above.

Jones in *Victory* bears a certain similarity to Brown who 'was supposed to be the son of a baronet'; Jones claims to be a 'gentleman'. Both carry over into the criminal world something of the airs of their former 'social sphere'. But Jones is not violent as Brown is, and, when violence is necessary, he directs his men to use it. The essential differences between Jones, Ricardo and Pedro are suggested by Heyst's description to Lena when she sees them for the first time from her bungalow: '. . . Here they are before you – evil intelligence, instinctive savagery arm in arm. The brute force is at the back . . .'. But the three desperadoes do not become symbols of these qualities. There are other similarly explicit attempts to endow them with a symbolic importance: Lena sees Ricardo as 'the embodied evil of the world' (when she employs duplicity to save Heyst); Jones regards himself as 'a sort of fate' (as he talks to Heyst shortly before he learns of Lena's presence on Samburan). An acceptable symbolic extension of meaning is almost impossible in their presentation because, in the first place, they do not come alive sufficiently as real human beings. Leavis thinks that they are 'a kind of Morality representation, embodiments of counter-potentialities',[11] but it seems to me that Conrad does not follow allegorical modes as Leavis suggests. When Shakespeare depicts the witches in *Macbeth*, he starts from contemporary popular belief and life, and presents them as embodiments of evil; he does not attempt to make the witches human and they remain moral forces throughout the play. Conrad's villains, however, are not allegorical figures of this type. Nor do they resemble figures from a Morality play like *Everyman*: the writer of such a play commences with moral concepts and, then, tries to lend them human interest. Conrad's method of portraying the desperadoes is not allegorical but symbolic. He begins with human beings[12] and, then, tries to invest them with a symbolic moral significance. But his effort in this direction is a failure, as I indicated above. M. C. Bradbrook is wrong to consider Jones 'the Living Skeleton, the Heart of Darkness';[13] none of the criminals gains a serious symbolic significance. Still, because they are not exactly like the villains of popular melodramatic fiction, say, of Peter Cheyney, Leslie Charteris or 'Sapper', who begin from nothing but melodramatic convention and remain within this convention, they offer an human interest. It is marked in their early appearances in Schomberg's hotel:

> The secretary retracted his lips and looked up sharply at Schomberg, as if only too anxious to leap upon him with teeth and claws.
> Schomberg managed to produce a deep laugh.
> 'Ha! Ha! Ha!'
> Mr Jones closed his eyes wearily, as if the light hurt them, and looked remarkably like a corpse for a moment. This was bad enough; but when he opened them again, it was almost a worse trial for Schomberg's nerves. The spectral intensity of that glance, fixed on the hotel-keeper (and this was most frightful), without any definite expression, seemed to dissolve the last grain of resolution in his character.
> 'You don't think, by any chance, that you have to do with ordinary people, do you? inquired Mr Jones, in his lifeless manner, which seemed to imply some sort of menace from beyond the grave.
> 'He's a gentleman', testified Martin Ricardo with a sudden snap of the lips, after which his moustaches stirred by themselves in an odd, feline manner.

The 'discomfiture' of the pusillanimous Schomberg and the breakdown of his 'resolution' appear completely human. Jones's quietly menacing

speech and demeanour as well as Ricardo's crude actions and sense of
social inferiority are realised as fully as if they were part of any domestic scene, lurid though they could easily have become. The key to
Conrad's descriptions of all three desperadoes is found in Schomberg's
reaction to them as 'a spectre, a cat, an ape' (shortly before he directed
their attention to Heyst). All their actions are too often conceived
within the framework of these three exaggerated analogies, and this
is partly why they soon begin to appear cardboard melodramatic
caricatures rather than human criminals. As they play a larger role
in *Victory* than all the other characters and as they play an important
role in its *dénouement*, the weakness in their presentation mars the
novel more than any other.

The various kinds of intrigue and villainy on the Malayan side of
the colonial context convey the same mixed impression of realism and
melodrama, but they are usually linked with political considerations.
These characteristics are exemplified by *Almayer's Folly*. The cunning
way by which Dain escapes the Dutch officers – the use of the dead
body of one of Dain's boatmen after dressing it as if it were his own
and battering its face – is a glaring and gruesome instance of melodrama. But the intriguing of Babalatchi and Lakamba – to get rid of
the Dutch influence with the help of the Arabs, to trade with the latter
and find out the location of Lingard's goldfield – is often put
realistically:

'If the Orang Blanda come here, Babalatchi, and take Almayer to
Batavia to punish him for smuggling gunpowder, what will he do,
you think?'

'I do not know, Tuan'.

'You are a fool', commented Lakamba, exultingly. 'He will tell
them where the treasure is, so as to find mercy. He will'.

Babalatchi looked up at his master and nodded his head with by
no means a joyful surprise. He had not thought of this; there was a
new complication.

'Almayer must die', said Lakamba, decisively, 'to make our secret
safe. He must die quietly, Babalatchi. You must do it'.

Babalatchi assented, and rose wearily to his feet. 'To-morrow?'
he asked.

'Yes; before the Dutch come. He drinks much coffee', answered
Lakamba, with seeming irrelevancy.

Babalatchi stretched himself yawning, but Lakamba, in the
flattering consciousness of a knotty problem solved by his own

unaided intellectual efforts, grew suddenly wakeful.

'Babalatchi', he said to the exhausted statesman, 'fetch the box of music the white captain gave me, I cannot sleep'.

A prominent feature of Babalatchi's appearance is his single eye, but this does not necessarily make him a melodramatic villain: 'a fine old one-eyed fellow called "Souboo"' was among Captain Sherard Osborn's Malayan seaman.[14] Both Babalatchi and Lakamba appear very human plotters. The unsuccessful 'statesman' is in low spirits and the usually inefficient chief is animated as he feels he has hit upon certain bright ideas. They speak of death and murder imperturbably; Lakamba casually suggests to Babalatchi a specific method of murder when he refers to Almayer's coffee-drinking habit. Murderous intrigue, as suggested above, was an ordinary occurrence in places such as Sambir. The primitive chief uses an opera of Verdi from a hand-organ as a lullaby, a kind of ironic situation to be had in developing societies coming into contact with the West.[15] Indeed, all Conrad's insights here come off as authentically Malayan drama. He is aware of a need to fashion an English equivalent for the Malayan vernacular of his characters. Terms like 'Tuan' and 'Orang Blanda' are obviously Malayan; they are part of a simple idiom which is differentiated from Standard English in its structures. It is an alien English which is alive and sounds natural. Hugh Clifford attempts to meet the same need when Panglima tries to dissuade Wan Beh from accompanying him through 'the rebel party' in *Wan Beh, Princess of the Blood*:

'Whither goest thou?' he asked.
'With thee, sweetheart', she said simply.
'Thou can'st not', said he shortly. . . .
. . . Malay-like his energy was not equal to arguing the point further. 'Let her be', he said to his followers. 'She for ever made trouble for me; it is her custom. What can one do? *Kras hati ta' takut mati* – the hard heart feareth not to die! Let her be'.

The speech of both characters has been fashioned crudely and appears extremely artificial. The English is stilted and full of archaisms. It is awkward to transliterate a Malay proverb and follow this with an English translation; indeed, such a thing would hardly occur in private conversation between Malayans.

The politics in Conrad's Malayan world is mainly intrigue. What are its directions and how accurate is Conrad's portrayal of them?

Arnold Kettle refers to Dain Waris and Hassim, and says: 'these young Malayan aristocrats are conceived as Polish rather than Malayan nationalists'.[16] V. S. Pritchett goes further along the same lines: he thinks that Conrad's Malayans 'are really transplantations from Polish history'.[17] Firstly, are the Malayans nationalists? Let us discuss this question mainly in relation to the Malayans in Patusan (*Lord Jim*). Dain Waris is content to accept unquestioningly Jim's foreign over-lordship as if it were in the natural order of things; the other members of his community hold Jim in even greater awe. Before Brown came to Patusan, it is Doramin alone who thinks in terms of a successor to Jim. To Doramin's mind, the issue of a successor arises only after Jim of his own accord decides to leave Patusan. Moreover, Doramin's 'secret ambition' is to see his son 'ruler of Patusan' – that is, as a tribal chief. He is disturbed by the possibility that Jim's stay, if permanent, may prevent his son's succession; but he never thinks of requesting or forc-ing the 'white lord' to step aside. When he shoots Jim in the last scene, he is executing tribal justice. Let us now look at the opponents of the Bugis. They accept Jim's sway and stop their usual active hostilities towards the Bugis. But the attitudes of their leaders, Tunku Allang and Kassim, change in response to the new situation created by the arrival of Brown and his men:

> Kassim disliked Doramin and his Bugis very much, but he hated the new order of things still more. It had occurred to him that these whites, together with the Rajah's followers, could attack and defeat the Bugis before Jim's return. Then, he reasoned, general defection of the townsfolk was sure to follow, and the reign of the white man who protected poor people would be over. Afterwards the new allies could be dealt with. They would have no friends.

Because the enemies of the Bugis share in the general awe of Jim, they wish to attack the Bugis in his absence and with the help of the newly-arrived Europeans. They are friendly with Cornelius because he, too, is against Jim. They are hostile to Jim and the other Europeans for purely tribal, not nationalist, reasons. The attitudes of the Malayans in Conrad's other settings are of a piece with those of the inhabitants of Patusan. Babalatchi and Lakamba in Sambir intrigue with the Arabs against the Dutch for tribal financial gain. Hassim and Immada revere Lingard as Dain Waris does Lord Jim; they require Lingard's help to fight for the rightful tribal succession in Wajo. Certain Malayans seem to reveal one of the basic characteristics of nationalists, opposition to alien rule: but this hostility is motivated by tribal considerations and cannot be considered nationalistic. Moreover, the Malayans were more often submissive to the Europeans than hostile; nor did they feel themselves to be on an equal footing with the Europeans. None of them reveals even a semblance of the other basic characteristic of nationalists, a sense of corporate identity. Conrad's Malayans think only in terms of their particular small tribe; although they live on or near the East coast of Borneo, they do not have a conception of belonging to the larger entity, Indonesia. But they are not tribalists. The need to be very conscious of and to defend the tribal order does not arise because it is not seriously endangered in Conrad's remote settings – not by the Dutch, not by individuals such as Almayer or Lingard or Lord Jim, not by a firm such as Stein's.

Conrad's Malayans, then, are tribal. Could one consider characters such as Dain Waris and Hassim 'aristocrats', as Kettle does? They are members of a privileged class by virtue of their ancestry and wealth. But theirs is the ruling class of tribal society – not an aristocracy in the usual sense of the term, a privileged class in 'democratic' or 'undemocratic' civilised society. Thus to use the term 'aristocrats' for members of a tribal ruling class is to misapprehend their social role and level of development.

Are there reasons to justify Kettle's point that they 'are conceived as Polish rather than Malayan nationalists'? Zdzislaw Najder describes succinctly the 'three major groups' of Polish nationalists in the nineteenth century:

First, the appeasers, who wanted to preserve Polish national identity but within the scope of the Russian Empire (their most prominent representative was Count Aleksander Wielopolski, 1803–77). Secondly, the 'Whites' who thought about rebuilding the Polish Kingdom of the pre-partition time without basically changing its internal structure and preserving its feudal outlook; they relied heavily on the hope of foreign, mostly French and British, support of the Polish cause. Thirdly, there were the 'Reds' of various shades, who linked the fight for national independence with programmes for social reforms (particularly land reform and the abolishment of serfdom) and counted rather on a successful armed uprising than on the results of international political manoeuvring. The appeasers were, of course, dead against the two other groups. However, even the two 'patriotic' groups, the Whites and the Reds, opposed each other violently, especially just before and in the early stages of the

January 1863 insurrection.[18]

All these kinds of Polish nationalists of upper-class background are very different from the tribal leaders in Conrad's kind of milieux. The Poles live in a feudal system; in fact, the 'appeasers' and the 'Whites' do not wish to change it. On the other hand, all the Malayans belong to a tribal system. The Polish 'Whites' and 'Reds' are nationalist; the 'appeasers' are aware of their 'national identity' and value it. The Malayans are not nationalist and not even conscious of a 'national identity'. The conflicts between, say, Doramin's group and Tunku Allang's group in Patusan or Belarab's group and Tengga's group in the Land of Refuge are tribal, not like the nationalist antagonism of the Polish groups. The Malayans believe in primitive religion; the organised religion with which they were coming into contact, was Islam. On the other hand, the Poles were Catholics, though Conrad himself rejected Catholicism. Thus, the Malayans and the Poles live and think in cultural contexts which are very dissimilar and at different stages in the evolution of different civilisations. Moreover, the Malayans in Conrad's kind of milieux could not be expected to be conscious of nationality or be nationalistic in any way, Polish or Malayan, because nationalism did not emerge in that part of the world until shortly after *Lord Jim* was first published (in *Blackwood's Edinburgh Magazine*, 1899): as J. D. Legge observes,

> The emergence of a nationalist movement in the first decades of the twentieth century was essentially a new phenomenon. There had been movements of resistance against the Dutch from time to time in the past – the Java War of 1825 or the struggle in West Sumatra in the 1820s and 1830s for example – and these, in retrospect, might seem to have been the forerunners of a later, more coherent, resistance to colonial rule. Indeed they have been so regarded by modern nationalists themselves, and the leaders of the early revolts have become heroes of the modern republic. More correctly, however, these were prenationalist movements, isolated, unco-ordinated responses to particular discontents, sporadic in character and reflective of fissures within Indonesian society as well as hostility to the spread of Dutch power.[19]

Thus nationalism could have entered *Victory* and *The Rescue*. But they, like the early novels, are set in more or less remote environments, and there were no articulated national feelings in such places: as

George McTurnan Kahin notes, 'long before and throughout the period of Dutch rule Java was the political and cultural centre of Indonesia and the supporter of most of its population'.[20]

Was Indonesian nationalism, when it did emerge, like Polish nationalism? The Indonesian nationalists were members of a tiny educated elite – as late as the 1930s the literacy rate in Indonesia was 6% – who were drawn from both the upper class and lower social strata. Three of the major factors which gave rise to nationalism and led to its development, were Dutch education, Islam and Marxism. Thus the Indonesian nationalists were markedly different from their Polish counterparts.

There is, then, no justification for thinking that Conrad's young Malayan leaders are 'aristocrats', that they 'are conceived as Polish rather than Malayan nationalists' and that his Malayans 'are really transplantations from Polish history'. His Malayans are conceived as Malayans in his particular selected environments at the specific chosen period. I agree with Kettle when he states that Conrad's 'feeling for the native peoples is sincere'. But Kettle proceeds to support the point in this way: 'Dain Waris in *Lord Jim*, Hassim in *The Rescue* are presented with the greatest sympathy and dignity, indeed they are among Conrad's few characters (apart from the women) who can be said to be idealised'.[21] Can we agree? Consider Dain Waris. Conrad introduces him through Marlow: 'Of small stature, but admirably well proportioned, Dain Waris had a proud carriage, a polished easy bearing, a temperament like a clear flame. His dusky face, with big black eyes, was in action expressive, and in repose thoughtful'. This description is somewhat 'idealised'; but the idealisation is Marlow's, not Conrad's. The author's realism is more pronounced and ironic earlier in the introductory passage:

> Of Dain Waris, his own people said with pride that he knew how to fight like a white man. This was true; he had that sort of courage – the courage in the open, I may say – but he had also a European mind. You meet them sometimes like that, and are surprised to discover unexpectedly a familiar turn of thought, an unobscured vision, a tenacity of purpose, a touch of altruism.

Marlow records a true insight of Conrad into the primitive Malayan mind, its sense of racial inferiority to the 'white' men. At the same time, Conrad exposes limitations of Marlow's amiable conservatism. Marlow has a racialist bias. He speaks highly of Dain because he sees in him certain qualities which he associates only with the Europeans, virtually because Dain does not seem to him a Malayan. He views Dain as Mrs Aphra Behn did Oroonoko, though much less crudely. First he focuses attention on Dain in particular. Then he widens his vision to take in Dain's whole race and the full extent of his racialism stands revealed. The Malayans were primitive but even among people at this level of development one would expect to discover, say, more than 'a touch of altruism sometimes'. Thus Conrad presents Dain through Marlow with critical realism. But is he effectively portrayed? In his case, Conrad sets himself a particularly difficult task of character-creation – Dain is very different from an ordinary Malayan (more so than Jewel) and not European – and is not equal to its demands. He brings Dain into the action occasionally but not dramatically, only descriptively as in this instance. Dain never speaks. Indeed, he seems to me the least alive and striking of the characters in *Lord Jim.*

Conrad's portrayal of Dain, then, is realistic but, on the whole, a failure. But what of Hassim? and Immada? Conrad himself introduces them:

> He was clad in a jacket of coarse blue cotton, of the kind a poor fisherman might own, and he wore it wide open on a muscular chest the colour and smoothness of bronze. From the twist of threadbare *sarong* . . . His upright figure had a negligent elegance. But in the careless face, in the easy gestures of the whole man there was something attentive and restrained.
>
> . . . . .
>
> . . . Her black hair hung like a mantle. Her *sarong*, the kilt-like garment which both sexes wear, had the national check of grey and red, . . . She walked, brown and alert, all of a piece, with short steps, the eyes lively in an impassive little face, the arched mouth closed firmly; . . .

Conrad describes them carefully, precisely and fully. In the case of Immada, for instance, he does not 'launch out' into a conventional 'glowing description' of a Malayan 'damsel' which Alfred Wallace parodies: 'The jacket or body of purple gauze would figure well in such a description, allowing the heaving bosom to be seen beneath it, while 'sparkling eyes', and 'jetty tresses', and 'tiny feet' might be thrown in profusely'.[22] This kind of commonplaceness mars Sherard Osborn's description of Baju-Mira[23] but not, as I said, Conrad's presentation of

Immada. Moreover, Conrad dramatises the characters of Hassim and Immada as in the scenes with them examined above. They are secondary characters portrayed successfully.

Of course, Conrad regards Dain Waris, Hassim and Immada very favourably but one cannot say, with Kettle, that they are 'idealised'. Conrad is also aware that Malayans suffer from certain deficiencies of character. He portrays these with much the same critical realism and with much the same degree of success as their virtues, as in the case of Babalatchi and Lakamba. We have noticed that he does not succumb to the current prejudices of the Clifford and Kidd type or, worse, of the Charles Kingsley and Frank Marryat type.[24] On the other hand, there were the minority views of, say, Alfred Wallace and Sir Frank Swettenham. Here is Wallace (in *The Malay Archipelago*):

> The higher classes of Malays are exceedingly polite, and have all the quiet ease and dignity of the best-bred Europeans. Yet this is compatible with a reckless cruelty and contempt of human life, which is the dark side of their character. It is not to be wondered at, therefore, that different persons give totally opposite accounts of them – one praising them for their soberness, civility and good nature; another abusing them for their deceit, treachery, and cruelty.[25]

Here is Swettenham (in *Malay Sketches*):

> The real Malay is a short, thick-set, well built man, with straight black hair, a dark brown complexion, thick nose and lips, and bright intelligent eyes. His disposition is generally kindly, his manners are polite and easy. Never cringing, he is reserved with strangers and suspicious, though he does not show it. . . .
>
> They [Malay women] are generally amiable in disposition, mildly – sometimes fiercely – jealous, often extravagant and, up to about the age of forty, evince an increasing fondness for jewellery and smart clothes. . . .[26]

Conrad's balanced awareness of the Malayans is a development on views such as these. In fact, Wallace's *The Malay Archipelago* was Conrad's 'intimate friend for many years' (in the words of Richard Curle).[27] From first-hand experience and reading he knows more about Malayans than about negroes and Chinese, and he is more interested in them. That is why he puts them into his fiction far more than the others. He presents these people alien to him with their alien speech in their alien context with a mixture of success and failure as in the case of the Europeans there.

His Malayan world is predominantly authentic in all its varied spheres. His degree of success and failure is explicable. He is able to rise above conventional Western prejudices against Malayans for much the same reasons as he is able to transcend those against Chinese, whereas he yields slightly to those against negroes. The prejudices against Malayans were less strong than those against negroes; among the favourable views of South-East Asians expressed by Europeans are those of Sherard Osborn on Nicodar Devi and Baju-Mira,[28] Fred McNair on the Maharajah of Johore,[29] and Graham Greene on the women of Indo-China.[30] Westerners knew of great Asian civilisations in the past; Malayan civilisations had not regressed into as primitive a stage as African ones, and Conrad had experienced the difference. Westerners suffered less from guilt about ill-treatment of Malayans than of negroes and Chinese: there was no slave or coolie trade in Malayans; Dutch rule in 'Indonesia' and British rule in 'Malaysia' were less harsh than other colonial regimes in Asia and Africa. Presumably it is because of this problem of guilt that Sherard Osborn betrays conventional prejudice against the Chinese, but considers his whole book, *My Journal in Malayan Waters*, an attempt to give 'a fair impression of the much-abused Malay'.[31] Thus, the same European could yield to conventional prejudices against one 'coloured' race but not other 'coloured' races, and different Europeans could have prejudices against different 'coloured' races, for historical reasons.

M. C. Bradbrook says: 'it would be generally agreed that Conrad's first three books [she is referring to *Almayer's Folly*, *An Outcast of the Islands* and the first efforts of *The Rescue*] show promise but not achievement. They are uneven because he was too close to the experience he used and also too close to his models'.[32] She is right in her judgement that Conrad's early endeavours show promise but not achievement, but her reasons do not seem to me correct. Conrad was not 'too close to the experience he used': 'the experience' in the East was gathered between 1883 and 1888; *Almayer's Folly* was published about seven years later. It is doubtful whether he thought in terms of 'models' as such (Bradbrook mentions Flaubert), though he was influenced by writers such as Flaubert and Maupassant.[33] The closeness to his 'models' or, more probably, his sources of influence was not decisively debilitating: weaknesses in his first efforts such as poor psychological 'exploration', conventional romance and melodrama are also found in his last novels, as we noticed above. The unevenness of his early fiction and his last Malayan novels should be related partly to their period of composition; in the case of the former, to his artistic immaturity and, in the case of the latter, to the unsteadiness of an artist past his prime. The conventional romance is partly a consequence of that disinclination to render intimacies common in nineteenth-century fiction. However, the artistic challenges involved in presenting various male–female relationships between people of different races, of different degrees of development and different character (Almayer and his wife, Willems and Aissa, Jim and Jewel) in alien environments call into play a degree of realism unusual for Conrad in this field. There is still another important cause for the unevenness of his Malayan fiction: Conrad did not know enough; his rhetorical vein reflects, and appears partly an attempt to conceal, an ignorance. We noticed at the beginning of this chapter that his experience of the East was slight. He had to depend heavily on books about it and pure imagination. This did not suit his kind of talent, which fed mainly on personal experiences and contacts. Norman Sherry has worked out much of the factual background of Conrad's Eastern works in *Conrad's Eastern World*, and it suggests that there is an even closer connection between the workings of Conrad's imagination and his personal experiences and facts than we have hitherto been aware of. Conrad's artistic difficulties increased because he, a writer from a European context, was presenting life in the Malay Archipelago, a developing environment alien to him, to a European reading public for whom it was even more alien.

Conrad himself was aware that he knew too little about Malaya: in a letter to Hugh Clifford in 1898, he says,

> I suspect my assumption of Malay colouring for my fiction must be exasperating to those who *know*. It seems as though you had found in my prose some reason for forgiving me. Nothing could be more flattering to a scribbler's vanity or more soothing to the conscience of a man who, even in his fiction, tries to be tolerably true.[34]

On the other hand, he was not unconscious of the solid reading behind his fiction; he wrote to William Blackwood on 13 December 1898 about an article by Clifford:

> I am inexact and ignorant no doubt (most of us are) but I don't think I sinned so recklessly. Curiously enough all the details about the little characteristic acts and customs which they hold up as

proof I have taken out (to be safe) from undoubted sources – dull, wise books.[35]

But his sense of his ignorance and of his want of first-hand experience were more deeply embedded in his consciousness as deficiencies affecting his art, particularly after he became more familiar with Clifford as a man and as a writer.

Before he met Clifford, he had reviewed his *Studies in Brown Humanity* in the *Academy* for 23 April 1898. Conrad seldom reviewed books but this review was meant (he told Clifford in a letter) as 'a tribute not only to the charm of the book but to the toil of the man; to the years of patient and devoted work at the back of the pages'.[36] In the review itself, he had praised Clifford as 'the embodiment of the intentions, of the conscience and might of his race'.[37] Clifford became one of his best friends and he later counted this friendship as 'amongst his precious possessions'.[38] In his 'memoir article' Clifford summarises aspects of their friendship relevant to my concerns:

> His lament was that, while I possessed unusual knowledge, I made of it an indifferent use; mine that though his style was a Miracle, his knowledge was defective; yet it was upon this unpromising foundation that a friendship was built up which endured without a falter for a quarter of a century, and ended only on that sad day in August, 1924, when I stood mourning at my old friend's graveside in the quiet Kentish cemetery where he lies sleeping.[39]

In the review mentioned above, Conrad said:

> Each study in this volume presents some idea, illustrated by a fact told without artifice, but with an effective sureness of knowledge. . . .
> Nevertheless, to apply artistic standards to this book would be a fundamental error in appreciation. . . . And this book is only truth, interesting and futile, truth unadorned, simple and straightforward. . . . One cannot expect to be, at the same time, a ruler of men and an irreproachable player on the flute.[40]

This view, both respectful and critical, was Conrad's habitual reaction to Clifford's work. Clifford said:

> . . . the author [of *Almayer's Folly*] had none but a superficial

acquaintance with the Malayan customs, language and character. . . .

. . . one who had not had the opportunity of entering into the life of the people of the country, as I and some of my friends had done, had been able in that first book to convey so much of the magic and singular charm possessed by Malaya and to limn the lives of the people with a force and imaginative touch which had never been equalled by any other writer.[41]

Although Clifford was scarcely treating Conrad's work as *literature*, his 'authoritative' criticism was bound to have effects on an author as hard on himself as Conrad was, still unestablished, and still rather isolated as a comparative newcomer to England. By the time he came to write *Lord Jim*, his confidence in his mastery of the Malayan experience seems to have been shaken. Consider Jim's comment on the ring given him by Stein: 'The ring was a sort of credential – ("It's like something you read of in books", he threw in appreciatively) and Doramin would do his best for him'. Introducing the Gentleman Brown episode, Marlow says: 'This astounding adventure, of which the most astounding part is that it is true, . . .'. Jim makes an observation to Marlow on the relationship of Dain Waris, Doramin and his wife: '"It's well worth seeing", Jim had assured me while we were crossing the river, on our way back. "They are like people in a book, aren't they?" he said triumphantly'. These remarks are meant to establish the 'foreignness' of Jim's and Marlow's reactions to an alien way of life. I think they also betray a doubt in Conrad about the convincingness not only of these particular items but also of all his Malayan material. He seems to be anticipating readers' objections to its authenticity. Those remarks are put into the mouths of Jim and Marlow not only as appropriate to their characters but also to forestall possible objections. His doubt of his own powers lies behind other aspects of his art: the Malayans speak much less than in his first two novels and Dain Waris not at all; he makes Jewel speak an English closer to the Standard than, say, Babalatchi and justifies it, rather than attempts to give her a Malayan English. In *Victory* the Malayans do not appear in terms of drama and hardly matter; in *The Rescue* they play a considerably less important part than in the early novels. These tendencies could be due either to a further flagging of his originally rather slight sense of Malay life, or to his awareness that he did not know enough to write well about the Malayans, or to both. In his prime, from 1901 to 1911, he never made the mistake of attempting to articulate themes with too little material to go on – although it has to be noted that *Nostromo* was composed from a minimum of what would usually be called first-hand experience.

The fact is that an artist's experience cannot be weighed solely by amounts of time spent or by his veritable presence in such-and-such a place. At times what Conrad calls 'most vivid impressions' and 'highly valued memories'[42] can trigger off perceptions of exceptional depth, apparently because they fit in with tendencies that his sensibility is already preoccupied with. This is the case with Conrad's interest in the ironies of hypocrisy and self-deception. In *Lord Jim* he writes: '. . . There were very few places in the Archipelago he had not seen in the original dusk of their being, before light (and even electric light) had been carried into them for the sake of better morality and – and – well – the greater profit, too'. Conrad is here describing Stein, not directly but through Marlow. The point is not the characterising of Stein but the Conradian irony – made clearer and more mordant by Marlow's reluctance to utter the key words at the end – regarding the hypocrisy of conservative English thinking about imperialism which Marlow typifies. He speaks of an altruistic moral ideal as the prime goal of empire-building; this acts as a cover for the chief motive of 'greater profit', and it also helps him to maintain his dignity in his own eyes and in the eyes of the public (at home and abroad), to salve his conscience, and to fool the credulous. Conrad also shows that Marlow is unaware of his dishonesty: the hesitancy in his speech is not the author's but the character's. Thus Conrad has dramatised, during the heyday of Empire, a national trait of his adopted country. Twenty years later Forster wrote:

> Hypocrisy is the prime charge that is always brought against us. The Germans are called brutal, the Spanish cruel, the Americans superficial, and so on; but we are perfide Albion, the island of hypocrites, the people who have built up an Empire with a Bible in one hand, a pistol in the other, and financial concessions in both pockets. Is the charge true? I think it is; but while making it we must be quite clear as to what we mean by hypocrisy. Do we mean *conscious* deceit? Well the English are comparatively guiltless of this; they have little of the Renaissance villain about them. Do we mean *unconscious* deceit? muddle-headedness? Of this I believe them to be guilty.[43]

In *The Rescue* Carter is credited with 'the clear vision of a seaman

able to master quickly the aspect of a strange land and of a strange sea'.
It is likely that Conrad himself had this 'clear vision of a seaman' and
that this is what enabled him so quickly to grasp essentials of life in the
Archipelago and in Latin America. He was perhaps helped also by his
Polishness. We have noticed his ability to rise above common imperial
attitudes, and we know that as a Pole he had suffered, with his family,
under the empire-building of the Tsars. In his autobiography he pays
tribute to

> the Polish temperament with its tradition of self-government, its
> chivalrous view of moral restraints and an exaggerated respect for
> individual rights: not to mention the important fact that the whole
> Polish mentality, Western in complexion, had received its training
> from Italy and France and, historically, had always remained, even
> in religious matters, in sympathy with the most liberal currents of
> European thought.[44]

This cultural heritage must have helped him to achieve his extraordinary liberal-mindedness. So, he considered, did his kind of aristocratic
origins:

> An impartial view of humanity in all its degrees of splendour and
> misery together with a special regard for the rights of the unpri-
> vileged of this earth, not on any mystic ground but on the ground of
> simple fellowship and honourable reciprocity of services, was the
> dominant characteristic of the mental and moral atmosphere of the
> houses which sheltered my hazardous childhood: – matters of calm
> and deep conviction both lasting and consistent, and removed as far
> as possible from that humanitarianism that seems to be merely a
> matter of crazy nerves or a morbid conscience.[45]

Because these Polish attitudes were 'matters of calm and deep conviction both lasting and consistent', we are justified in finding in his
Polishness at least some of the roots of his extraordinarily humane and
keen awareness of realities in other countries dominated from abroad.
The political aspects of his Polish background appear explicitly in the
opening of 'Prince Roman':

> '. . . Of course the year 1831 is for us an historical date, one of these
> fatal years when in the presence of the world's passive indignation
> and eloquent sympathies we had once more to murmur '*Vae Victis*'

and count the cost in sorrow. Not that we were ever very good at calculating, either, in prosperity or in adversity. That's a lesson we could never learn, to the great exasperation of our enemies who have bestowed upon us the epithet of Incorrigible. . . .'

The speaker was of Polish nationality, that nationality not so much alive as surviving, which persists in thinking, breathing, speaking, hoping, and suffering in its grave, railed in by a million of bayonets and triple-sealed with the seals of three great empires.[46]

Here Conrad reveals his anger at the indifference of the world to Poland's plight, his sympathetic sense of her inherent weakness, of her subjection, of her valiant but abortive striving. Nationalism was a prominent part of Conrad's family tradition; the Korzeniowskis were 'Reds', while the Bobrowskis were generally 'appeasers'. These Polish interests and feelings of Conrad could have found a psychological release and a congenial field for expression in the developing countries of the Far East because of the similarity of their predicament under imperialism. V. S. Pritchett suggests that 'Conrad seems to have turned the Polish exile's natural preoccupation with nationality, history, defeat and unavailing struggle, from his own country to these Eastern islands'.[47] What Pritchett does not note is that in Conrad's Malayan fiction, though the Malayans, the subject people, are more or less important in all the works except *Victory*, it is the Europeans, the members of the 'ruling race' and his fellow 'white' men, who matter most; that though the roles of 'Tuan Jim' and the 'Rajah Laut' have a social significance, the most important themes are always personal and not political; and that in his remote milieux at that particular time there was nothing like the national struggles against imperialism found in Poland. Thus Conrad's Polishness is relevant, in a rather indirect and unverifiable way, to a consideration of his Malayan fiction; but the East evokes new independent interests and emphases.

5 Conrad's African tales: ironies of progress

King Leopold: '... It is all the same old thing – tedious repetitions and duplications of shop-worn episodes; mutilations, murders, massacres, and so on, and so on, till one gets drowsy over it'.

Mark Twain, *King Leopold's Soliloquy* (1907 ed.).

'Before the Congo I was only a simple animal', Conrad had told Edward Garnett. The Congo, certainly, made him think deeply about life. But how did the Congo itself, so disturbingly enlightening by his own confession, impinge on his imagination? Let us start, chronologically, with *An Outpost of Progress* and move on to *Heart of Darkness*.

Conrad said: '*An Outpost of Progress* is the lightest part of the loot I carried off from Central Africa'.[1] The critics (for instance, A. J. Guerard and J. I. M. Stewart) concur.[2] Does this view lead to an underestimate or not?

Let us consider Conrad's description of the trading post of Kayerts and Carlier in the interior of Congo: 'And stretching away in all directions, surrounding the insignificant cleared spot of the trading post, immense forests hiding fateful complications of fantastic life, lay in the eloquent silence of mute greatness'. This is the wordy and imprecise rhetoric characteristic of Conrad when he is not a master of his subject. But the story opens differently:

> There were two white men in charge of the trading station. Kayerts, the chief, was short and fat; Carlier, the assistant, was tall, with a large head and a very broad trunk perched upon a long pair of thin legs. The third man on the staff was a Sierra Leone nigger, who maintained that his name was Henry Price.

Conrad takes the reader directly to his setting and introduces his three chief characters, Kayerts, Carlier and Makola. The ironic stance implies a controlling intelligence, and the terseness of the prose has an immediacy of impact. The ironic humour becomes marked as Conrad moves from the 'short and fat' Kayerts to Carlier. The image evoked by 'perched' suggests an uneasy comic balance of Carlier's 'very broad trunk' on 'a long pair of thin legs'. The element of comedy in the description suggests the ineptness of the two Europeans. In the introduction of Makola, 'maintained' suggests his bland confidence in sticking to his name despite its oddness. It is the kind of language used here which is the staple of the tale; there are only traces of the weak style.

Conrad's theme is the perils of petty trading on the fringes of an empire. The title, *An Outpost of Progress*, recurs as a key *leitmotiv* and suggests his approach to his subject. It is unmistakably ironic; the irony works by playing off the conventional, lofty associations of the phrase against the squalid, perilous reality. But is the promise of the opening fulfilled? This is a scene soon after Kayerts and Carlier have been left in charge of their outpost:

> They chatted persistently in familiar tones. 'Our station is prettily situated', said one. The other assented with enthusiasm, enlarging volubly on the beauties of the situation. Then they passed near the grave. 'Poor devil!' said Kayerts. 'He died of fever, didn't he?' muttered Carlier, stopping short. 'Why', retorted Kayerts with indignation, 'I've been told that the fellow exposed himself recklessly to the sun'. . . .

Conrad brings to life dramatically the excessive rosy talkativeness and *camaraderie* of Kayerts and Carlier as an attempt to suppress their fears and dissatisfactions. But what immediately precedes this scene is commentary, and commentary of this kind:

> They were two perfectly insignificant and incapable individuals, whose existence is only rendered possible through the high organisation of civilised crowds. . . . But the contact with pure unmitigated savagery, with primitive nature and primitive man, brings sudden and profound trouble into the heart. . . .

Conrad's analysis here is not prejudiced as in Benjamin Kidd's argument (quoted above) that 'the white man tends to sink slowly to the level around him'. Yet Conrad does not go deeper. Indeed, much of the narrative is over-general and undramatic.

An Outpost of Progress has its drawbacks and is confined by the limits of petty trading. But it is more than a preliminary exercise; it suggests the kind of talent that, in *Heart of Darkness*, could take on a

theme in which the perils of petty trading in an outpost const
a minor aspect.

In *Heart of Darkness*, Conrad presents the imperial entang⌣ents
of Western civilisation and primitive culture as these are skirted by a
certain type of Englishman, Marlow. We can still say, with Conrad,
'the subject is of our time distinctly – though not topically treated'.[3]
Why use Marlow? Detachment (springing from his Continental
literary background, from his aristocratic origins and from his temperament) is the necessary essence of Conrad's technique, and he often
achieves it partly with the help of narrators. In *Heart of Darkness*, he
uses the same narrator as in *Lord Jim*, but with a difference. In *Lord
Jim*, Marlow was relating the experiences of someone else; here he is
recounting his own. That is, Conrad is employing the fictional convention of the first-person narrator. His 'early Polish readings' in the
gaweda, the kind of Polish story 'told by some clearly defined person',[4]
may have influenced him to use this convention. But a more potent
influence would have been, probably, the yarns of seamen: Conrad's
career in the Merchant Service mattered greatly to him as a man and
as a writer; the narrators of *The Secret Sharer* and *The Shadow-Line*
are young captains; Marlow himself is a seaman. Still, Marlow is
'wanderer, too';[5] and in *Heart of Darkness*, it seems to me likely that
the most powerful influence on the narrative convention would have
been the mode of the 'sahib' recounting his colonial experiences. This
mode was established in *Blackwood's Edinburgh Magazine*,[6] to which
Conrad contributed *Karain*, *Youth*, *Lord Jim* and *Heart of Darkness*
itself.[7] Marlow talks of his connection with the Belgian Congo because
of 'his propensity to spin yarns'.[8] The 'propensity' is released in a
situation conducive to it, which appropriately forms the opening of the
tale – Marlow on board a yawl in the Thames at dusk with four cronies
joined by 'the bond of the sea' who were 'tolerant of each other's yarns
– and even convictions'. Marlow's tale does not spring from the pressure of inner compulsion as, say, the 'Rime' of Coleridge's Ancient
Mariner. But the experiences in it do matter to him and he relives them
as he narrates them.

Marlow's portrayal is part of Conrad's theme and his suitability as
a narrative vehicle is crucial to its presentation. It is Marlow who
utters these words as he ruminates on his experiences at the Central
Station:

You know I hate, detest, and can't bear a lie, not because I am straighter than the rest of us, but simply because it appals me. There is a taint of death, a flavour of mortality in lies – which is exactly what I hate and detest in the world – what I want to forget. It makes me miserable and sick, like biting something rotten would do. Temperament, I suppose.

Marlow's confession of his uprightness and his explanation for it ring true; indeed, his tone always sounds honest. Our acceptance of his probity is one reason why we accept his narrative as authentic.

That Marlow is a certain type of Englishman is also important. These are observations and reflections of his in the waiting-room of the Belgian imperial company:

Deal table in the middle, plain chairs all round the walls, on one end a large shining map, marked with all the colours of a rainbow. There was a vast amount of red – good to see at any time, because one knows that some real work is done in there, a deuce of a lot of blue, a little green, smears of orange, and, on the East Coast, a purple patch, to show where the jolly pioneers of progress drink the jolly lager-beer. However, I wasn't going into any of these. I was going into the yellow.

Conrad takes care to see to it that Marlow takes into account all the colonial countries; on the map, the red must stand for the British, the blue for the French, the green for the Portuguese, the orange for the Spanish, the purple for the Germans, and the yellow for the Belgians. The Empire of his own country evokes a warm response from Marlow which the other empires do not, and he mentions one specific reason for it. But is he a conventional imperial-minded Englishman? A little earlier, he contemplated imperialism in general:

I was thinking of very old times, when the Romans first came here, nineteen hundred years ago – . . . But darkness was here yesterday. . . . Or think of a decent young citizen in a toga – perhaps too much dice, you know – coming out here in the train of some prefect, or tax-gatherer, or trader even, to mend his fortunes. . . . He has to live in the midst of the incomprehensible, which is also detestable. And it has a fascination, too, . . . Mind, none of us would feel exactly like this. What saves us is efficiency. But these chaps were not much account, really. They were no colonists; their administration was merely a squeeze, and nothing more, I suspect. They were conquerors, and for that you want only brute force – nothing to boast of, when you have it, since your strength is just an accident arising from the weakness of others. They grabbed what they could get for the sake of what was to be got. It was just robbery with violence, aggravated murder on a great scale, and men going at it blind – as is very proper for those who tackle a darkness. The conquest of the earth, which mostly means the taking it away from those who have a different complexion or slightly flatter noses than ourselves, is not a pretty thing when you look into it too much. What redeems it is the idea only. An idea at the back of it; not a sentimental pretence but an idea; and an unselfish belief in the idea – something you can set up, and bow down before, and offer a sacrifice to. . . .

Conrad sees the interaction of imperialism and primitive life historically. Marlow puts the imperialism of the British in line with that of the Romans. It was a prominent and longstanding British imperial tradition to admire the Roman Empire and emulate it: one of Thomas Sprat's arguments in 1667 for 'a great Reformation in the manner of our Speaking and Writing' was that 'purity of Speech and greatness of Empire have in all Countries still met together' and he cited the Ancients;[9] Cecil Rhodes 'liked to picture himself as [Roman] emperor!'[10] But Marlow is humane: he condemns the Romans in a way that reflects the minority critical attitudes towards them of, say, D. H. Lawrence who saw their 'brute force' (to use Marlow's words) in wiping out 'the Etruscan existence as a nation and a people';[11] Marlow trenchantly criticises 'the conquest of the earth'. Still, he finds justification for British imperialism in its 'efficiency' and its 'idea'. Marlow's language carries suggestions of which he is not aware. Terms such as 'saves' and 'redeems' imply an uneasy consciousness in him of unsatisfactory features even in British imperialism and in their attempted vindication an unconscious hypocrisy. This is one of the traits which he betrayed in *Lord Jim*; it is so deep-seated that it remains despite his maturing Congo experience. With fine insight, Conrad suggests through the ritual implications of Marlow's concluding words that an idealisation of imperialism is an attempt to justify an element of inhumanity which is common to both civilised and primitive societies. The action which follows implicates the British Empire in its exposure of the evils of imperial entanglements. In this context, Conrad is critically projecting Marlow; Marlow is not the kind of 'self-dramatisation' on the part of the author which Walter Allen takes him to be;[12] in fact, Conrad himself enters this tale as a member of

Marlow's company, his audience. Thus, it seems to me wrong to quote Marlow's remark, 'There was a vast amount of red – good to see at any time because one knows that some real work is done in there', as an expression of an opinion of the author and take it as evidence of Conrad's 'loyalty to the British Empire', as Arnold Kettle does.[13] The elegantly spoken and thoughtful side of Marlow, evident in the comparison of Roman and British imperialism, seems to overlap somewhat with Conrad himself; so do the touches of vague elevated language, which from the very beginning enter the tale when Conrad tries to render the deep reaches of the entanglement of cultures. But if we consider Marlow's personality as a whole, we see that Conrad is essentially projecting a character. Indeed, the words that immediately follow those quoted by Kettle reinforce this point; here Conrad is clearly and deliberately rendering the idiom of a character, a rather extravert middle-class Englishman who is Marlow, not his own idiom which is that of an aristocratic European *deraciné*. Marlow's honesty and humanity qualify him to be a suitable narrator. But is his usefulness limited by his imperial-mindedness in respect of Britain? Conrad is able to treat this side of Marlow critically just as he does other aspects. Marlow provides one way by which he can bring Britain into his concerns. Moreover, he sends Marlow 'into the yellow'. He can plausibly employ Marlow to convey his theme as fully as he understands it partly because Marlow's national sentiment would not be on the defensive, as an hindrance to clear-sightedness and frankness, in confronting the imperial involvements of a foreign country, Belgium.

Marlow is an excellent narrative vehicle partly because he is British, and we can appreciate this all the more if we look at him from another angle. All the imperial powers are guilty of atrocities. The French, the Spanish and the Belgians chopped off the hands of indigenous people as a punishment. In France, torture was a legal instrument of justice until the First World War, and the French were more callous towards subject people; it is not long since they used torture on the Algerians. There was a shattering drop in the African population of the Congo under the Belgians. The early imperial activities of the British were not less inhuman than those of the other countries. We have noticed their trafficking in slaves and their less cruel, later trade in coolies. William Knighton's 'sketches' bring in the brutal side of British imperialism in mid-nineteenth century Ceylon:

'. . . Every man is a magistrate on his own estate, you know,' he [Siggins] continued, 'and therefore, as long as the man is working for you, you have a right to do what you like with him – that is, anything short of killing'.

'A new doctrine, truly', said Mouat, coming as near a laugh as he ever permitted himself, 'but one very often acted upon, I believe.'[14]

But generally by the turn of this century British imperialism had become so experienced and so self-enriching that it was able to rectify the worst features of imperialism. Thus, Marlow is a spokesman from a country with this imperial tradition. With no adequate sense of the past, the present state of the British Empire tends to confirm his distorted view of it, his racial and cultural prejudices. This is perfectly convincing and is also representative: for instance, both T. S. Eliot and George Orwell thought along such lines.[15] Marlow's national blindness is part of Conrad's theme, and Conrad has selected a person from the right imperial country, Britain, who could see clearly and humanely the imperial entanglements of a foreign country whose empire was comparatively recent and whose excesses were uncorrected. Moreover, Conrad has also chosen a kind of imperial environment in which the essentials of his theme would 'stand out with particular force and colouring' (to use his own words quoted above).

Marlow's journey into imperial involvements begins in Brussels, the headquarters of the Belgian empire, not in the Congo itself. The scene when he bids farewell to his aunt is by no means irrelevant:

In the course of these confidences it became quite plain to me I had been represented to the wife of the high dignitary, and goodness knows to how many more people besides, as an exceptional and gifted creature – a piece of good fortune for the Company – a man you don't get hold of every day. Good heavens! and I was going to take charge of a two-penny-half-penny river-steamboat with a penny whistle attached! It appeared, however, I was also one of the Workers, with a capital – you know. Something like an emissary of light, something like a lower sort of apostle. There had been a lot of such rot let loose in print and talk just about that time, and the excellent woman, living right in the rush of all that humbug, got carried off her feet. She talked about 'weaning those ignorant millions from their horrid ways', till, upon my word, she made me quite uncomfortable. I ventured to hint that the Company was run for profit.

'You forget, dear Charlie, that the labourer is worthy of his hire,' she said brightly.

Conrad introduces conventional Western notions of imperialism (these were naturally more prominent in the metropolitan countries than in the colonies) through the aunt; in *An Outpost of Progress*, he did the same thing undramatically through 'some old copies of a home paper' found by Kayerts and Carlier. Marlow's sensible honesty becomes clearer as Conrad employs him to expose the falsity of these conceptions. Marlow can see the difference between the exaggerated view of his job and its real pettiness, between the sentimental idealism centring around imperialism and the economic basis of it. Conrad dramatises the actual working of the head office of an imperial company. There are the memorable figures of the two unconcerned women at the door knitting black wool, who go with such an office. There is Conrad's presentation of the medical examination with its suggestions of callousness in the operations of the company, of possible derangement and death of its employees. The whole city, in fact, seems to Marlow 'a whited sepulchre'. Its deathlike attributes link up with the inhumanity in the Empire, and Conrad suggests how the attributes of the metropolitan country are founded on imperialism.

When Marlow leaves Brussels for the Congo, the realities *en route* are as much an integral part of the portrayal of imperial entanglements as the realities in Belgium and in the Congo itself:

Now and then a boat from the shore gave one a momentary contact with reality. It was paddled by black fellows. . . . They had faces like grotesque masks – these chaps; but they had bone, muscle, a wild vitality, an intense energy of movement, that was as natural and true as the surf along their coast. They wanted no excuse for being there. They were a great comfort to look at. For a time I would feel I belonged still to a world of straightforward facts; but the feeling would not last long. Something would turn up to scare it away. Once, I remember, we came upon a man-of-war anchored off the coast. There wasn't even a shed there, and she was shelling the bush. It appears the French had one of their wars going on thereabouts. . . .

We gave her her letters (I heard the men in that lonely ship were dying of fever at the rate of three a-day) and went on. We called at some more places with farcical names, where the merry dance of death and trade goes on in a still and earthy atmosphere as of an overheated catacomb; . . .

That the faces of the 'black fellows' seem like 'grotesque masks' to

Marlow suggests that he is a racial-minded foreigner. This aspect of supposed unreality stresses, by contrast, their oneness with their own environment. The naturalness and reality of the Africans differ strikingly from the alienness and frightening absurdity of the man-of-war. The juxtaposition illuminates and accounts for Marlow's grave inner disturbance and, at the same time, lights up and gives substance to 'the merry dance of death and trade'. It is also important to notice that realities outside Marlow are more in the picture than his own reactions. This is typical of the opening phases.

When the action moves on to the Congo, Conrad presents the imperial entanglements of Western civilisation and primitive culture in the developing environment itself. Marlow's condensed view of imperialism, 'a flabby, pretending weak-eyed devil of a rapacious and pitiless folly', is placed in the thick of these realities and is validated by them dramatically. The physical details are made to typify the whole system. Marlow observes this: 'I avoided a vast artificial hole somebody had been digging on the slope, the purpose of which I found it impossible to divine. It wasn't a quarry or a sandpit, anyhow. It was just a hole . . .'. Then this; '. . . I discovered that a lot of important drainage pipes for the settlement has been tumbled in there. There wasn't one that was not broken. It was a wanton smash-up . . .'. After that:

> Black shapes crouched, lay, sat between the trees leaning against the trunks, clinging to the earth, half coming out, half effaced within the dim light, in all the attitudes of pain, abandonment, and despair. Another mine on the cliff went off, followed by a slight shudder of the soil under my feet. The work was going on. The work! And this was the place where some of the helpers had withdrawn to die'.

Conrad powerfully suggests meaninglessness, costly disorder and gross inhumanity, respectively, by the selection and juxtaposition of these strikingly presented realities rather than by way of commentary on the part of Marlow. The outer realities matter more than Marlow's inner state. Conrad's voice rises as he goes on to present the plight of the labourers.

> Near the same tree two more bundles of acute angles sat with their legs drawn up. One, with his chin propped on his knees, stared at nothing, in an intolerable and appalling manner: his brother phantom rested its forehead, as if overcome with a great weariness; and all about others were scattered in every pose of contorted collapse,

as in some picture of a massacre or a pestilence. . . .

This dramatised portion derives its power partly from the metaphorical suggestions of dehumanised beings and partly from the visual exactness. Conrad's realism controls his compassion so that there is no lapsing into sentimentality. This scene is characteristic of Conrad's presentation of the Congolese. He does not go deep into their lives and, from the external standpoint of a visitor, presents them as victims of imperialism who remain anonymous to him.

After describing 'the grove of death', Marlow speaks of himself: 'I didn't want any more loitering in the shade, and I made haste towards the station'. This is all that he says solely about himself. He quickly gets on to realities outside:

> When near the buildings I met a white man, in such an unexpected elegance of get-up that in the first moment I took him for a sort of vision. I saw a high starched collar, white cuffs, a light alpaca jacket, snowy trousers, a clear necktie, and varnished boots. . . .
>
> I shook hands with this miracle, and I learned he was the Company's chief accountant, . . .

The disorder and horror Marlow has met, become more remarkable by forming both a glaring contrast to the juxtaposed figure of the spruce accountant and his books 'in apple-pie order', and a telling complement to the 'muddle' elsewhere in the station. The presentation of these realities is convincing partly because it is made through a narrator who is describing first-hand experiences with an air of casualness. Moreover, the proximity of such incongruities is perfectly natural in a colonial context; Roger Casement observes in 'The Congo Report' (11 December 1903):

> . . . When I visited the three mud huts which serve the purpose of the native hospital, all of them dilapidated, and 2 with the thatched roofs almost gone, I found 17 sleeping sickness patients, male and female, lying about in the utmost dirt. . . .
>
> In somewhat striking contrast to the neglected state of these people, I found within a couple of 100 yards of them, the Government workshop for repairing and fitting the steamers. Here all was brightness, care, order, and activity, and it was impossible not to admire and commend the industry which had created and maintained in constant working order this useful establishment.[16]

Whereas the action of *An Outpost of Progress* takes place in a single setting, the structure of *Heart of Darkness* is provided by Marlow's journey to and from the heart of Africa. Thus, Conrad can render his much more inclusive theme in terms of a whole range of realities. As Marlow penetrates deeper into the Congo, he observes more aspects of imperial entanglements. He indignantly describes the Eldorado Exploring Expedition as a base private attempt at plunder; Conrad ironically implies his criticism through the euphemism of the designation itself. Through Marlow, he is preoccupied with the key imperial agencies, the public companies and governments, which are shown as essentially no better; the suggested difference is chiefly that they operate on a larger and more organised scale. At the Central Station, Marlow meets a small exclusive society of European traders and agents:

> However, they were all waiting – all the sixteen or twenty pilgrims of them – for something; and upon my word it did not seem an uncongenial occupation, from the way they took it, though the only thing that ever came to them was disease – as far as I could see. They beguiled the time by backbiting and intriguing against each other in a foolish kind of way. There was an air of plotting about that station, but nothing came of it, of course. It was as unreal as everything else – as the philanthropic pretence of the whole concern, as their talk, as their government, as their show of work. The only real feeling was a desire to get appointed to a trading-post where ivory was to be had, so that they could earn percentages. They intrigued and slandered and hated each other only on that account, – but as to effectually lifting a little finger – oh, no.

In his 'Congo Diary', Conrad had noted: 'Prominent characteristic of social life here; people speaking ill of each other'.[17] The term 'pilgrims', which Marlow uses consistently for them, is a significant *leitmotiv*; its idealistic associations ironically sound, among other things, their competitive greed. Their senseless dilatoriness is shown as part of their sterile mentality. Amidst the pretences, their desire for ivory is unmistakably real and prominent. 'Ivory' also becomes a *leitmotiv* in the tale. Ivory is to the Congo what silver is to Costaguana in *Nostromo*. It is the actual raw wealth which private individuals, colonial companies and imperial powers covet, as well as a symbolic centre for their self-aggrandising motives. These observations of Marlow are acute, but they are made from the outside and are general. He does not enter as such into colonial society and does not talk in detail about any particular individual. His own predicament figures in a minor way.

Marlow appears in several works of Conrad, but in all of them he is not, to use Virginia Woolf's description, a subtle, refined, and fastidious analyst'.[18] He was that in *Lord Jim*, but it seems to me that in *Heart of Darkness* he is extraordinary in his powers of observation, not in his attempts at analysis. In fact, as we shall notice, Conrad presents Marlow as a narrator who partially understands his experiences. Thus, the most fundamental irony of the tale is that Marlow is narrating experiences whose full import – as it emerges through prose rich in implication, through the fine selection and arrangement of scenes – he is unaware of. Conrad secures the objectivity he needs partly with the help of this ironic method, partly by employing a narrator, and partly by making Marlow relate his tale in retrospect. Conrad's detachment has to be particularly resolute in this tale because he is dealing with Congo realities which he found both profoundly disturbing and enlightening, as they would be for a European such as him.

Marlow's journey in the Congo is strictly along the river. He does not penetrate into less accessible areas. But because the river is the main highway for the country, Conrad can present an impressive range of imperial involvements and a wealth of more or less fundamental insights into them. He does not systematically organise the realities of the tale to bring out a thesis. They enter the story in a way such that they could be credibly encountered during the kind of journey which Marlow undertakes. They fit in with each other to form a coherent, culturally profound impression of the entanglement of Western civilisation and primitive culture. Douglas Hewitt argues that 'the story is primarily concerned with the effect of the country [Africa] and of Kurtz on Marlow'; Albert J. Guerard thinks that 'the story is not primarily about Kurtz or about the brutality of Belgian officials but about Marlow its narrator'.[19] But it seems to me that Marlow's role as a character in his own right is of secondary importance; his character does not matter as does, say, Fielding's in *A Passage to India*. He is mainly a vehicle through which Conrad conveys the entanglements of Western civilisation and primitive culture; these form the main theme. We noticed that Conrad's approach is from the outside; he does pick out specific realities but he does not go deep into any one of them; they are important, not so much in their own right, as in their contribution to his general theme. As in the phases already discussed, the realities outside Marlow bulk much larger than his own role and are more important. And, as we shall see later in more detail, in this tale he is not the subtle psychologist critics have made him out to be.

Let us now discuss Kurtz and go more deeply into Marlow's role; they are the only characters important as individuals in the tale. Kurtz is placed in the heart of Africa. His character and European civilisation which he stands for, are thus subject to their most severe test. In one way, we see the disintegration of the European values which he held at the beginning of his career. This is suggested summarily by the immediate contrast between his report for the International Society for the Suppression of Savage Customs ('It gave me the notion of an exotic Immensity ruled by an august Benevolence') and his *postscriptum* ('Exterminate all the brutes!'). Kurtz's humanity, however theoretical and romantic it might sound, contrasts with his later racialism and savagery. The *postscriptum* has to be taken very seriously because it figures not merely as a safety valve of an exhausted, defeated idealist but as a principle of action. Still, in other ways, Conrad suggests that Kurtz's case is extremely complex. To his European disciple in the Congo, he is virtually an all-comprehending sage who 'could be very terrible' but cannot be judged as 'an ordinary man'. In a way, he is a contrast to his follower. His kind of maturity makes him vulnerable, whereas the latter is 'indestructible' partly (in Marlow's view, 'solely') 'by virtue of his few years and of his unreflecting audacity'. Conrad weaves the relationship of Kurtz and his disciple even more closely into the texture of the tale; Marlow reflects: 'If it had come to crawling before Mr Kurtz, he crawled as much as the veriest savage of them all'. Marlow is critical of the adoration of both the disciple and the Africans. But their notions of Kurtz suggest certain worthy qualities in him, though Conrad does not suggest that they are fully sound; their views are not fully discredited or drastically devalued by Marlow's, as we shall notice later. The strain of living in the wilderness makes Kurtz ill twice and saps his strength. But his response to the wilderness never becomes simple. As a European, Kurtz hates the wilderness and, at the same time, is lured by it. The attraction is stronger than the dislike and could at times even compel him to forget his European identity.

Let us now examine further how Marlow records the entanglements of Western civilisation and primitive culture in the interior of the Congo, especially Kurtz's case. He sketches the approach to Kurtz's outpost:

But suddenly, as we struggled round a bend, there would be a glimpse of rush walls, of peaked grass-roofs, a burst of yells, a whirl of black limbs, a mass of hands clapping, of feet stamping, of bodies swaying, of eyes rolling, under the droop of heavy and motionless

[handwritten marginal note: Kurtz contrast to Russian]

foliage. The steamer toiled along slowly on the edge of a black and incomprehensible frenzy. The prehistoric man was cursing us, praying to us, welcoming us – who could tell? We were cut off from the comprehension of our surroundings; we glided past like phantoms, wondering and secretly appalled, as sane men would be before an enthusiastic outbreak in a madhouse. . . .

Conrad uses this kind of rhetoric whenever he deals with the deep reaches of imperial entanglements – and most prominently during the Kurtz phase because it is then that this aspect is central. The first half of the extract above is in lurid jingoistic prose: by portraying the Africans as if they are constantly in a state of 'incomprehensible frenzy', it denies their normal activities; this kind of distortion of indigenous life was commonly employed as a justification of annexation in the name of civilisation. These words could come from Marlow. But the language soon shades into the vague awe-creating literary prose of Conrad rather than the conversational idiom of Marlow. Marlow confesses his incomprehension and this is credible; but Conrad's kind of prose does not convey this effectively. Marlow describes his surroundings thus: 'And this stillness of life did not in the least resemble a peace. It was the stillness of an implacable force brooding over an inscrutable intention'. This is the same kind of literary prose as that in the earlier excerpt.

Let us now turn to the important human experiences. At the beginning of the tale Marlow comments on his meeting with Kurtz:

It was the farthest point of navigation and the culminating point of my experience. It seemed somehow to throw a kind of light on everything about me – and into my thoughts. It was sombre enough, too, – and pitiful – not extraordinary in any way – not very clear either. No, not very clear. And yet it seemed to throw a kind of light.

Here Conrad conveys, through an idiom appropriate to Marlow, a convincing impression of his narrator groping to find out the significance of the Kurtz episode to him. The episode is 'the culminating point' of Marlow's experience. It is a crucial phase in the tale, as I have already suggested: it deals with the entanglement of Western civilisation and primitive culture in the most remote of places and the human dilemmas in those conditions particularly for the European. Marlow, in fact, finds himself striking up an enduring relationship with Kurtz who appears to him degenerated and demented. Conrad had earlier suggested that they have something temperamentally in common. Marlow turns to the 'nightmare' of Kurtz 'for relief' from the 'nightmare' of the other colonial employees because it is more honest though more unsettling. The term, 'nightmare', suggests appropriately the disturbing unfamiliarity of Marlow's experiences and his inability to come to terms with them. But they themselves have to be satisfactorily defined for us by Conrad. Marlow analytically comments:

> You can't understand. How could you? – with solid pavement under your feet, surrounded by kind neighbours ready to cheer you or to fall on you, stepping delicately between the butcher and the policeman, in the holy terror of scandal and gallows and lunatic asylum – how can you imagine what particular region of the first ages a man's untrammelled feet may take him into by the way of solitude – utter solitude without a policeman – by the way of silence – utter silence, where no warning voice of a kind neighbour can be heard whispering of public opinion? These little things make all the great difference. When they are gone you must fall back upon your own innate strength, upon your own capacity for faithfulness.

Presumably, the pressures of 'utter solitude' and 'utter silence' are too much for Kurtz's 'inner strength' and 'capacity for faithfulness'. Marlow's reasoning is bare, general and slanted. It is of a piece with Benjamin Kidd's analysis of 'the white man sinking slowly to the level around him', Conrad, however, does not provide a deeper and specific analysis. Marlow speaks of 'the awakening of forgotten and brutal instincts' in Kurtz, of 'gratified and monstrous passions', of 'certain midnight dances ending with unspeakable rites which were offered up to Mr Kurtz'. But the objective realities of these African experiences enter the drama only slightly and unsatisfactorily. One such instance occurs when Marlow's steamer is about to leave the outpost with Kurtz aboard:

> I pulled the string time after time. They broke and ran, they leaped, they crouched, they swerved, they dodged the flying terror of the sound. The three red chaps had fallen flat, face down on the shore, as though they had been shot dead. Only the barbarous and superb woman did not so much as flinch, and stretched tragically her bare arms after us over the sombre and glittering river.

The suggestion for 'gratified and monstrous passions' is meagre; the woman's action takes the form of a grand-opera pose.

The element of weakness in Conrad's presentation of African realities can be related to his attitudes towards and knowledge of them. We have noticed that he has certain conventional attitudes towards the negroes and knew little about them and that consequently he cannot portray negroes as Joyce Cary can. If we consider African realities in particular, we see that neither in *An Outpost of Progress* nor in *Heart of Darkness* does he penetrate deep into African culture, as Cary does. Conrad did visit the Congo, and Richard Curle has shown that the earlier phases of *Heart of Darkness* are based closely on the author's own Congo journey.[20] Conrad's 'Congo Diary' is sketchy, and covers only the first two months of his four-month stay in the Congo, but it is unlikely that a European of his character would have got to know his carriers or other Africans, let alone African culture. Jocelyn Baines points out that in the Congo during Conrad's visit there was an agent named Georges Antoine Klein who was reported to be sick and 'in the manuscript of the story Conrad starts by writing Klein and then changes to Kurtz'.[21] But Norman Sherry thinks that Kurtz was modelled on Arthur Eugene Constant Hodister more than on Klein. Hodister was in the Congo during 1890 and Klein was working under him. Sherry says that Hodister's 'character, charisma and success suggest that he was at least in part the inspiration for Kurtz', yet adds 'I do not believe that Conrad ever met Hodister but I believe that he had heard of him through gossip and hearsay'.[22] So it is not certain how much personal experience and information contributed to Conrad's portrait of Kurtz. As for the factual basis of Kurtz's secrets, by 1899 there were available a number of careful and substantial works by eminent anthropologists, such as Sir Edward Burnett Tylor's *Primitive Culture* (1871) and Sir James George Frazer's *The Golden Bough, A Study in Magic and Religion* (1890), which dealt among other things with the kind of realities which Conrad tries to handle in the tale. Indeed, a critic, Stephen A. Reid, using Frazer's *The Golden Bough*, has suggested that 'Kurtz's unspeakable rites and secrets concern (with whatever attendant bestiality) human sacrifice and Kurtz's consuming a portion of the sacrificial victim'.[23] But this seems to me speculation which is not sufficiently based on Conrad's type of art. The realities of the Kurtz phase in the tale are far from clear and the main reason for this is probably that Conrad himself had much less first-hand or even second-hand knowledge (though the latter was abundantly available) than his kind of imagination needed. In a letter to R. B. Cunninghame Graham, he confessed that he knew much less than Roger Casement:

'He could tell you things! Things I've tried to forget: things I never did know. He has had as many years of Africa as I months – almost'.[24]

Though the Kurtz phase is to Marlow 'the culminating point' of his experience, it is Kurtz who matters to the reader more than Marlow as far as the tale is concerned. The episode reaches a climax with Kurtz's death. His final cry, 'The horror! The horror!', is interpreted by Marlow as 'complete knowledge' and 'a moral victory', as a rejection of 'going native'. Critics usually follow Marlow's inference; to J. I. M. Stewart, it can signify 'an act of contrition'.[25] But it seems to me that Kurtz's cry can no less validly be understood as a recoil from the whole mess of European rapacity and brutality in Africa into which he is being taken back: it is necessary to remember, first, that Kurtz desires to remain permanently in the heart of Africa and, secondly, that certain aspects of civilised behaviour do, as presented, appear horrors. Both interpretations can stand, just as Marlow's view of Kurtz and his disciple's view of him do not cancel out each other. There is an essential ambiguity in Conrad's presentation of Kurtz. His ironic first-person narrative mode permits, indeed, lends itself to, this kind of equivocalness and non-commitment.

Now let us pay more attention to Marlow. We noticed his chauvinistic blindness, his degree of conventionality, his honesty and humanity. He is extremely observant, but he is not unflinching. Not long after his arrival at the Central Station, he says: 'I went to work the next day, turning so to speak, my back on that station. In that way only it seemed to me I could keep my hold on the redeeming facts of life'. This kind of action and attitude are characteristic of him. The work of navigation is a telling contrast to the discomposing imperial realities; he turns to this work for relief and to help maintain his balance. He adopts the same kind of attitude aboard the steamer as it approaches Kurtz's outpost: he is disturbed by the 'suspicion' that the primitive Africans ashore are 'not inhuman' but he soon sidesteps this by 'helping to put bandages on those leaky steam-pipes'. He is not the kind of person whose psyche is liable to be affected in a deep and complex way by his experiences; indeed, he guards against this, though he does find his experiences deeply disturbing and contributing to his maturation. But he himself is mainly a narrative vehicle and his value in this respect is enhanced because he only half understands his experience; to echo the *Four Quarters*, he had the experience but (at least partially) missed the meaning.

We noted that to Marlow the Kurtz episode is 'the culminating point' of his experience, and for a very long time critics (Hugh Clifford,

F. R. Leavis, M. C. Bradbrook, J. I. M. Stewart and Norman Sherry among them)[26] have implicitly or explicitly considered it the climax of the tale, too, presumably making here the common error of taking Marlow and Conrad to be one. But it seems to me that the climax of *Conrad's* tale is the final phase in Europe. Marlow's African journey ends at the key place from where he set out – the headquarters of the Congo Empire, Brussels. The section is pitched on a lower key than those in Africa. This is appropriate, perhaps necessary, not merely to a tale drawing to its close, but to convey and underline its final wisdom. When Marlow meets Kurtz's Intended, the presentation is somewhat sentimental, but the conclusion as a whole is not more spoilt than the Kurtz phase. Here is Marlow in Brussels:

> I found myself back in the sepulchral city resenting the sight of people hurrying through the streets to filch a little money from each other, to devour their infamous cookery, to gulp their unwholesome beer, to dream their insignificant and silly dreams. They trespassed upon my thoughts. They were intruders whose knowledge of life was to me an irritating pretence, because I felt so sure they could not possibly know the things I knew.

Here he is in the house of the Intended: 'The tall marble fireplace had a cold and monumental whiteness. A grand piano stood massively in a corner; with dark gleams on the flat surfaces like a sombre and polished sarcophagus'. The prominent suggestions of darkness and death in Europe link up with the same suggestions in the African phases to imply how the prosperity in the metropolitan country is based on inhumanity in the Empire. This effect was achieved in the same way between the opening and the African phases which followed. The parallel makes for valid emphasis. Conrad is showing up, ironically, the unawareness of people in the metropolitan country and that there are even more 'things' than Marlow knows. The ironies at the end are of a piece and cohere with those that went before. Here is Marlow talking to Kurtz's Intended.

> 'And you admired him', she said. 'It was impossible to know him and not to admire him. Was it?'
> 'He was a remarkable man', I said, unsteady. Then before the appealing fixity of her gaze, that seemed to watch for more words on my lips, I went on, 'It was impossible not to –'
> 'Love him', she finished eagerly, silencing me into an appalled

dumbness.

Marlow speaks a deliberately ambiguous language which he mistakenly thinks adequately fits reality and, at the same time, does not destroy what he thinks are the illusions of the woman. The Intended speaks erroneously of Kurtz in Africa purely in terms of her impression of him 'before the Congo'. Conrad's ironic mode implies a criticism of both views and, at the same time, accommodates both. Through Marlow's account of his return to 'the sepulchral city' during which he refers to physical details such as the fireplace with 'a cold and monumental whiteness', a piano like a 'sarcophagus', even the woman's perfect yet pallid skin, Conrad is able to suggest, without any forcing of the symbolism, that the secure opulence of Europe is able to maintain itself intact only by a radical ignorance of, an unbridgeable distance from, the raw savageries which ultimately pay for it.

Conrad contemplates the particular imperial entanglements of Belgium and the Congo in a universal light. He does not mention Belgium, Brussels and the Congo (the country and the river) by name; this helps to give his theme the widest possible application. The man-of-war 'firing into a Continent', which Marlow sees on his voyage to the Congo, is French. Kurtz is presented as a representative of European civilisation as a whole ('All Europe contributed to the making of Kurtz'). Conrad connects Britain, past and present, to his theme. We observed that Conrad implicates the Romans, too. The tale ends with a shift of scene to the men on the yawl in the Thames:

> Marlow ceased, and sat apart, indistinct and silent, in the pose of a meditating Buddha. Nobody moved for a time. 'We have lost the first of the ebb', said the Director, suddenly. I raised my head. The offing was barred by a black bank of clouds, and the tranquil waterway leading to the uttermost ends of the earth flowed sombre under an overcast sky – seemed to lead into the heart of an immense darkness.

Conrad himself takes over the narrative from Marlow. In this final vision, the Thames, the symbol of British imperial activity and, by extension, of worldwide imperial activity, itself appears to him 'to lead into the heart of an immense darkness', to go in the same direction as the Congo. Imperial entanglements are symbolically implied to represent a black tendency in civilisation itself.

In *Heart of Darkness*, Conrad is not able to render well the entanglement of Western civilisation and primitive culture in its deepest reaches; he is not quite equal to the deepest issues which he raises. But what he achieves in the tale is substantial enough to make it a masterpiece whose relevance extends beyond the Belgian-Congolese involvements at a particular period in history to today's imperial entanglements and permanent cross-cultural problems.

6 Conrad's Nostromo: *the morality of 'material interests'*

The fact is you want more scepticism at the very foundation of your work. Scepticism, the tonic of minds, the tonic of life, the agent of truth, – the way of art and salvation.

Conrad, letter to John Galsworthy, 11 November 1901.

With *Typhoon,* completed in January 1901 about two years after *Heart of Darkness,* Conrad reached maturity as an artist. He was then capable of moving on to *Nostromo* (September 1904), one of the greatest novels in English. He developed with the extraordinary rapidity of a great artist. His creative interests continue to be found outside Britain, this time in Latin America. Costaguana is a developing country, but it is different from the Malay Archipelago and the Congo. The latter are colonies, whereas the former is politically independent ('the great Liberator Bolivar' had seen to that) while belonging to the financial 'empire' of the Holroyds and Sir John.

Conrad concentrates on a single historical phase of Costaguana – the period which begins with Charles Gould's development of the silver mine and ends with the founding of the Occidental Republic; but Conrad recreates the past sufficiently for his purposes and goes as far back as the rule of Guzman Bento; he includes a glimpse of the future, too. While it embraces the whole of Costaguana (and more) in its significance, the drama of *Nostromo* centres on one province, Sulaco. Characteristically for Conrad, Sulaco is an isolated setting and the whole environment (its geography, history, economy, politics and society) is brought to life. The opening of the novel is typical of Conrad's rendering of the setting and shows nothing of the strained, vague exoticism which mars his presentation of Malayan realities in *Almayer's Folly* and *An Outcast of the Islands.* The setting is established with an eye to precise realistic detail and an apparent ease, though Conrad said (in a letter to Edward Garnett): 'Nostromo is finished; a fact upon which my friends may congratulate me as upon a recovery from a dangerous illness'.[1] He highlights the main bearings of the locale – Punta Mala, Azuera, the Isabels, Golfo Placido, Cordillera and Higuerota. Jerry Allen thinks that 'the setting was Colombia and the isthmus, Cartagena and Panama and Cólon'.[2] It is true that the fictive realities appear specifically Latin American, but they do not seem to me to belong to particular Latin American regions. There is a certain generalising quality in Conrad's presentation of them, as in his rendering of Malayan realities. The same impression is conveyed by the human context. In fact, Costaguana is a whole country which Conrad creates in his imagination. In his view it 'is meant for a South American state in general'[3] and it is realised as such. Thus, our discussion of *Nostromo* is a discussion of Conrad's reaction to South America as a whole.

He has selected as his central theme the evil human effects of economic imperialism, a major social phenomenon in independent developing countries. Of course, Conrad does not use the term 'economic imperialism'; it became current only recently, when thinkers in the developing countries themselves worked out the terms and concepts necessary in their own struggles for independence. But it is economic imperialism that he is contemplating so profoundly, about half a century before thinkers came to terms with it. Conrad's term for it is 'material interests'. The term is less specific and is in keeping with his period. It is the kind of ordinary phrase that could plausibly rise to the lips of people quite often as it does in the case of the characters in this novel. It receives an extraordinarily rich specific significance from the unfolding action.

During the opening, Conrad unobtrusively introduces his main theme while he sketches his setting – through the story of the two *gringos*. It acts as a kind of traditional *exemplum* of the evil consequences of greed. It serves as a *leitmotiv* till the end of the novel: Nostromo thinks of it when he becomes a slave of the silver he has stolen. In one way, the *exemplum* intensifies Nostromo's, and the reader's, sense of Nostromo's 'moral ruin'[4] which ironically contrasts with his appearance of success. In another way beyond Nostromo's consciousness, it suggests that the web of modern economic imperialism, in which Nostromo gets entangled, develops from a weakness besetting this part of the world, rich in precious metal. Thus, the story of the *gringos* is a meaningful *leitmotiv* and suggests the closely woven texture of the novel.

But the major centre of interest lies elsewhere; Conrad himself indicates it (in a letter to Dr Ernst Bendz): 'I will take the liberty to point out that Nostromo has never been intended for the hero of the Tale of the Seaboard. Silver is the pivot of the moral and material events, affecting the lives of everybody in the tale'.[5] Silver is the 'precise correlative' in the novel for 'material interests', as against the view of Arnold Kettle who suprisingly does not recognise it as such.[6] But how appropriate and effective a 'correlative' is it? Michael Wilding argues:

> And with something as complex as 'the rationale of modern economics and politics', a blanket symbol like silver can never surely be adequate. There is something strangely unmodern about the conception of using a central symbol like silver; it is almost medieval in the attitude of mind, like *Pearl*, or Langland's Lady Mede, and we have already noted *The Faerie Queene*-like iconography of the description of Nostromo. What is especially strange is that such symbolisation should be used, and used so centrally, in a novel dealing with the political, social and economic themes of the modern world.
>
> By choosing a silver mine and by using the silver of the mine as his central image, Conrad has confused the issue of capitalist imperialism.[7]

Wilding is unable to appreciate Conrad's symbol because he misapprehends the nature of the microcosm of the novel. The silver is in part a traditional symbol, but this enhances its value; like the story of the *gringos*, it serves to connect modern acquisitiveness with long-standing greed. It may not be an appropriate symbol for the stock-market of a developed country; but it is in its major aspect a perfectly modern symbol of imperialism which completely suits a part of an economic empire; this is what Costaguana is. The silver is not allegorical. It is the actual raw wealth of a country which private individuals, colonial companies and imperial powers covet (it acts like copper in Katanga or like rubber in Malaya and Ceylon), at the same time as it is a symbolic centre for their self-aggrandising motives. This specific historical interest, which underlies the highly concrete art of the novel, quite disappears if one treats it as 'a picture of the modern world in microcosm'. The erroneous approach is customary among critics; it is followed not only by Wilding but also by Walter Allen, Douglas Hewitt and Robert Penn Warren.[8]

Captain Mitchell summarises his view of the silver mine during his recital of the Sulaco Revolution: 'A great power, this, for good and evil, Sir. A great power'. This is a representative commonplace view. The very fact that it is expressed by the rather dull Mitchell suggests ironically that it is not the true import of the action. During the early phases of the main action, the mine does appear, in a way, 'a great power for good'. Costaguana is politically unstable; it could have four governments in six years; 'the tyranny of Guzman Bento' is followed by a 'fatuous turmoil of greedy factions'. During this 'turmoil', Charles Gould begins to develop the mine. The domestic entrepreneur, Gould, has foreign (English) affiliations and he needs the support of a foreign investor, Holroyd. The economic enterprise, the mine, needs a political agent at Sta Marta; it tactfully and extensively bribes those with political influence to be left in peace. These insights into an economic 'colony' are authentic. They indicate that Conrad has the kind of intelligence necessary to present the kind of central theme in *Nostromo*. But it is more important to the success of the novel that Conrad has the ability to dramatise insights of this kind. Let us consider the luncheon scene on board the *Juno*:

> 'My husband wanted the railway', Mrs Gould said to Sir John in the general murmur of resumed conversations. 'All this brings nearer the sort of future we desire for the country, which has waited for it in sorrow long enough, God knows. But I will confess that the other day, during my afternoon drive when I suddenly saw an Indian boy ride out of a wood with the red flag of a surveying party in his hand, I felt something of a shock. The future means change – an utter change. And yet even here there are simple and picturesque things that one would like to preserve'.
>
> . . . .
>
> 'The honour of the country is in the hands of the army. I assure you I shall be faithful to it'. He [General Montero] hesitated till his roaming eyes met Sir John's face, upon which he fixed a lurid, sleepy glance; and the figure of the lately negotiated loan came into his mind. He lifted his glass. 'I drink to the health of the man who brings us a million and a half of pounds'.
>
> He tossed off his champagne, and sat down heavily with a half-surprised, half-bullying look all round the faces in the profound, as if appalled, silence which succeeded the felicitous toast. Sir John did not move.
>
> 'I don't think I am called upon to rise', he murmured to Mrs Gould. 'That sort of thing speaks for itself'. But Don José Avellanos came to the rescue with a short oration, in which he alluded pointedly to England's goodwill towards Costaguana – 'a goodwill', he continued, significantly, 'of which I, having been in my time accredited to the court of St James, am able to speak with some

knowledge'.

Conrad puts imperial 'exploitation' bluntly and dramatically in the foreground when General Montero proposes a toast to money. He shows how Sir John is nonplussed and how, being an experienced businessman, he diplomatically turns to genteel conversation with Mrs Gould. Through Mrs Gould, Conrad points to the social change brought about by imperialism. He also conveys an irony beyond her consciousness through Montero's toast – that the social change is a byproduct of 'exploitation'. He brings in through Avellanos the most loudly proclaimed motive of imperialism, altruism, and ironically suggests its hollowness through the pomposity of the character and the already-established fact of 'exploitation'. Thus, Conrad transmutes into drama an all-sided understanding of imperialism, an understanding of the multiplicity of ironies in the roles of the imperialists.

The roles of Charles Gould and his wife make the chief contribution to the impression of social promise held out by the mine at the start. Though Holroyd is a hard-headed investor, Gould is not an imperialist at this stage. He is a creole, though he does not become really naturalised; he remains more English than Costaguanan. His wife and he react to his father's ultimately fatal attitudes in this way: 'It was as if they had been morally bound to make good their vigorous view of life against the unnatural error of weariness and despair. If the idea of wealth was present to them it was only so far as it was bound with that other success'. He tells her:

> . . . What is wanted here is law, good faith, order, security. Anyone can declaim about these things, but I pin my faith to material interests. Only let the material interests once get firm footing, and they are bound to impose the conditions on which alone they can continue to exist. That's how your money-making is justified here in the face of lawlessness and disorder. It is justified because the security which it demands must be shared with an oppressed people. A better justice will come afterwards. . . .

Thus, Gould's motives in developing the mine are half privately moral and half patriotically social. His wife cannot share his public motive: she is much more a foreigner; she was born outside Costaguana and has no long-standing family connection with it. But she does share his private moral idealism. And, in fact, by adapting himself to the corruptness of Costaguana politics, Gould realises his aims *partially*: 'Security seemed to flow upon this land from the mountain-gorge. The authorities of Sulaco had learned that the San Tomé mine could make it worth their while to leave things and people alone'. The mine as '*imperium in imperio*' is a constantly-struck chord. It becomes 'the fountain of honour, of prosperity and peace'.

To achieve his intentions *fully*, however, Gould finds that adjustment to political reality is not enough:

> The extraordinary development of the mine had put a great power into his hands. To feel that prosperity always at the mercy of unintelligent greed had grown irksome to him. To Mrs Gould it was humiliating. At any rate, it was dangerous. In the confidential communications passing between Charles Gould, the King of Sulaco, and the head of the silver and steel interest far away in California, the conviction was growing that any attempt made by men of education and integrity ought to be discreetly supported.

'The Ribierist party whose watchwords were honesty, peace, and progress' is typical of an 'economic colony' and assumes power in a manner characteristic of such a country. It represents a movement for political improvement spearheaded by the Europeanised upper class, the Blancos; the mass of the people are politically very immature and have no say in government. The change has to be brought about by a revolution, which needs the help of the army – the army of General Montero, a man different from the Ribierist leaders, a crude power-hungry politician masquerading as a general. The change also requires, and is exploited by, imperialist power: the 'tacit approval [of Holroyd] made the strength of the Ribierist movement'. But the Ribierist regime is short-lived. Because the country is not yet developing, there is a dearth of leadership and drive. 'The life and soul of the party', Don José Avellanos, is very old and feeble. Ribiera is a 'scrupulous constitutionalist', but he is a 'man of delicate and melancholy mind, physically almost a cripple, coming out of his retirement into a dangerous strife at the call of his fellows'. Don Juste Lopez, the President of Sulaco, is not less inept than Ribiera. A dictatorship (this time with laudable aims) is necessary because the country is not ripe for representative government. It is overthrown by a 'military revolt' engineered by General Montero and his brother, Pedro. Characteristically for such a country, it is the army that often makes, maintains and breaks governments; this is evident in the careers of General Ne Win in Burma, General Ayub Khan in Pakistan, General Suharto in Indonesia, Lt. Gen.

Olusegun Obasanjo in Nigeria, Brigadier Afrifa in Ghana, General Castello Branco in Brazil and General Moreales Bermudez in Peru. When Pedro Montero enters Sulaco, 'the President of the Provincial Assembly' comes out 'bravely to save the last shread of parliamentary institutions (on the English model)'. The irony works on the surface in the use of 'bravely' and deepens when we come to 'on the English model'. It does not merely suggest the superficial incongruity of English-type institutions in an alien and developing country, but also a certain basic unsuitability in them. As in Costaguana, parliamentary systems on the English model have failed in several developing countries in recent times and have been ironically replaced by their very negation, one-party states or virtual dictatorships; this has happened in Burma, Pakistan, Tanzania, Ghana and Nigeria, after the Second World War. Of course, the content of government matters more than the form and some of these one-party states or virtual dictatorships, like the Blanco regimes in Costaguana, have tried, in appreciable degrees, to serve the mass of the people. It is an irony, characteristic of developing politics, that tyrants use the name of 'democracy' as a mask. Pedro Montero 'was going to take possession of Sulaco in the name of Democracy'; Guzman Bento had referred to his dreadful tyranny as 'the democratic form of government'. In the real world, Ayub Khan and Sukarno called their autocratic regimes 'guided democracy' and 'basic democracy', respectively.

Irving Howe points out that 'through his extraordinary insight, Conrad came upon a basic pattern of Latin American politics'; he indicates how the politics of *Nostromo* parallel the politics of Cuba from the 1930s to the 1950s.[9] But it seems to me that Conrad's achievement is greater. Developing countries in the West and in the East have much in common, and Conrad in artistic terms hits upon a paradigm of the economics, the politics, and their interrelations, of all 'economic colonies'. The scale of his vision entails a perspective into the future. The final phase of the main public drama is the founding of the Occidental Republic. It achieves a 'flourishing and stable condition', mainly because of the Gould Concession. Public opinion recognises the importance of the Concession and favours it wholly at first. But the glimpses into the future suggests contrary tendencies:

'We have worked for them; we have made them, these material interests of the foreigners', the last of the Corbeláns uttered in a deep, denunciatory tone.
'And without them you are nothing', cried the doctor

[Monygham] from the distance. 'They will not let you'.

'Let them beware, then, lest the people, prevented from their aspirations, should rise and claim their share of the wealth and their share of the power', the popular Cardinal-Archbishop of Sulaco declared, significantly, menacingly.

Conrad validly suggests the transitional nature of semi-colonial capitalism. But he goes on to endorse Dr Monygham's and Mrs Gould's views of the future. Here is Monygham's view:

There is no peace and no rest in the development of material interests. They have their law, and their justice. But it is founded on expediency, and is inhuman; it is without rectitude, without the continuity and the force that can be found only in a moral principle. Mrs Gould, the time approaches when all that the Gould Concession stands for shall weigh as heavily upon the people as the barbarism, cruelty, and misrule of a few years back.

Here is Mrs Gould's view: 'She saw the San Tomé mountain hanging over the Campo, over the whole land, feared, hated, wealthy; more soulless than any tyrant, more pitiless and autocratic than the worst Government; ready to crush innumerable lives in the expansion of its greatness'. In his recoil from the material facts of modern life, Conrad is of his age and in line with the nineteenth-century tradition of warning against the inhuman effects of unbridled industrial and technical growth – the tradition of Cobbett, Carlyle, Dickens, Ruskin and Morris. It is only a minority even today who have come to terms positively with modern developments; David Craig is one of them:

Now, it would be foolish to burke the truth that the rapid disruption started by the Industrial Revolution undermined, and actually demoralised, the masses who were uprooted from the country and flung into the towns. But there are ways and ways of viewing this change – defeatist ways and constructive ways. . . . when we speak of immemorial ways of life, we must remember how cramped a range of vocations they offered: consider the release of wider human talents made possible by the growth of technology and of organisation. . . . I have suggested that it is futile to draw up an overall comparison between the old and contemporary types of culture. This is partly because we are now as we are; we have the means we now have; it is these alone that we can use. Therefore the only positive course is to cooperate with the hopeful present trends.[10]

The public drama in *Nostromo* goes with several significant personal themes. This is possible because of Conrad's admirable grasp of the complex interrelations between the individual and society in an 'economic colony'. Wilding, however, is unable to appreciate this:

> We move not through an interrelated society in *Nostromo* but from group to group. *Middlemarch*, at the opposite pole, shows a society in which individuals are involved with each other by their social ties; but at the same time the gulfs – between the businessmen and the country set, for instance – are clearly there. In Sulaco there are only gulfs.[11]

English provincial society in *Middlemarch* and Costaguanan society are so different as to make Wilding's comparison valueless. It is true that there are 'only gulfs' between groups in Sulaco society, but this is part of Conrad's triumph; he has portrayed accurately the society of a country in a state of wildly uneven development. At the same time, he is aware of the interrelations of the social and personal aspects of human behaviour *within each group*. Charles Gould begins to develop the mine out of motives part social and part personal; before long, he is possessed by his public role as owner of the mine. This isolates him from his wife and destroys his private marital life. We find Mrs Gould's social service particularly touching because it is, in one way, a substitute, and a poor one at that, for a close personal relationship with her husband. Conrad is also aware that a whole complex of motives, personal and social, could converge on a single important event and *cross the gulfs between social groups*. This awareness is exemplified by his presentation of the removal of the silver from the Sulaco harbour. Decoud accurately records in his pocketbook the different motives of Gould and his wife: 'Don Carlos's mission is to preserve unstained the fair name of his mine; Mrs Gould's mission is to save him from the effects of that cold and overmastering passion, which she dreads more than if it were an infatuation for another woman'. Nostromo, 'a man of the People' (as Conrad calls him in his 'Author's Note' to the novel),[12] is entrusted with the actual job of saving the silver and he accepts it for the sake of personal prestige. Decoud as he sees himself, is 'the man with a passion, but without a mission'; he proposes to use the silver for a public task, to help establish a separate Occidental Republic, but this overt public purpose is a means to achieve a wholly personal aim, to win Antonia for himself.

Conrad examines diverse and representative values, which are important and even fundamental, in relation to 'material interests'. The frailty of Gould's idealism is implied in the way he succumbs to the silver and allows it to estrange him from his wife. But he does have a certain extraordinary strength which enables him to run the mine, undaunted by the difficulties of a country such as Costaguana. Holroyd is a typical American investor: '. . . We shall run the world's business whether the world likes it or not. The world can't help it – and neither can we, I guess'. His sense of religion is corrupted by 'material interests': ' ". . . he looked upon his own God as a sort of influential partner, who gets his share of profits in the endowment of churches" [Mrs Gould]'. Nostromo, however, belongs to a different social sphere and is a very different kind of person. At first, the prominence of silver in his appearance underlines ironically his desire to live for the sake of public prestige and remain above the struggle for wealth. The vulnerability and inadequacy of his values are revealed during the episodes after the removal of the silver from the Sulaco harbour. He becomes disenchanted with his role; he acquires a bitter sense of himself as a mere tool of others, a bitter sense of the ill-treatment of the people by the wealthy and of a possible bleak future for idealistic vanity as first suggested by Teresa. As Conrad observes (in his 'Author's Note' to the novel), Nostromo's 'conviction of having been betrayed is bewildered';[13] it gives rise to a resentment which makes him steal the silver. As 'a faithful and lifelong slave' to the silver, he himself feels the ironies of his changed role: he is aware of the 'moral ruin' of his fidelity and incorruptibility as well as aware of the respect and trust accorded to him as Captain Fidanza. He dies a victim of the silver. On his death, Linda utters a piercing 'cry of undying passion', and Conrad writes: '. . . the genius of the magnificent Capataz de Cargadores dominated the dark gulf containing his conquests of treasure and love'. In a sense, Nostromo captured the silver, but, in another sense, it conquered him; hence the irony of 'conquest of treasure'. In a sense, he won love on the island; he conquered both Giselle and Linda. But, in another sense, he was not complete conqueror. Slavery to the silver makes him officially accept Linda as his betrothed, though he preferred Giselle. He betrays Linda and makes love to Giselle secretly; but it is Linda who is going to remember him. The final irony is that it is his 'conquests of treasure and love' that have brought about his death. These ironies contribute to make this conclusion of the novel in keeping with its whole drift of deep scepticism.

'Material interests', then, as they appear realistically and symbolically in the form of the silver, are a potent source of corruption. But what of Giorgio Viola, Captain Mitchell and Don Pepe? Their values are not corrupted by the silver. Viola remains 'the idealist of the old humanitarian revolutions' (as Conrad regards him in his 'Author's Note' to the novel).[14] Captain Mitchell retains the values of the Merchant Service – discipline, sobriety and solidity. Don Pepe is the loyal retired military man. But Viola is an old man, and an immigrant, who cannot affect or take part in the affairs of the country. Captain Mitchell (like Captain MacWhirr) and Don Pepe are rather dense, and they actively support the 'material interests'.

Decoud is very different. His sceptical mind is intelligent. He is an acute analyst of character and also an acute analyst of the state of his country: '. . . Now the whole land is like a treasure-house, and all these people are breaking into it, whilst we are cutting each other's throats . . .'. Conrad also suggests the limitations of Decoud's kind of scepticism. His love for Antonia is presented as a healthy, positive development; it rescues him from the barren side of his scepticism because it evokes warm, stable feelings and gives him a sense of purpose in life. The insufficiency of his scepticism is underlined most forcefully when it fails him on the Great Isabel at the moment of his greatest need: 'Solitude from mere outward condition of existence becomes very swiftly a state of soul in which the affectations of irony and scepticism have no place'. He commits suicide in the Placid Gulf: 'A victim of the disillusioned weariness which is the retribution meted out to intellectual audacity, the brilliant Don Martin Decoud, weighted by the bars of San Tomé silver, disappeared without trace, swallowed up in the immense indifference of things'. Wilding argues that the silver as a symbol is 'pointless and even misleading here'.[15] But it seems to me purposive. It is true that Decoud is not corrupted by the silver but the meaning of the symbol at this point is not to indicate corruption. Rather, it helps to convey how Decoud has been ruined by allowing himself to get involved in the affairs that flow from the silver mine.

Among the important characters, Dr Monygham and Mrs Gould have the values which are both least unbalanced and least vulnerable to corruption by the silver. Monygham is intelligent but cynical. His betrayal of friends under severe torture is to him a serious falling short of an ideal of conduct (to us, an impossibly high one) 'fit and proper for an officer and a gentleman'. He is isolated, not generally trusted or liked. The semi-colonial situation has permanently maimed him in several ways. His self-rehabilitation – after he proves his worth to himself in leading Sotillo astray – makes him more socially accepted without redeeming the 'crabbed' despondency and severity of his outlook. The silver itself does not corrupt him but he serves its cause: he is doing this when he leads Sotillo astray; his devotion to Mrs Gould is devotion to a person connected with the affairs of the mine.

Mrs Gould represents personal relations and sensitive humanity. She shares the personal side of her husband's idealistic view of the mine, but, unlike him, she is not possessed by the silver. Still, she is not an effective force. She can win the devotion of Monygham, but cannot retain the love of her husband or save him from the evil side of the silver. She remains *deraciné* and lonely. She is not usually led astray as such by the silver, but it affects her; she loses her balance and comes to hate it; it cuts off her husband from her; and she serves its cause. She is even driven to hide the news of Montero's victory from her husband on Decoud's advice till the silver comes down from the mine.

'Material interests', then, affect all the characters and test their values, all of which emerge as more or less qualified. 'Material interests' pervade the whole texture of life in the 'economic colony' and constitute the essence of such an environment. Conrad presents them magnificently as the centre of his novel. He has selected a whole range of representative personal tendencies and representative modes of social behaviour, and presented them in interrelation so as to suggest a whole society in flux. This impression is created partly by a cinematic method of montage, of bold and skilful shifts of time, scene and focus. At the very beginning of the novel, we are given a glimpse of the defeated Ribiera; soon after we are shown some of the fighting around that time; when these scenes are followed by a presentation of the beginnings of the Ribiera regime, the juxtaposition suggests meaningfully the movement of history; it ironically introduces a sense of futility into the hopes of the Ribierists and a sense of sombreness into the fears raised by General Montero. Similarly, when Sulaco is threatened by Sotillo and Montero, Conrad inserts a flashback to Monygham's past under Bento; it suggests the dreadful nature of the future if the Monteros succeed and enhances the worthiness of Gould's attempt to oppose them. Conrad also uses changes of viewpoint and style in the same kind of way: at one time we have the luncheon scene aboard the *Juno* with its dramatic presentation; at another, Decoud putting down his sceptical view of the action in his pocketbook; at still another, Captain Mitchell relating events in his fussy uncomprehending manner. The power in Conrad's presentation of the theme of 'material interests' depends a great deal on his use of symbolism – the telegraph, the railway and, above all, the silver. It is only at the very end that the symbolism seems, at times, a trifle factitious.

Till he wrote *Nostromo*, Conrad had not handled more than six or seven important characters in a single work. Here he controls about three times that number. They represent virtually a cross-section of society and so fulfil a necessary condition if he is to dramatise a historical phase, a period in the life of a whole society. He combines generalising and specifying methods of presentation. The various sections of society are treated as groups; at the same time, he spotlights certain figures in the groups; these figures are treated as types or, in the case of the important characters, as individuals who are representative. Holroyd and the engineer-in-chief are types, of the American investor and the commercial-minded foreign technician, respectively. The Goulds are realised as individuals who represent the class of enterprising settlers in a country ripe for development. Conrad knows that in such a country the settlers are in a minority, that they have an importance far exceeding their number, that they comprise a variety of individuals. Gould is one kind of settler, Captain Mitchell another, and Monygham a third. Characteristically for a semi-colony, the settlers and the foreigners form an exclusive upper-class society, together with the Europeanised Costaguanan aristocrats. Characteristically again, it is almost exclusively the rich aristocrats, such as Don José Avellanos, Antonia, Decoud and Corbelán, who are politically conscious and lead the poverty-stricken mass of the people. As Costaguana is embroiled in political struggle, Conrad brings in a number of politicians such as the maniacal Bento, the brutish fighter General Montero, the superficially refined and perversely romantic (he imagines himself a second Duc de Morny) Pedro Montero, the inept 'constitutionalists' Ribiera and Don Juste Lopez. In his attempt to devalue *Nostromo*, Wilding objects: 'the people are not shown at all except as coloured extras'.[16] He disregards Nostromo's role as an individual who is a representative of the people; he rises from the cargadores, as Zapata rose from the Mexican peasantry; he is outstanding among the workers and belongs to them. And Nostromo is obviously a major character. Admittedly, the life of the people, as conveyed through characters such as Nostromo and the Violas, enters the drama much less than the life of the upper classes, but this is perfectly in keeping with the dynamics of a backward country. In this kind of society, most people are too poor, ill-educated and powerless to influence appreciably social conditions under which they themselves live.

One critical issue remains: the question of characterisation. It seems to me that Conrad characterises to the degree necessary in a novel whose prime concern is with experiences of a public kind. Most of the characters, in particular the leading ones, exist, in the first place, for what they are and, by extension, for what they represent. It is true that they do not have depths or complexities which are highly developed on the psychological plane; but at the same time their psychologies are not, as Jocelyn Baines thinks, 'on the whole crude, blurred or unconvincing'.[17] Conrad has focused on a few key traits in them; this, in fact, makes for clarity and physical presence. But he has not simplified their psychologies to the point of crudeness and implausibility. We have noticed that Charles and Emilia Gould, Decoud, Nostromo and Monygham are developing characters. Conrad does not shirk artistic problems such as presenting Decoud's psychological state on the Great Isabel:

> On the tenth day, after a night spent without even dozing off once (it had occurred to him that Antonia could not possibly have ever loved a being so impalpable as himself), the solitude appeared like a great void, and the silence of the gulf like a tense, thin cord to which he hung suspended by both hands, without fear, without surprise, without any sort of emotion whatever. Only towards the evening, in the comparative relief of coolness, he began to wish that this cord would snap. He imagined it snapping with a report as of a pistol – a sharp, full crack. . . .

Decoud's personality disintegrates under the pressure of silence and solitude. In *Heart of Darkness*, Marlow had ascribed what he considered to be Kurtz's deterioration to these same pressures. In *Nostromo*, Conrad is more specific, more sensitive and more powerful. With the help of the extended images of the void and cord, he conveys Decoud's difficult state with concrete force. In general the degree of psychological simplification Conrad employs is not a limitation because, while it allows him to make his characters sufficiently real, his major concerns are elsewhere, in the life these people share in their society. It is the social aspects that are rendered in their depths and complexities and this is what gives an impression that most of the characters, in particular the leading ones, are presented in the round. These points are brought out by scenes such as this one in Gould's room during an early stage in the development of the mine:

'Ah, if one only knew how far you mean to go', said his wife, inwardly trembling, but in an almost playful tone.

'Any distance, any length, of course', was the answer, in a matter-of-fact tone, which caused Mrs Gould to make another effort to repress a shudder.

She stood up, smiling graciously, and her little figure seemed to be diminished still more by the heavy mass of her hair and the long train of her gown.

'But always to success', she said persuasively.

Charles Gould, enveloping her in the steely blue glance of his attentive eyes, answered without hesitation:

'Oh, there is no alternative'.

He put an immense assurance into his tone. As to the words, this was all that his conscience would allow him to say.

Here Conrad dramatises how the silver is coming between the Goulds. This intimate scene is at the same time part of social life. Conrad presents the scene objectively and movingly, though it is not deeply moving. His detachment is a strength; it helps him to deal objectively and intelligently with turbulent contemporary affairs. Of course it also reduces the immediate emotional power of his fiction. Whether we are reading an intimate scene or a public one like the luncheon scene aboard the *Juno*, we see the characters as figures in a drama which we watch from the outside, without getting deeply moved, but with a greatly enhanced awareness of how lives interact in a state of social ferment.

7 Difficulties of connection in India: Kipling and Forster

> Come inside India, accept all her good and evil: if there be deformity
> then try and cure it from within, but see it with your own eyes,
> understand it, think it over, turn your face towards it, become one
> with it.
>
> Rabindranath Tagore, *Gora* (1924).

1. COLONIAL NEUROSES

Margery Perham, the distinguished authority on imperial affairs, has
spoken of her feelings when she was about to enter Somaliland for the
first time:

> I had an overwhelming spasm of recoil, of something more than
> physical fear. I referred to this in one of my Reith Lectures: a
> revulsion against the thought that I, so white, so vulnerable, so
> sensitive, so complex, was about to commit myself to that continent
> across the water, one among tens of thousands of strange, dark,
> fierce, uncomprehending people, and live away on that far frontier,
> utterly cut off from my own race. It was like a nightmare. I suppose
> it was racial fear. It passed.[1]

This kind of nightmarish experience was a characteristic aspect of
European life in the colonies, and I propose to examine its presence in
Kipling's earliest stories and Forster's *A Passage to India*. Probably,
'racial fear' is only a part of this experience; the cultural fear of the
alien and the invaders' fear of their subjects are more or less important
causes.

It is natural that this aspect of colonial life should have occupied
Kipling's mind at the beginning of his literary career just as it was a
part of Conrad's concerns in his first two (Malayan) novels and in his
African tales. Louis L. Cornell argues that Kipling's four earliest
stories were 'a false start and that it was through newspaper sketches,
not grotesque tales, that the main course of his development was to

lie'.[2] But it seems to me that 'the main course of his development' was only partly through 'newspaper sketches'; it *was* partly through these stories of nightmarish experience that he arrived at the body of his work, which focused mainly on the ordinary world of Anglo-India. The development of Kipling's interest from nightmarish experience to ordinary experience is logical: he moves from a kind of colonial experience which tends to strike a sensitive alien like Margery Perham, Conrad or himself with immediate force, to experience which impinges later on the consciousness of such a person. Moreover, Cornell's epithet, 'grotesque', does not accurately describe the earliest stories of Kipling.

There are more reasons why these stories are an integral part of Kipling's development as an artist, reasons which affect their quality. These stories illustrate the kind of unevenness despite consistent care which, W. W. Robson observes, is one feature of Kipling's work at any period of his career.[3] In all of them Kipling, like Conrad, employed narrators partly for the sake of an objectivity which became characteristic and a condition of artistic success, though it did not consistently guarantee it in his case. These stories reveal a typical economy. This probably derives mainly from his habit, as he himself confesses in his autobiography, of 'shortening his Anglo-Indian tales, first to his own fancy after rapturous re-readings and next to the space available'[4] – that is, a habit formed by considerations of artistic effect and journalistic exigence.[5] Kipling's fictive economy at times contributes to and at other times detracts from the power of his stories; these stories about nightmarish experiences are no exception. In 'The Gate of the Hundred Sorrows' (1884), he treats most fully and centrally the opium-addiction stage of Gabral Misquitta's life, but he artfully introduces a compressed account of Misquitta's whole life to bring out the full import of his deterioration. But in 'The Dream of Duncan Parrenness' (1884) he condenses too much. The story is an allegory about a European's maturation after a nightmare, set in India in the eighteenth century when Warren Hastings was Governor-General. This extremely swift maturation passes through three stages: Parrenness's future self takes from him his 'trust in man', his 'faith in women' and as much as remained to him of his 'boy's soul and conscience'. The whole process is rendered with an extreme conciseness which is partly responsible for the impression of slickness created by the development of the action.

The basic narrative mode of all the stories is the same – that of the 'sahib' recounting his experiences in the colonies. But the quality of the language in each and also the quality of the experiences, though all are broadly nightmarish, are diverse. As a Eurasian deteriorating in a colony, Misquitta in 'The Gate of the Hundred Sorrows' is a representative figure and belongs with such characters as Conrad's Almayer and Willems, Cary's Gollup in *Mister Johnson*:

> How did I take to it? It began at Calcutta. I used to try it in my own house, just to see what it was like. I never went far, but I think my wife must have died then. Anyhow, I found myself here, and got to know Fung-Tching. I don't remember rightly how that came about; but he told me of the Gate and I used to go there, and, somehow, I have never got away from it since. Mind you, though, the Gate was a respectable place in Fung-Tching's time, where you could be comfortable and not at all like the *chandookhanas* where niggers go. No; it was clean, and quiet, and not crowded. Of course, there were others beside us ten and the man; but we always had a mat apiece, with a wadded woollen headpiece, all covered with black and red dragons and things, just like the coffin in the corner.
>
> At the end of one's third pipe the dragons used to move about and fight. I've watched 'em many and many a night through. I used to regulate my Smoke that way, and now it takes a dozen pipes to make 'em stir. Besides, they are all torn and dirty, like the mats, and old Fung-Tching is dead.

An 'I' introduces the story at the beginning as that told entirely by Misquitta when he was at death's door. As the story unfolds itself, it becomes clear that Misquitta had become fatally addicted to opium. At this point, he is halfway through his account when Kipling introduces one of his flashbacks to an earlier period of his life. It coheres with the rest as a natural part of one of his open answers to the series of implied questions from the 'I', answers which compose the whole story. This flashback is one of his rather hazy recollections of the origins of his addiction, which the reader finds suggestive. Through it Kipling shows up Misquitta's deterioration in depth and, at the same time, ensures that the story is unfailingly in character. On the other hand, it is equally appropriate that Misquitta describes precisely the stage of opium-addiction because it comes later and grips his mind: he evokes the very experience of the increased addiction to opium-smoking. Through this kind of conversational idiom, Kipling presents Misquitta's case from the addict's standpoint as well as implies his own through suggestions in the language and organisation beyond the narrator's consciousness. Here Kipling suggests how Misquitta's fate is of his own making though he does not face this squarely, how he clings incongruously to his sense of superiority as a sahib when both his character and his opium den have declined. The deterioration of the den parallels and intensifies his own. Kipling uses Misquitta's expression of happiness over his poor allowance of 'sixty rupees fresh and fresh every month' as a kind of refrain which suggests an abortive attempt to appease a nagging sense of failure beneath his protestations of contentment and indifference. His last hopes are in keeping with and suggest movingly the irretrievable wreck which he has become: 'One of these days, I hope, I shall die in the Gate. . . . I should like to die like the bazar-woman – on a clean, cool mat with a pipe of good stuff between my lips. . . .'

Not all the nightmarish experiences of Europeans in colonies arise because of or are conditioned by that complex of colonial fears which I noted at the beginning of the chapter. The 'dream' of Duncan Parrenness is couched in a archaic prose to suit its period, but it remains rather artificially sterile. The dream remains artistically flimsy and is not related to those fears. In 'The Phantom Rickshaw' (1885), a much better story than 'The Dream of Duncan Parrenness', Kipling subtly suggests that Jack Pansay's 'delusion', which Pansay himself puts down in a 'blood-and-thunder magazine diction',[6] reflects a kind of schizophrenia caused mainly by his sense of guilt over his affair with Mrs Keith-Wesington. It is not presented as an experience which is typically or specially colonial.

In 'The Strange Ride of Morrowbie Jukes' (1885), however, Kipling presents a colonial kind of experience, 'going native', which appears nightmarish to a sahib. The sahib, Jukes, narrates his own story and the author introduces it. He vouches for its truth, but indicates that Jukes 'has touched it up in places and introduced Moral Reflections' presumably from his present healthy and maturer state in ordinary Anglo-India. The latter point is clear in the story, but the former is qualified by the story itself. Jukes is, certainly, true to his experience, but the experience itself is half-fantasy. The authorities of the Village of the Dead remain a mystery and the armed boat, which guards the only almost totally unknown way of escape from the Village through the swamp, is inexplicably rather strange. But these are suitable correlatives for Jukes's nightmarish experiences – of being ruthlessly hemmed in by 'native' life and of inner discomposure because of an overturning of his notion of what social roles should be and were in a colony. The European as conqueror holds the 'native' in subjection basically through force which appears nakedly during 'rebellion', but here the roles are reversed:

> As I led Pornic over the sands I was startled by the faint pop of a
> rifle across the river; and at the same moment a bullet dropped with
> a sharp '*whit*' close to Pornic's head. . . . Was ever a respectable
> gentleman in such an *impasse*?
>
> The treacherous sand-slope allowed no escape from a spot which
> I had visited most involuntarily, and a promenade on the river
> frontage was the signal for a bombardment from some insane native
> in a boat. I'm afraid that I lost my temper very much indeed.
>
> Another bullet reminded me that I had better save my breath to
> cool my porridge; . . .

Kipling captures the kind of slightly forced playfulness which a sahib
would come out with in this kind of situation, and the shooting is
described exactly. The fantasy works because it stylises into an extreme
form the actual essence of the coloniser's position.

Juke's experience is half-real in an extremely grim way. He has to
live among Hindu outcasts on the verge of death in a tiny barren
village in a crater. He has no alternative but to live on a staple diet of
crows and sleep in a filthy hole in a sandbank. Thus he is placed in
extremely primitive and difficult circumstances which test the very
essentials of his kind of character. Kipling renders ironically a range of
feelings within Jukes arising from a tension between his ingrained
sense of superiority as 'a Sahib, a representative of the dominant race',
which is absurd for one in his situation, and a sense of inescapable
degradation.

> One does not protest against the doings of a den of wild beasts; and
> my companions were lower than any beasts. While I ate what
> Gunga Dass had provided, a coarse *chapatti* and a cupful of the foul
> well-water, the people showed not the faintest sign of curiosity –
> that curiosity which is so rampant, as a rule, in an Indian village.
>
> I could even fancy that they despised me. At all events they
> treated me with the most chilling indifference, and Gunga Dass was
> nearly as bad. I plied him with questions about the terrible village,
> and received extremely unsatisfactory answers.

Jukes's experience is brought to a focus mainly through his interaction
with Gunga Dass. He had known the Indian earlier as a Government
servant with among other things 'unctuous speech'. But Dass now

treats him differently. Indeed none of the Hindus place him on his accustomed sahib's pedestal. His case is in some ways similar to and in others different from Dass's. The latter feels that his present state is a humiliation particularly because he is conscious of his past as a 'Brahmin and proud man', as a high caste and a proud man. He reconciles himself with difficulty to life in the Village, but Jukes finds it impossible to do this. The differences in their positions in Anglo-India matter here. The perils which await a person such as Jukes are indicated concretely when he learns of the Englishman who had died there and sees his remains. These carefully woven significances arise from the action whose realistic aspect, like its fantastic one, is rendered in precise detail. This is equally true of the everyday activities such as eating, and of the social attitudes that arise. It brings the story potently to the senses so that we lose the sense that it is half-fantasy. Indeed, it raises it to the level of a symbolic dramatisation of aspects of 'ruling race' and 'native' psychology in a colony.

In *A Passage to India* (1924), Forster also deals with the subject of colonial neurosis. In this respect, Adela Quested and Mrs Moore in the Marabar Caves have physical, psychological and cultural affinities with Jukes in the crater. The visit to the caves is the crux of the whole action, and their nightmarish experiences during and after it are an important part of the novel's significance. Adela imagines that Aziz had tried to rape her in a cave. Forster suggests that Aziz did not do so but he leaves vague what actually happened to Adela in there. The question as to what happened is as irrelevant as 'How many children had Lady Macbeth?' What matters is that in a situation of social and racial friction there can be smoke without a fire, 'it begins to be almost impossible to distinguish a real from a fancied injury'[7] (to quote from James Baldwin's analysis of the negro problem in American society in *The Fire Next Time* – a problem which has clear colonial analogues). The British and the Indians gather as though they were two opposed armies, as Forster suggests in the novel. The British as alien invaders feel a nightmarish sense of beleaguerment, and Forster metaphorically suggests that even nature seems to them murderously menacing because they have projected their own kind of fear onto it. Adela herself is haunted by an echo after her experience in the cave and this is a definite sign of neurosis. The echo disappears after she clears Aziz of the charge and this suggests that it is associated in her unconscious mind partly with a doubt as to his culpability and a related sense of guilt, a sense that she has brought the experience on herself.

Thus Forster is able to render the nightmarish kind of experiences of Europeans in colonies with a psychological and social depth which Kipling achieves in the best of his earliest stories, 'The Strange Ride of Morrowbie Jukes'. Yet Forster also sees a philosophical dimension to this kind of experiences which the young Kipling does not. The Marabar Caves themselves are important in this respect:

> . . . They were sucked in like water down a drain. Bland and bald rose the precipices; bland and glutinous the sky that connected the precipices; solid and white, a Brahminy kite flapped between the rocks with a clumsiness that seemed intentional. Before man, with his itch for the seemly, had been born, the planet must have looked thus. The kite flapped away . . . Before birds, perhaps . . . And then the hole belched and humanity returned.

Nature is presented accurately and strikingly in terms of human reactions to it, and is linked to the human action. Forster unobtrusively introduces symbolic suggestions of life as being puny in a world which has come to pass through a long mindless evolution; the sense of the material world as 'viscous', as so much clogging stuff devoid of values, anticipates Sartre. Suggestions of this kind begin to converge on Mrs Moore. It is mainly through her that Forster presents his deepest insights into philosophical rather than social matters. And, of course, he has selected a European for this kind of role because he is unable to see things from a fully accustomed and indigenous viewpoint.

> A Marabar cave had been horrid as far as Mrs Moore was concerned, . . . she had always suffered from faintness, and the cave had become too full, because all their retinue followed them. Crammed with villagers and servants, the circular chamber began to smell. She lost Aziz in the dark, didn't know who touched her, couldn't breathe, and some vile naked thing struck her face and settled on her mouth like a pad. She tried to regain the entrance tunnel, but an influx of villagers swept her back. She hit her head. For an instant she want mad, hitting and gasping like a fanatic. For not only did the crush and stench alarm her; there was also a terrifying echo.
> Professor Godbole had never mentioned an echo; it never impressed him, perhaps.

It is a European, not an Indian, who is prone to have experiences of this kind. On a realistic level, Forster renders the reactions of an elderly European woman. At the same time, he suggests symbolically a surreal sense of the unreality of the world of fact.

> The echo in a Marabar cave is . . . entirely devoid of distinction. Whatever is said, the same monotonous noise replies, and quivers up and down the walls until it is absorbed into the roof. 'Boum' is the sound as far as the human alphabet can express it, or 'bou-oum', or 'ou-boum', – utterly dull. Hope, politeness, the blowing of a nose, the squeak of a boot, all produce 'boum'.

The echo is real and, at the same time, a recurring symbol of a sense of nullity. It goes with that sense of life as being puny and these two kinds of symbolism intensify each other.

> The crush and the smells she could forget, but the echo began in some indescribable way to undermine her hold on life. Coming at a moment when she chanced to be fatigued, it had managed to murmur, 'Pathos, piety, courage – they exist, but are identical, and so is filth. Everything exists, nothing has value'. If one had spoken vileness in that place, or quoted lofty poetry, the comment would have been the same – 'ou-boum'. If one had spoken with the tongues of angels and pleaded for all the unhappiness and misunderstanding in the world, past, present, and to come, for all the misery men must undergo whatever their opinion and position, and however much they dodge or bluff – it would amount to the same, the serpent would descend and return to the ceiling. Devils are of the North, and poems can be written about them, but no one could romanticise the Marabar because it robbed infinity and eternity of their vastness, the only quality that accommodates them to mankind.

For an instant the prose here deteriorates into false rhetoric ('Devils are of the North and poems can be written about them'); devils are found in the mythology of cultures at least as far south as Sri Lanka and Bali. This apart, the nullity and pettiness of life are presented with power and particularity. It is an outstanding characteristic of this phase of the novel that the real and the symbolic interpenetrate, and Forster thereby succeeds in the difficult task of rendering philosophical considerations with the concreteness of immediate experience. From one aspect Mrs Moore reflects the depressed sense of an absence of solidly accepted or acceptable system of values which haunts the modern European mind. In this respect Forster is in the line from Hardy (for instance, *Jude the Obscure*) and Nietzsche ('God is dead.

God remains dead. And we have killed him'), through to existentialism and the Absurd (for instance, *Waiting for Godot*).

Mrs Moore's wisdom is appreciated neither by the British nor by the Indians. Adela thinks that 'the old lady had turned disagreeable and queer' after the episode at the Caves. Aziz is attached to her emotionally, but she is 'nothing' to him in an intellectual sense. Her apotheosis as 'Esmiss Esmoor' by the mass of the Indians reflects a spontaneous religious reaction, which is primitive. She is presented by Forster with critical realism. We noticed that her elderliness matters; here is a part of the scene immediately after her experience in the cave: 'As each person emerged she looked for a villain, but none was there, and she realised that she had been among the mildest individuals, whose only desire was to honour her, and that the naked pad was a poor little baby, astride its mother's hip'. Forster suggests that she has made too much of her experience. Here she is leaving India:

> As she drove through the huge city which the West had built and abandoned with a gesture of despair, she longed to stop, though it was only Bombay, and disentangle the hundred Indias that passed each other in its streets. The feet of the horses moved her on, and presently the boat sailed and thousands of coconut palms appeared all round the anchorage and climbed the hills to wave her farewell. 'So you thought an echo was India; you took the Marabar caves as final?' they laughed. 'What have we in common with them, or they with Asirgarh? Good-bye!'

Forster suggests that it is because Mrs Moore is an outsider that she finds it impossible to understand India, though he is aware that it is an extremely complex country. Her view is deeper than the conventional 'mysterious-East' kind of view, but is still limited. Mrs Moore's character is a development from Mrs Wilcox's in *Howards End*, but, unlike Mrs Wilcox, she comes alive as both fully real and richly symbolic. The nightmarish kind of experiences of Europeans in colonies provide one way by which Forster is able to make a 'passage to more than India'[8] (to use Walt Whitman's phrase). He taps the same vein as the young Kipling; yet he attempts and achieves a much larger structure of experiences and significances than the latter.

2. BASIC COLONIAL CONFLICTS

Kipling is free of imperial limitations in his earliest stories but when we consider the work in which he contemplates relationships between

British and Indians in the ordinary world of Anglo-India, we ought to grasp how extremely difficult it is for an Englishman to get beyond the mental habits of his people, whether he is based in England or in India. For this was the age of Joseph Chamberlain and Cecil Rhodes. Chamberlain said: 'In the first place, I believe in the British Empire and, in the second place, I believe in the British race. I believe that the British race is the greatest of governing races that the world has ever seen'.[9] Rhodes wrote: 'We are the first race in the world, and, more of the world we inhabit, the better it is for the human race'.[10] In India, colonial sentiments, including racialism, appeared unmistakably during the storm over the Ilbert Bill (1882) which sought to put Europeans on the same legal footing as Indians. European agitation compelled the Viceroy, Lord Ripon, to draft a compromise whereby Europeans could ask for a jury half of whose members were of their own race. The British were thus anxious to maintain their racial identity in the colonial environment.

Kipling's early poetry is relevant to this matter. It has been pointed out that the notorious line from 'The Ballad of East and West' (1889):

Oh, East is East, and West is West, and never the twain shall meet –

is followed by

But there is neither East nor West, Border, nor Breed, nor Birth,
When two strong men stand face to face, though they come from the
ends of the earth.[11]

This may look like evidence of an absence of racialism in Kipling as Jack Dunman and M. Tarinayya think;[12] Kipling might seem to be advocating the razing of barriers between human beings. But these lines are typical of his early, not of his later, poetry; and he limits his liberalism to 'strong men', to men of action strong in limb and courage whom he characteristically admired. Both the Indian Border thief and the British Colonel's son are such men. These lines, uttered by the author, form the moral of this simple ballad. Kipling does not state or imply that the Indians and the British are equal as human beings. 'Gunga Din' (1892 or earlier), a 'barrack-room ballad', is wholly a monologue spoken by a British soldier. Through him Kipling presents a relationship between such a person and an Indian servant which appears worse than a feudal relationship between a European lord and a European serf. Probably, the servant matters to both Kipling and the soldier essentially because he is a 'strong man', like the Border thief and the Colonel's son:

> An' for all 'is dirty 'ide
> 'E was white, clear white, inside
> When 'e went to tend the wounded under fire!

Kipling captures exactly the kind of idiom and attitudes an uneducated soldier would adopt. The idiom, which is public and colloquial, lends itself to reading aloud and recitation. The attitudes fit in with popular opinions. They are based on assumptions which are partly traditional and partly imperial: 'white' has been traditionally a term of approval, and in imperial times it was associated with the Europeans to indicate (rather imprecisely) the colour of their skin and to stand for a conception of them as the sole bearers of civilisation. But at the end Kipling permits the soldier to strike an attitude which, though rather unconventional, would jolt the blimps:

> Though I've belted you and flayed you,
> By the livin' Gawd that made you,
> You're a better man than I am, Gunga Din!

Kipling's more conventional attitudes and the popular vein in his poetry soon dominate his poetic practice. Not long after 1892 he began to use '*The Times* as a platform for major poems' (in Charles Carrington's phrase).[13] He steps into Tennyson's shoes as the spokesman and prophet of the Establishment. In 'A Song of the White Man' (1899), he welcomes the Boer War and is clearly imperialistic:

> Now, this is the cup the White Men drink
> When they go to right a wrong,
> And that is the cup of the old world's hate –
> Cruel and strained and strong.

The cup of life is a vague and hackneyed symbol, and the rhythm is mainly a kind of jingle. This kind of uplift – potent because it is indefinite – caters to the 'average' mind and receives the 'average' response, whether this is forthcoming from the reader of *The Times* or from the sections of the people who had served in the Army or at least fallen for the jingoist mystique purveyed by the Harmsworth Press. When Kipling celebrates 'the White Man's burden', he 'reminds one of

a man cheering to keep his courage up'.[14] What makes A. E. Rodway
say this is no doubt the forced rhetoric of the versification. Unfortunately, such work is not sensitive enough for the latter-day reader
to gauge whether Kipling looks glumly ahead to the collapse of
Empire because human arrangements necessarily fall apart or because
the British ascendancy could already be seen to be in jeopardy.
'Recessional' (1897) was meant to be a major poem about the Empire.
It was written to mark Queen Victoria's Diamond Jubilee and was
first published in *The Times*. It is a *locus classicus* for an examination
of Kipling's maturest vision in poetry of imperial matters, including
race relations.

> Far-called, our navies melt away;
>   On dune and headland sinks the fire:
> Lo, all our pomp of yesterday
>   Is one with Nineveh and Tyre!
> Judge of the Nations, spare us yet,
> Lest we forget—lest we forget!
>
> If, drunk with sight of power, we loose
>   Wild tongues that have not Thee in awe,
> Such boastings as the Gentiles use,
>   Or lesser breeds without the Law –
> Lord God of Hosts, be with us yet,
> Lest we forget – lest we forget!

Kipling contemplates the British Empire in a historical light and
foresees its inevitable dissolution. What is breathtaking is the sense
we are palpably meant to get that it is extraordinarily noble for the
poet of the master-race to concede this inevitability. He was intelligent
enough to criticise extreme jingoism; for example, in 'The Flag of their
Country' (*Stalky and Co*) he suggests that there is considerable truth
in the schoolboys' view of Mr Raymond Martin M.P. as 'a Flopshus
Cad, an Outrageous Stinker, a jelly-bellied Flag-flapper'. But the implications of 'lesser breeds without the Law' are no less characteristic.
The notorious phrase is obscure. It could refer to any, some or all, of
the beings whom Kipling considers outside the pale of civilised order –
the Indians in general, or the Germans (as George Orwell and
Michael Edwardes think),[15] or the *Bandar-log* in *The Jungle Book* or
even the Wolves when they broke away from Akela and the Jungle
Law to follow Shere Khan and their own unbridled appetites. The
implication is that the British are the norm of a people within the Law,

even that they are uniquely endowed with the qualities necessary to carry out best the tasks of imperialism. By the same token the 'lesser breeds' are the people of the developing countries – classed as 'breeds' because the spokesman of the dominant people cannot help thinking of the subject races in animal terms.

Rodway argues that 'in Kipling's case no distinction between poetry and prose is necessary' and refers to works in both genres which have qualities in common.[16] But it seems to me that the remarkable works in each class – by which I mean both the works of rare skill *and* those that have become proverbial – make it plain that it was in his fiction that Kipling was keenly aware of social and psychological fact, whereas in his poetry he was apt to surrender to the imperial wave. In an early story such as 'Lispeth' (*Plain Tales from the Hills*), the embryo of this awareness is unmistakable. Lispeth is half servant, half companion to the wife of the Chaplain of Kotgarh. She rescues an injured young Englishman.

> She explained to the Chaplain that this was the man she meant to marry; and the Chaplain and his wife lectured her severely on the impropriety of her conduct. Lispeth listened quietly, and repeated her first proposition. It takes a great deal of Christianity to wipe out uncivilised Eastern instincts, such as falling in love at first sight.

Kipling's balanced criticism of both the Indian and the British characters is conveyed through an anonymous narrator who characteristically laces matter-of-fact presentation with sardonic comment. Here he suggests that his Indian 'heroine' is naive. At the same time he sympathises with and respects her impulsiveness. His humour at the expense of the conventionality of the British missionaries is deservedly tart.

> Being a savage by birth, she took no trouble to hide her feelings, and the Englishman was amused. When he went away, Lispeth walked with him up the hill as far as Markanda, very troubled and very miserable. The Chaplain's wife, being a good Christian and disliking anything in the shape of fuss or scandal – Lispeth was beyond her management entirely – had told the Englishman to tell Lispeth that he was coming back to marry her. 'She is but a child, you know, and, I fear, at heart a heathen,' said the Chaplain's wife. So all the twelve miles up the Hill the Englishman with his arm round Lispeth's waist, was assuring the girl that he would come back and

marry her; and Lispeth made him promise over and over again.

Thus the action develops in terms of human behaviour as influenced by the social and cultural differences between the Indian woman and the British. Kipling ironically suggests that it is the Christian and civilised characters who are two-faced and cruel whereas the primitive 'heathen' is open and trusting, though not fully confident. The English traveller quickly forgets Lispeth, but she clings to his promise and suffers. At 'a profitable time', the Chaplain's wife informs Lispeth of 'the real state of affairs'. She is shocked and later tells the Chaplain's wife: 'I am going back to my own people, . . . You have killed Lispeth. There is only left old Jadéh's daughter – the daughter of a *pahari* and the servant of *Tarka Devi*. You are all liars, you English'. 'Lispeth' (29 November 1886) was first published in the *Civil and Military Gazette* just as 'Yoked with an Unbeliever' (7 December 1886) was. But whereas in the latter story Phil Garron's association with Dunmaya is an interlude in his relationship with Agnes Laiter and is part of an undramatic 'magazine-ish' story, in the former Lispeth's affairs form its core and are presented interestingly though on a very small scale. Lispeth's actions, unlike Bisesa's in 'Beyond the Pale' (January 1888), are always psychologically consistent; Bisesa is said to be 'a widow, about fifteen years old, as ignorant as a bird', but she incongruously acts as a resourceful charmer would.

The East–West relationships in the very early stories – between Lispeth and the English traveller, between Dunmaya and Phil Garron, between Bisesa and Trejago, between Georgina (a Burmese) and Georgie Porgie in 'Georgie Porgie' (3 March 1888) – do not usually come off. The ironies of inter-racial love in a colonial context as Kipling has them are such that it is the morally better 'natives' who suffer more than the British. The failures are a consequence of the interaction of the characters but behind this are premises such as these: 'A man should, whatever happens, keep to his caste, race, and breed. Let the White go to the White and the Black to the Black. Then, whatever trouble falls is in the ordinary course of things – neither sudden, alien, nor unexpected'. These explicit generalisations are imperial and form the opening of 'Beyond the Pale' (*Plain Tales from the Hills*).

Where the Queen's Law does not carry, it is irrational to expect an observance of other and weaker rules. The men who run ahead of the cars of Decency and Propriety, and make the jungle ways straight, cannot be judged in the same manner as the stay-at-home folk of the ranks of the regular *Tchin.*

These imperial presuppositions act virtually as excuses for Georgie Porgie's treachery. Still, during the main actions of the interesting stories such as 'Lispeth' and 'Georgie Porgie' Kipling appears to remove his blinkers, though they practically predetermine the general drift of the fiction.

In a story written a little later, 'Without Benefit of Clergy' (1890), he develops the theme of race relations on a larger scale.

'But if it be a girl?'

'Lord of my life, it cannot be. I have prayed for so many nights, and sent gifts to Sheikh Badl's shrine so often, that I know God will give us a son – a man-child that shall grow into a man. Think of this and be glad. My mother shall be his mother till I can take him again, and the mullah of the Pattan mosque shall cast his nativity – God send he be born in an auspicious hour! – and then, and then thou wilt never weary of me, thy slave'.

'Since when hast thou been a slave, my queen?'

This is the opening of the story. It introduces the reader immediately to the tensions in the relationship between Holden, an English administrator, and Ameera, his Indian mistress. His confidence in the permanence of his love and her sense of insecurity appear understandable feelings. But they speak a rather stilted English which includes archaisms and conventionally exotic-romantic terms. The impact of the scene is reduced by Kipling's failure to shape an effective equivalent for the Indian vernacular – which is a weakness even in his best work of fiction, *Kim* (1901). Kipling goes on to economically elaborate the position of Holden, Ameera and her mother, and sketches their differing attitudes to a baby. When Tota is born, Holden as a sahib 'could not feel that it was a veritable son with a soul', but he does become 'full of riotous exultation, alternating with a vast tenderness directed towards no particular object'. On the other hand, Ameera, though she considers herself inferior to him, regards the baby as a normal son of both of them; she is happy partly because she thinks that the baby will cement her relationship with Holden. Ironically, he had earlier 'every hour of the night pictured to himself the death of Ameera' and 'a dread of loss' even impels him to perform the Muslim 'birth-sacrifice' to protect Tota from harm, but the baby dies of 'the seasonal autumn fever': 'The delight of that life was too perfect to endure. Therefore it was taken away as many things are taken away in India – suddenly and without warning'. Holden and Ameera 'touched happiness again, but this time with caution'. Soon after, a cholera epidemic occurs in the plains during a period of hot weather. Her intense but insecure love for Holden makes Ameera stay there by his side, though he did his best 'to persuade Ameera to go away with her mother to the Himalayas'. She is fatally stricken by the disorder. Unlike the chief British characters in the very early stories such as the traveller in 'Lispeth' and Georgie Porgie, Holden is aware of the fate of his 'native' partner and is saddened by it. To 'round off' the misfortunes of Holden and Ameera, their house is to be 'pulled down' though Holden, who has been suddenly ordered to relieve a dying colleague, wants to 'keep it on'.

Alan Sandison argues that 'the main character in the Indian stories is not the tired, tough, dedicated administrator nor the resourceful subaltern; the principal role is, in fact, played by India itself'. He implicitly accepts Kipling's view of India as having a central and inherent destructiveness.[17] But it seems to me that in some of the stories such as 'Lispeth' and 'Georgie Porgie' this view of India does not enter importantly and that, as we have noticed, their themes develop in terms of the interaction of the human characters in a particular social context with certain imperial premises behind the general drift. In stories such as 'Without Benefit of Clergy', 'At the End of the Passage' and 'The Story of Muhammad Din', India does appear something like Fate as in Hardy's novels (remember the sudden deaths of Tota and Ameera) though it is the human characters who play the substantial roles. This, in fact, detracts from the varying degrees of social and psychological depth of these stories, even of 'Without Benefit of Clergy'. It looks as though certain facts in a developing country such as India – difficulties of acclimatisation for Europeans, more disease and shorter life-expectancy than in developed countries – have been exaggerated by Kipling into a myth (the country itself as having a quality of malignancy) to support his imperial bias. This myth is central to his view of colonial officials.

It is understandable that not many of Kipling's works deal with relationships between the ruled and the rulers. As Louis L. Cornell notes, 'the passage of time brought with it an increasing estrangement between the races in British India throughout the nineteenth century', and this 'pattern' was particularly marked after the 'Mutiny'.[18] Moreover, such relationships as were struck were usually between superior and inferior social orders as in Kipling – between a regimental *bhisti* (Gunga Din) and a soldier or (a not rare social happening) between Indian mistress and European master. Kipling boldly deals with intimate inter-racial relationships between sexes, an aspect of life in a colony which Forster skirts in *A Passage to India*. Kipling's works have it, just as Forster's novel does, that Easterners and Westerners in a colony do not usually connect. But whereas in Kipling this failure derives basically from imperial views of his, in Forster it derives from a realistic view of human nature in a colonial context. Furthermore, Forster is not fatalistic and does not think that connection is impossible. Fielding and Aziz remain firm friends though their friendship is fraught with misunderstanding, anxiety, suspicion and the like which rise credibly given the differences in their characters and socio-cultural affiliations. Both are exceptional among their fellow nationals, but Forster has it positively that human nature on the side of both the colonisers and colonised can rise to their level. Of course, Aziz proves himself to be an equal of Fielding and the Englishman treats him as such, in a way typical of the educated Indian who by the 1920s was being 'respected as a man' by exceptional Europeans.[19]

A Passage to India is a classic work of fiction on the theme of race relations. Frederick C. Crews argues that 'the central question of the novel is that of man's relationship to God, it is a novel in which two levels of truth, the human and the divine, are simultaneously explored'; John Colmer thinks that it 'is a novel that explores the difficulties men face in trying to understand each other and the universe; it is not primarily concerned with questions of rule and race'.[20] Crews and Colmer represent the drift of recent criticism of *A Passage to India*. The philosophical considerations in the novel (examined above) are important, but to regard them as forming its central theme is to miss the main life of the fiction. The novel is rooted in its colonial context, though its significance is not limited to it. The racial and social connections of each character, whether British or Indian, matter in his or her affairs within or outside his or her group; these connections matter in the conversation, actions, thoughts and feelings of everyone. The theme of race relations bulks much larger than the philosophical considerations and the latter forms an integral part of it. Forster does not rate philosophical matters as intrinsically more important than social matters.

When he wrote *A Passage to India*, he had Conrad and Kipling behind him. His novel is set in the same developing country as Kipling but when we consider his reaction to it, we shall see that he is akin to Conrad rather than to Kipling. He was deeply concerned with imperial realities long before his novel appeared, at least ten years before he first went to India in 1912. In October 1903 a circle of Liberals founded *The Independent Review*, and Forster contributed short stories and non-political essays to it.[21] The journal was edited by Edward Jenks with an editorial council comprising Goldsworthy Lowes Dickinson, F. W. Hirst, C. F. G. Masterman, G. M. Trevelyan and N. Wedd. As Forster says in *Goldsworthy Lowes Dickinson*, the journal was 'founded to combat the aggressive Imperialism and the Protection campaign of Joe Chamberlain; and to advocate sanity in foreign affairs and a constructive policy at home'.[22] Forster identifies himself with other Liberals and says that the journal appeared to them 'a light rather than a fire, but a light that penetrated the emotions'.[23] Thus, at the turn of the century he is aware of imperialism in a liberal spirit.

This gets into *Howards End* (1910), which is set in Britain during the heyday of its Empire. During this period, British business was particularly closely connected with the Empire and Forster is so alert to this fact as to make his major representative of the world of business, Mr Wilcox, have imperial commercial interests. Here is Margaret at the offices of the Imperial and West African Rubber Company:

> And even when she penetrated to the inner depths, she found only the ordinary table and Turkey carpet, and though the map over the fireplace, did depict a helping of West Africa, it was a very ordinary map. Another map hung opposite, on which the whole continent appeared, looking like a whale marked out for blubber, and by its side was a door, shut, but Henry's voice came through it, dictating a 'strong' letter. She might have been at the Porphyrion, or Dempster's Bank, or her own wine merchant's. Everything seems just alike in these days. But perhaps she was seeing the Imperial side of the company rather than its West African, and Imperialism always had been one of her difficulties.
>
> 'One minute!' called Mr Wilcox on receiving her name. He touched a bell, the effect of which was to produce Charles.

This office is like the head office of the Belgian imperial company with its map which Conrad presents through Marlow in *Heart of Darkness*. Forster suggests trenchantly, through the image of the whale in particular, the wide-ranging acquisitiveness of imperialism and, at the same time, suggests how even rubber extraction, with its inhuman methods, looks from the metropolitan country as respectable as any other business. Thus, in *Howards End*, we have the embryo of the radical vision of imperial realities that is fully developed in *A Passage to India*.

Forster's artistic development was helped by the deep impact of the First World War on him; it was at this time that his mind became fully 'politicised', as we can see in some of the most trenchant pieces in *Abinger Harvest* like 'Me, Them, and You', 'A Voter's Dilemma' and 'Our Graves in Gallipoli'. His stay in the 'protectorate' of Egypt from November 1915 to January 1919 added to his first-hand knowledge of imperial affairs. His radical understanding of them with respect to that particular country is evident in his pamphlet, *Egypt* (1920), written for the Labour Research Department.

Forster, then, has a developing intelligence with regard to imperial realities. Naturally, his two visits to India, in 1912–13 and in 1921, play the chief role in this development and provide the experiences that go into *A Passage to India*. He considers his experience of Dewas State Senior 'the great opportunity of my life'.[24] It certainly was this, artistically.

Kipling called his most ambitious Indian work *Kim*, but Forster calls his novel *A Passage to India*. This title itself suggests the scale of his work – to live up to it, the novelist would have to present a wide range of experience representative of the subcontinent and at the same time it suggests that the view will be that of incomers, birds of passage, rather than an indigenous one.

As we have noticed, in an imperial situation the importance of the 'ruling race' greatly exceeds their number. Thus Forster is right to present it as such. Let us consider a scene typical of this side of the novel – Mrs Moore and Adela at the Club soon after their arrival:

'Why, the kindest thing one can do to a native is to let him die', said Mrs Callendar.

'How if he went to heaven?' asked Mrs Moore, with a gentle but crooked smile.

'He can go where he likes as long as he doesn't come near me. They give me the creeps'.

'As a matter of fact I have thought what you were saying about heaven, and that is why I am against missionaries', said the lady who had been a nurse.

. . . . .

Her [Adela's] impressions were of no interest to the Collector; he was only concerned to give her a good time. Would she like a Bridge

Party? He explained to her what that was – not the game, but a party to bridge the gulf between East and West; the expression was his own invention, and amused all who heard it.

'I only want those Indians whom you come across socially – as your friends'.

'Well, we don't come across them socially', he said, laughing. 'They're full of virtues, but we don't, and it's now eleven-thirty, and too late to go into the reasons.'

There can be no Club in outposts like Conrad's Sambir and Patusan, but it was (to use Leonard Woolf's words) 'a symbol and centre of British imperialism' in places like Chandrapore or, to move into real places under the British around this period, Lahore and Kandy.[25] Forster, then, rightly presents it as such and rightly focuses on it often in his presentation of the European side of the action. It has been observed by critics (Virginia Woolf and F. R. Leavis among them) that Forster, characteristically for his pre-War novels, employs a mode of social comedy coming down from Jane Austen.[26] But in this novel he is doing something radically original in using it to dramatise social realities in a colony. In this scene the satirical comedy has the aim of exposing the European side of these realities. The norms necessary for his criticism are formed by his liberal values which he expounds elsewhere:

Tolerance, good temper and sympathy – they are what matter really, and if the human race is not to collapse they must come to the front before long. . . .

I have, however, to live in an Age of Faith – the sort of epoch I used to hear praised when I was a boy. It is extremely unpleasant really. It is bloody in every sense of the word. And I have to keep my end up in it. Where do I start?

With personal relationships. Here is something comparatively solid in a world full of violence and cruelty. . . .[27]

It is on the firmness with which Forster holds these liberal values and on the accuracy, the sensitiveness with which he records their violation that the effectiveness of his comedy depends. In this scene he successfully confronts the attitudes of newcomers such as Mrs Moore and Adela with those of the 'veterans'; Adela's well-meaning *naiveté* is played off against the exclusive superiority and callousness of Mrs Callendar, the nurse, and Turton. In a way, Adela embodies Forster's liberal values; so do Mrs Moore and Fielding. Through them, Forster performs the necessary task of embodying his touchstones in character and, at the same time, presents them objectively as distinctive individuals. In fact, as in *Howards End*, his liberal values are part of his themes. The values are the same as in the pre-War novels, but in *A Passage to India* they are developed to cope with a colonial situation, necessarily more inflammable and more drastic in its conflicts than a developed country. Thus here it is not only personal relations which count; race relations are even more important.

In the scene quoted above, Forster dramatises differences in attitude towards the Indians among the British and suggests the gulfs between the two races. Let us turn now to his direct presentation of the gulfs, for example the Bridge Party:

> When they took their leave, Mrs Moore had an impulse, and said to Mrs Bhattacharya, whose face she liked, 'I wonder whether you would allow us to call on you some day'.
> 'When?' she replied, inclining charmingly.
> 'Whenever is convenient'.
> 'All days are convenient'.
> 'Thursday . . .'
> 'Most certainly'.
> 'We shall enjoy it greatly, it would be a real pleasure. What about the time?'
> 'All hours'.
> 'Tell us which you would prefer. We're quite strangers to your country: we don't know when you have visitors', said Miss Quested.
> Mrs Bhattacharya seemed not to know either. Her gesture implied that she had known, since Thursdays began, that English ladies would come to see her on one of them, and so always stayed in. Everything pleased her, nothing surprised. She added, 'We leave for Calcutta to-day'.
> 'Oh, do you?' said Adela, not at first seeing the implication. Then she cried, 'Oh, but if you do we shall find you gone'.
> Mrs Bhattacharya did not dispute it. But her husband called from the distance, 'Yes, yes, you come to us Thursday'.
> 'But you'll be in Calcutta'.
> 'No, no we shall not', he said something swiftly to his wife in Bengali. 'We expect you Thursday'.
> 'Thursday . . .' the woman echoed.

Mrs Bhattacharya's complete verbal compliance (later, the Bhattacharyas do not keep to their agreed appointment), divorced from her feelings and plans, reflects the political difference between rulers and subjects and also the cultural difference between Europeans and Indians: the exactitudes of industrial society have not sunk into India and altered the traditional approach to human relations and human intercourse. The speech of the Indians and that of the English register a difference in emotional and factual content. The two kinds of speech are finely differentiated in idiom, too. The Indians' speech is of particular interest. Without descending to crude babuism, Forster gives them a language slightly but distinctly different from Standard English in idiom and content; it realises the fact that English is to them an alien tongue springing from an alien culture. In this respect, Forster's artistic problem is different from Leonard Woolf's in *The Village in the Jungle*; let us consider this piece from a conservation among Sinhalese village women at the tank in Beddagama:

'Nanchohami, your tongue is still as sharp as chillies. Punchi Menika has gone with my brother, and Hinnihami is busy in the house'.

'Punchi Menika wants but three things to make her a man. I pity you, Karlinahami, to live in the house of a madman, and to bring up his children shameless, having no children of your own. They are vedda children, and will be vedda women, wandering in the jungle like men'.[28]

Woolf has to fashion an English equivalent for the Sinhalese spoken by almost all his characters, and does so. Here the speech is rooted in the jungle context through local references; the non-English turns of phrase echo Sinhalese idiom. On the other hand, Forster has to render an Indian kind of English spoken by his Westernised Indian characters, and does so.

Relations between races are more important than relations within races in this novel. In the Bridge Party scene Forster is presenting a formal occasion. In Aziz's house the contact between British and Indian is more intimate. After one of Fielding's completely candid remarks,

The Indians were bewildered. The line of thought was not alien to them, but the words were too definite and bleak. Unless a sentence paid a few compliments to Justice and Morality in passing, its grammar wounded their ears and paralysed their minds. What they said and what they felt were (except in the case of affection) seldom the same. They had numerous mental conventions, and when these were flouted they found it very difficult to function.

Forster notices that 'what they said and what they felt were (except in the case of affection) seldom the same', and puts it as if it were always and everywhere true of Indians. It seems to me that it applies most characteristically to the relations between colonised peoples and their colonisers; Forster is observing such a relationship from the point of view of a British incomer. Even given some limitation of viewpoint he can still present the situation in a fully dramatic mode:

And those Englishmen who are not delighted to be in India – have they no excuse?' he asked.

'None. Chuck 'em out'.

'It may be difficult to separate them from the rest', he laughed.

'Worse than difficult, wrong', said Mr Ram Chand. 'No Indian gentleman approves chucking out as a proper thing. Here we differ from those other nations. We are so spiritual'.

'Oh, that is true, how true!' said the police inspector.

'Is it true, Mr Haq? I don't consider us spiritual. We can't co-ordinate, we can't co-ordinate, it only comes to that. . . . So we go on, and so we shall continue to go, I think, until the end of time'.

'It is not the end of time, it is scarcely ten-thirty, ha, ha!' cried Dr Panna Lal, who was again in confident mood. 'Gentleman, if I may be allowed to say a few words, what an interesting talk, also thankfulness and gratitude to Mr Fielding in the first place teaches our sons and gives them all the great benefits of his experience and judgement –'

At the end of the scene Fielding is shown as wryly anticipating his fellow Englishmen's opinion of his behaviour – 'making himself cheap as usual'. Thus, whether they meet formally or informally, the British and the Indians find it hard to connect. Now let us turn to the purely Indian side of the action. Consider the scene, early on, when important Indian characters are discussing a central question in the novel 'as to whether or no it is possible to be friends with an Englishman':

'It is impossible here. Aziz! The red-nosed boy has again insulted me in Court. I do not blame him. He was told that he ought to insult me. Until lately he was quite a nice boy, but the others have got hold of him'.

'Yes, they have no chance here, that is my point. They come out intending to be gentlemen, and are told it will not do. Look at Lesley, look at Blakiston, now it is your red-nosed boy, and Fielding will go next.... I give any Englishman two years, be he Turton or Burton, it is only the difference of a letter. And I give any Englishwoman six months. All are exactly alike. Do you not agree with me?'

'I do not', replied Mahmoud Ali, entering into the bitter fun, and feeling both pain and amusement at each word that was uttered. 'For my own part I find such profound differences among our rulers. Red-nose mumbles, Turton talks distinctly, Mrs Turton takes bribes, Mrs Red-nose does not and cannot, because so far there is no Mrs Red-nose'.

Here Forster sees the attitudes of the Westernised Indians from their point of view and from the same critical liberal standpoint he occupies in the case of the British. These attitudes of the Indians appear the inverse of the attitudes of the British in the scene at the Club discussed above; both sets arise from the colonial situation and work against *rapport*. The remarks in this dialogue are palpably sincere: in spite of Forster's later comment, there is here no gap whatsoever between 'what they said and what they felt'. As so often Forster's insight is sounder and more exact in the dramatic mode than when he is offering to catch in one wise remark the truth of a tangled class or racial matter. Now let us turn to the Indians and their own concerns. Consider the reactions of these Muslims to news that Professor Godbole is ill:

'If this is so, this is a very serious thing: this is scarcely the end of March. Why have I not been informed?' cried Aziz.

'Dr Panna Lal attends him, sir'.

'Oh, yes, both Hindus; there we have it; they hang together like flies and keep everything dark. . . .'

Thus Forster presents in rich detail the condition of India as a deeply divided country. This kind of context throws into relief his extended presentations of attempts at *rapport*. First examine the relationship of Ronny and Adela. They first meet 'among the grand scenery of the English Lakes'. Their relationship never becomes deep. They find it difficult to maintain it in India partly because of important differences in character (Adela is liberal-minded whereas Ronny is not) and partly because of the demands of Anglo-India. Their growing estrangement stops temporarily after the journey in Nawab Bahadur's car: 'Her hand touched his, owing to a jolt, and one of the thrills so frequent in the animal kingdom passed between them, and announced that all their difficulties were only a lovers' quarrel'. It is because their relationship is shallow that slight physical contact is sufficient to renew it. But Adela's fairness in clearing Aziz of the charge in the trial scene puts an end to it: 'He really could not marry her – it would mean the end of his career. Poor lamentable Adela . . .'. Their relationship enacts the difficulties of establishing personal relations among the Europeans when there is want of conformity to colonial values, as in the case of Adela. Her rather naive honesty has failed to bring her close to either the Indians she wanted to meet or the Englishman she wanted to marry.

The relationship of Fielding and Aziz is the most important one in the novel, quite naturally because race relations are Forster's prime concern. Fielding is a liberal of a different quality from Adela; he has a seasoned intelligence. Indeed, he is the character closest to Forster himself, but the author is able to portray him objectively: through his motto, 'I travel light', Forster critically suggests both a detached independence and an absence of responsibility to anyone other than himself. It is these qualities that result in his being the only Englishman resident in Chandrapore who consistently develops relationships with Indians instead of keeping exclusively to his fellow nationals. His friendship with Aziz develops rapidly because of Aziz's capacity to feel; Aziz shows him his dead wife's photograph: 'Fielding sat down by the bed, flattered at the trust reposed in him, yet rather sad. He felt old. He wished that he too could be carried away on waves of emotion'. Forster shares Lawrence's sense of modern civilisation blunting emotion. Here Fielding has the 'undeveloped heart' which Forster regards as typical of the Englishman.[29] Aziz has the capacity to feel which Forster, in real life, associated with an unnamed Indian friend[30] and with the Maharajah of Dewas State Senior,[31] and which he clearly considers typical of what we may call pre-industrial life.[32] The relationship of Fielding and Aziz does not take a simple, even course from the start. It is subject to strain partly because of differences in temperament which arise from differences in the shaping culture:

> 'He – he has not been capable of thought in his misery, naturally he's very bitter', said Fielding, a little awkward, because such remarks as Aziz had made were not merely bitter, they were foul. The

underlying notion was 'It disgraces me to have been mentioned in connexion with such a hag'. . . . This had puzzled and worried Fielding. Sensuality, as long as it is straightforward, did not repel him, but this derived sensuality – the sort that classes a mistress among motor-cars if she is beautiful, and among eye-flies if she isn't – was alien to his own emotions, and he felt a barrier between himself and Aziz whenever it arose.

The severest strains put on their friendship, however, derive from the disturbed, even neurotic, colonial environment: this is evident in the events after Adela's experience at the Marabar Caves. A person like Fielding is able to be singularly just in the face of simmering inter-racial hostility and of racial sentiments whipped up by the British over Adela's case. This is Forster's presentation of Fielding as he leaves the Club after openly stating his views:

> And he felt dubious and discontented suddenly, and wondered whether he was really and truly successful as a human being. After forty years' experience, he had learnt to manage his life and make the best of it on advanced European lines, had developed his personality, explored his limitations, controlled his passions – and he had done it all without becoming either pedantic or worldly. A creditable achievement, but as the moment passed, he felt he ought to have been working at something else the whole time – he didn't know at what, never would know, never could know, and that was why he felt sad.

Fielding's thoughts are put in the language of an ordinary sensible person. Forster carefully makes him unheroic and real. He elects to be on the side of the Indians but his racial connection to Adela does not permit him to remain comfortably on that side; after the hearing at court, he has to take care of her:

> The English always stick together! That was the criticism. Nor was it unjust. Fielding shared it himself, and knew that if some misunderstanding occurred, and an attack was made on the girl by his allies, he would be obliged to die in her defence. He didn't want to die for her, he wanted to be rejoicing with Aziz.

Aziz neurotically suspects that Fielding's later concern for Adela is motivated by a selfish desire for marriage and breaks off his friendship when he mistakenly believes that Fielding has married her. The ironies of Fielding's position increase after he gets married; it is he and the daughter of Mrs Moore, another kind of liberal, who are (at least partially) absorbed by Anglo-India. These are some of Fielding's reflections during his 'last free intercourse' with Aziz:

> All the stupid misunderstandings had been cleared up, but socially they had no meeting-place. He had thrown in his lot with Anglo-India by marrying a countrywoman, and he was acquiring some of its limitations, and already felt surprise at his own past heroism. Would he to-day defy all his own people for the sake of a stray Indian? Aziz was a memento, a trophy, they were proud of each other, yet they must inevitably part.

Is this quite convincing? Marriage brings a responsibility new to him, but do we not feel that on the basis of his earlier independence Fielding *is* the kind of man who could 'defy all his own people' again? Furthermore, this integrity of his has been dramatised strongly, whereas we are merely told about this alleged change. This is in keeping with the bald reflection Forster puts in earlier: Fielding believes that 'if he had been either ten years younger or ten years longer in India, he would have responded to McBryde's appeal, for all the Europeans 'to hang together' during the crisis after the Marabar Caves episode. Forster seems to have momentarily lapsed into the unconvincing in his over-anxiety to be realistic, to avoid making Fielding a hero.

But in the conclusion Forster puts all his themes convincingly. He presents them here in fully dramatic terms:

> 'Oh, shut up', he said. 'Don't spoil our last hour with foolish questions. Leave Krishna alone, and talk about something sensible'.
> ' They did. All the way back to Mau they wrangled about politics. Each had hardened since Chandrapore, and a good knock-about proved enjoyable. They trusted each other, although they were going to part, perhaps because they were going to part. Fielding had 'no further use for politeness', he said, meaning that the British Empire really can't be abolished because it's rude. Aziz retorted, 'Very well, and we have no use for you', and glared at him with abstract hate. Fielding said 'Away from us, Indians go to seed at once. Look at the King-Emperor High School! Look at you, forgetting your medicine and going back to charms. Look at your poems'.

This is a moment of complete candour. Aziz and Fielding are testing the quality of their feelings for each other, and through this interplay Forster unobtrusively introduces his broader social themes – race relations, the inadequacy of religion and politics. Each man in turn, almost consciously letting the momentum of the argument sweep him along, comes out with statements which he knows misrepresent his wisest self – violent nationalism on the one hand, great-power superiority on the other. By this entirely dramatic means, Forster is able to catch the swaying and clashing forces that lead on into the future of India as a nation (or rather, as three nations) without in the least taking away from the individuality of his characters.

Aziz grew more excited. He rose in his stirrups and pulled at his horse's head in the hope it would rear. Then he should feel in a battle. He cried: 'Clear out, all you Turtons and Burtons. We wanted to know you ten years back – now it's too late. If we see you and sit on your committees, it's for political reasons, don't you make any mistake'. His horse did rear. 'Clear out, clear out, I say. Why are we put to so much suffering?. . . .

'Who do you want instead of the English? The Japanese?' jeered Fielding drawing rein.

'No, the Afghans. My own ancestors'.

'Oh, your Hindu friends will like that, won't they?'

. . . . .

Then he shouted: 'India shall be a nation! No foreigners of any sort! Hindu and Moslem and Sikh and all shall be one! Hurrah! Hurrah for India! Hurrah! Hurrah!'

India a nation! What an apotheosis! Last comer to the drab nineteenth-century sisterhood! Waddling in at this hour of the world to take her seat! She, whose only peer was the Holy Roman Empire, she shall rank with Gautemala and Belgium perhaps! Fielding mocked again. And Aziz in an awful rage danced this way and that, not knowing what to do, and cried: '. . . we shall drive every blasted Englishman into the sea, and then' – he rode against him furiously – 'and then', he concluded, half kissing him, 'you and I shall be friends'.

'Why can't we be friends now?' said the other, holding him affectionately. 'It's what I want. It's what you want'.

But the horses didn't want it – they swerved apart; the earth didn't want it, sending up rocks through which riders must pass single file; the temples, the tank, the jail, the palace, the birds, the carrion, the Guest House, that came into view as they issued from the gap and saw Mau beneath: they didn't want it, they said in their hundred voices, 'No, not yet', and the sky said, 'No, not there'.

Forster has developed the right historical perspectives in portraying a divided India. Aziz's ill-digested mixture of patriotism and xenophobia is characteristic of nationalist-inclined India; his kind of English – by turns schoolboyish, bookish, and spontaneously apt – suggests the kind of mixture it is. The good-humoured jibing of Fielding has serious point and Forster, by a clever use of indirect speech ('India a nation!' etc.), gives it more objective weight than if it had been wholly the character's. The point – the difficulty which this divided country has in becoming a nation as such – is supported by Aziz's own sense of India's divisions and, indeed, Forster is being prescient. He has been proved right by such happenings as the partition of the subcontinent and religious massacres in 1947 and the Indo-Pakistani clashes ever since. The latter section of the passage focuses on race relations. The details of the external setting work both realistically and symbolically to suggest that the impossibility of inter-racial relationships is in the very nature of things at this particular time in this particular context. Forster, however, leaves open a possibility of reconciliation between races (. . . 'No, not yet', . . . 'No, not there'). His basic spirit is very clear here – a seasoned, disillusioned but humane confronting of the deeply unsatisfactory social and political realities of India as an understandable (to a point) part of the total human state. Sound personal and race relations are considered very desirable and very necessary, but their difficulty and failure are faced. Given his view, it is irrelevant for us to ask him for 'solutions' or 'positives'; his view does not allow of them. In this respect, he has left behind one of the important weaknesses in his earlier work: we can contrast this with the unsatisfactoriness of his 'solution' in *Howards End* which I discuss in the last chapter.

A Passage to India gives the impression of a microcosm of society in India under the British Empire in the first quarter of this century. This impression convinces the reader because Forster's characters are individuals or types who represent a wide range of sections in society. Of course, it is not a complete cross-section; for example, on the British side there is no one not of the middle class (no ordinary soldiers for example, only majors and subalterns) and on the Indian side there are no farmers or shopkeepers. The sections represented, say, by the British nurse in a Native State or the Indian punkah-puller, enter the novel only slightly. Forster judiciously focuses on the life of those who influence appreciably the workings of society and show them up – the less important British officials and residents, 'the educated Indians who were weaving, however painfully, a new social fabric' and the visitors who produce an impact. These must have been the kinds of people he himself knew best, from his position as private secretary to a maharajah. The leading characters are sharply individualised; for instance, among the Indians, the emotional sensitive Muslim, Aziz, the imperturbable Hindu, Professor Godbole, and the cynical aggressively anti-British Hamidullah; among the British, Fielding, Adela and Mrs Moore with different kinds of liberal minds, Turton with his hardened superciliousness towards the Indians. But none of them is presented in the proportions of a hero or a heroine, like Cary's Louis Aladai or Aissa or Conrad's Lord Jim. All are given an importance commensurate with the needs of Forster's social themes.

Nirad C. Chaudhuri has argued that this novel 'presents all the Indians in it either as perverted, clownish, or queer characters. There are few delineations of the Indian character which are more insultingly condescending to self-respecting Indians, Muslim and Hindu, than those of this book'.[33] On the other hand, top Anglo-Indian opinion regarded the novel as a libel upon the British in India: 'Another time he [Bapu Sahib] got some amusement out of *A Passage to India*. He dined at the Viceregal Lodge at Delhi soon after it has been published, and found that it was ill thought of there . . .'.[34] First consider the question of the justness of Forster's portrayal of the Indians with reference to Aziz. Aziz's character, certainly, has its valuable and attractive side: we noticed his emotional capacity; to Adela, presumably trying to discount her own recognition of his attractiveness, he is 'a handsome little Oriental'. He is in no way a paragon:

> Yes, he did want to spend an evening with some girls, singing and all that, the vague jollity that would culminate in voluptuousness. Yes, that was what he did want. . . .
>
> . . . . .
>
> But he must not bring disgrace on his children by some silly escapade. Imagine if it got about that he was not respectable! His professional position too must be considered, whatever Major Callendar thought.

And, of course, Indians in real life, too, have shortcomings: these are betraying words of Chaudhuri himself:

> Aziz would not have been allowed to cross my threshold, not to

speak of being taken as equal. Men of his type are a pest even in free India. Some have acquired a crude idea of gracious living or have merely been caught by the lure of snobbism, and are always trying to gain importance by sneaking into the company of those to whom this way of living is natural.[35]

Aziz, then, has a plausible mixture of 'virtues' and 'vices'. Turn now to the question of the justness of Forster's portrayal of the British. Fielding will not do as an example because he is exceptional and because, as a teacher, he does not govern the Indians, though he belongs to the 'ruling race'; and it is specifically 'the virtues of English governing-class character' which Forster is supposed to have denied. Take a police official:

> Mr McBryde, the District Superintendent of Police, was the most reflective and best educated of the Chandrapore officials. . . . Aziz was led off weeping. Mr McBryde was shocked at his downfall, but no Indian ever surprised him, because he had a theory about climatic zones. The theory ran: 'All unfortunate natives are criminals at heart, for the simple reason that they live south of latitude 30. They are not to blame, they have not a dog's chance – we should be like them if we settled here'.

In real life, too, there were such officials: George Orwell is known for his fellow-feeling for the dispossessed, but even he as a policeman in Burma thought that 'the greatest joy in the world would be to drive a bayonet into a Buddhist priest's guts' and that 'feelings like these are the normal by-products of imperialism; ask any Anglo-Indian official, if you can catch him off duty'.[36] Similar attitudes appear also at the other end of the political spectrum; Churchill has said:

> It is alarming and also nauseating to see Mr Gandhi, a seditious Middle Temple lawyer, now posing as a fakir of a type well-known in the East, striding half-naked up the steps of the Viceregal palace, while he is still organising and conducting a defiant campaign of civil disobedience, to parley on equal terms with the representative of the King-Emperor.[37]

Forster, then, is evidently accurate in his portrayal of the British rulers as prone to quite virulent racialism. Moreover, there is no bias in the mixture itself of 'virtues' and 'weaknesses' which Forster ascribes to the

Indians and to the British. For example, McBryde and Fielding are
shown to be no different as men from Aziz:

> He [McBryde] held up Aziz's pocket-case. 'I am going through the
> contents. They are not edifying. Here is a letter from a friend who
> apparently keeps a brothel'.
> 'I don't want to hear his private letters'.
> 'It'll have to be quoted in Court, as bearing on his morals. He was
> fixing up to see women at Calcutta'.
> 'Oh, that'll do, that'll do'.
> McBryde stopped, naively puzzled. It was obvious to him that
> any two sahibs ought to pool all they knew about any Indian, and
> he could not think where the objection came in.
> 'I dare say you have the right to throw stones at a young man for
> doing that, but I haven't. I did the same at his age.'
> So had the Superintendent of Police, but he considered that the
> conversation had taken a turn that was undesirable. He did not like
> Fielding's next remark either.

Of course, Forster's sense of human frailty is keener than his sense of
human powers; this applies to all the characters, both Indian and
British. Indeed, critics of Forster's fairness, on the Indian side and on
the British side, are unconsciously paying a tribute to his all-sided
scrupulousness. Consider further the related objections to particular
espisodes; Chaudhuri says:

> Of one implied charge I will definitely acquit them. Mr Forster
> makes the British Officials of Chandrapore nervous about the ex-
> citement of the Muharram to the extent of making the women and
> children take shelter in the club, and after the trial of Aziz he makes
> them reach home along by-ways for fear of being manhandled by a
> town rabble. Of this kind of cowardice no British official in India
> was to my mind ever guilty, . . .[38]

There are, however, attitudes and clues in abundance to show that this
kind of nervousness is a characteristic of the colonial position; Churchill says:

> When the nation finds that our whole position is in jeopardy, that
> her whole work and duty in India is being brought to a standstill,
> when the nation sees our individual fellow-countrymen scattered

about, with their women and children, throughout this enormous land, in hourly peril amidst the Indian multitudes, when, at any moment, this may produce shocking scenes, then I think there will be a sharp awakening, then, I am sure, that a reaction of the most vehement character will sweep this country and its unmeasured strength will once more be used. That, Sir, is an ending which I trust and pray we may avoid, but it is an ending to which, step by step and day by day, we are being remorselessly and fatuously conducted.[39]

R. Palme Dutt notes: 'The British Chief of Staff, Sir Henry Wilson, had to report to the Cabinet in January 1919 . . . that the only policy was to "get our tropps out of Europe and Russia, and concentrate all our strength in *our* coming storm centres, England, Ireland, Egypt, India"'.[40] This was the year of the Amritsar massacre.

Of course, it is impossible to verify the truth of Forster's fictional world at first hand because it is placed in a period of history over fifty years past, but there is sufficient evidence to suggest that it is authentic. In any case, is it not axiomatic that if the art of the work is of unquestionable quality on its own plane, then it verifies itself and thenceforth demands to be used *along with* the documentary data as part of the historical evidence?

Forster, then, has certainly made the passage to India. But it is virtually impossible for even an incomer like Forster to be completely above the view of a European outsider. This is true of *The Hill of Devi*[41] and even of *A Passage to India*:

'Do you know what the name of that green bird up above us is?' she [Adela Quested] asked, putting her shoulder rather nearer to his.
    'Bee-eater'.
    'Oh, no, Ronny, it has red bars on its wings'.
    'Parrot', he hazarded.
    'Good gracious no'.
    The bird in question dived into the dome of the tree. It was of no importance, yet they would have liked to identify it, it would somehow have solaced their hearts. But nothing in India is identifiable, the mere asking of a question causes it to disappear or to merge in something else.[42]
. . . . .
Unfortunately, India has few important towns. India is the country, fields, fields, then hills, jungle, hills, and more fields. The branch line

stops, the road is only practicable for cars to a point, the bullock-carts lumber down the side tracks, paths fray out into the cultivation, and disappear near a splash of red paint. How can the mind take hold of such a country? Generations of invaders have tried, but they remain in exile.[43]

Here we see a sophisticated and intelligent outsider doing little more than elaborate on the view of superficial outsiders embodied in the appropriately stupid phrase 'mysterious East'. It did not occur to me that the East could be considered 'mysterious' until I read Western writings about it. To me, Sri Lanka has never appeared mysterious; neither has India, partly no doubt because of cultural links between the two countries. In the final sentences of the latter passage Forster does seem to half-realise that it is the ignorance of the invaders that makes the country seem bafflingly mysterious; it is surely all the more inconsistent to turn the mystery into an objective quality of the country itself. This apart, his basic spirit is very different from majority opinion at that time as expressed in a speech of Churchill's on 12 December, 1930:

The truth is that Gandhi-ism and all it stands for will, sooner or later, have to be grappled with and finally crushed. It is no use trying to satisfy a tiger by feeding him with cat's meat. The sooner this is realised, the less trouble and misfortune will there be for all concerned.[44]

Forster belongs with the Liberals and socialists; with those who founded *The Independent Review*; with such people as Annie Besant and Ramsay MacDonald before he came into office. Ramsay Mac-Donald said:

Thus political India evolves. No people can be freed from chains unless it has done something to strike them off, unless it feels their weight and their dishonour in its heart, unless its attainments in intelligence and in the things which create and uphold dignity have won the sympathy of men. India has met these tests.[45]

In the year of *A Passage to India*, Annie Besant wrote:

India will never again be peaceful and connected until she stands a free nation amid the other free nations of the Commonwealth. She may be driven into revolt and separation by despair, to the injury of both nations. Short of this, she will never again cease to struggle until she is free. She will be a constant menace to the safety of an Empire which holds her in subjection; but she will be a faithful and loyal friend if the bonds of love and mutual service bind the two countries, and will be Britain's strongest defence and bulwark in the years to come.[46]

Mrs Besant's moralistic idealism betrays the weak side of the liberal tradition. We noticed that it mars William Arnold's *Oakfield*. Forster does not fully shed it. Mrs Moore thinks as she argues with Ronny after the Bridge Party: 'One touch of regret – not the canny substitute but the true regret from the heart – would have made him a different man, and the British Empire a different institution'. Fielding says to Adela not long after the trial: '. . . Indians know whether they are liked or not – they cannot be fooled here. Justice never satisfies them, and that is why the British Empire rests on sand'. We may take it that Mrs Moore and Fielding have the author behind them here: they are presented as wise and reliable witnesses and those sentences are indistinguishable from Forster's own aphorisms. In these instances, Forster is betraying a tendency we noticed earlier: he is over-neatly and with well-meaning unreality simplifying complexities of an inescapably social kind. He had expressed the same view before. In an article of 1922, after citing a case where an English Collector had affronted Indian opinion on a seemingly trifling matter, he wrote:

India to-day is a chopping sea, and this social question is only one of its currents. There are Mohammedans and Hindus; there is Labour and Capital; there are the native princes and the constitutionalists. Where the sea will break, what wave will uprise, no man can say; perhaps in the immediate future the chief issue will not be racial after all. But isolating the question, one may say this: firstly, that responsible Englishmen are far politer to Indians now than they were ten years ago, but it is too late because Indians no longer require their social support; and, secondly, that never in history did ill-breeding contribute so much towards the dissolution of an Empire.[47]

This is the besetting tendency of the earnest outsider – to imagine that mass conflicts (in this case between invaders and indigenous peoples) have been brought about by individual thoughtlessness and may be resolved by individual decencies. But in *A Passage to India* this kind of view cannot deflect the general tendency of the drama, which is to put before us a complex of entanglements – of entrenched loyalties, racial conflict and half-thwarted desires for a better level of human interaction – which of their nature could only be resolved by the kind of long-term change that is foreseen in those closing pages of the novel.

8 D. H. Lawrence: primitivism?

> We cannot help it if we are born as men of the early winter of full Civilisation, instead of on the golden summit of a ripe Culture, in a Phidias or Mozart time. Everything depends on our seeing our own position, *our destiny*, clearly on our realising that though we may lie to ourselves about it we cannot evade it. He who does not acknowledge this in his heart, ceases to be counted among the men of his generation, and remains either a simpleton, a charlatan, or a pedant.
>
> Oswald Spengler, *The Decline of the West, Form and Actuality* (trans. C. F. Atkinson).

Lawrence experienced primitivist tendencies, and these tendencies urged him to visit Ceylon, Australia and Mexico. His reaction to New Mexico and Mexico is very different from Forster's reaction to India. In our discussion of it, the concepts of primitivism are important. Because the term, 'primitivism', is often used in a loose, derogatory way, we must first clarify these concepts as they occur in the history of ideas.

There are two major primitivist views – chronological primitivism and cultural primitivism. The chronological side is a view of history based on the hypothesis that man's finest or happiest days were at the beginning of history. Several important theories are derived from this as to the course of man's subsequent deterioration. The Theory of Undulation conceives the course of history as wave-like in form, as cyclical, while the Theory of Progressive Deterioration looks upon history as a steady downward movement. Cultural primitivism seems to spring consciously or unconsciously from the dissatisfaction of the civilised with their own kind of civilisation. At a simple level, it manifests itself as a hankering after the primitive or the unfamiliar and as a reaction against the usual and the known. At a deeper level, it is a belief of men in a sophisticated and complicated society that a less sophisticated and simpler life is better. Both chronological and cultural primitivism accept nature and the natural, in their various senses, as a norm of human behaviour.

Lawrence's fascination with developing peoples – as it emerges in his Australian novel, *Kangaroo* (1923), and, far more prominently, in his Mexican works such as *St. Mawr* (1925), *The Princess* (1925), *The Woman Who Rode Away* (1928) and *The Plumed Serpent* (1926) – will be examined in relation to traditional primitivist thought. Its origins are discernible in his European works preceding them and this will be discussed first. In his last (European) novel, *Lady Chatterley's Lover*, he put explicitly important aspects of his view of European history:

> This is history. One England blots out another. The mines had made the halls wealthy. Now they were blotting them out, as they had already blotted out the cottages. The industrial England blots out the agricultural England. One meaning blots out another. The new England blots out the old England. And the continuity is not organic, but mechanical.[1]

Lawrence is a chronological primitivist in his view of European history. He considers the 'blotting out' of 'the old England', of 'the organic community', as a loss; 'and the continuity is not organic, but mechanical'. At the same time he accepts this as an inevitable stage in the inexorable working out of history.

His critical acceptance of modern industrial civilisation makes it possible for him to contemplate its disorders very steadily and very acutely. His contemplation of it is at its widest in *Women in Love* (1920), and involves the fullest use of the art of fiction. Gerald Crich and Gudrun Brangwen are 'born in the process of destructive creation'. In Gerald, this is shown in a dominance of will, a will which is more subtle and, therefore, more dangerous than the deranged will of Hermione Roddice. At the very beginning, he confesses his inability to strike a healthy, abiding relationship with a woman. 'Coal Dust' (Chapter 9) brings out in symbolic terms that his will is inimical to life; when spontaneous life, as found in the mare, shies away from his type of modernity, as represented by the railway, he would assert his inhuman will over her and press her down bleeding. His kind of condition is suggested by Lawrence in *Psychoanalysis and the Unconscious*: 'The tortures of psychic starvation which civilised people proceed to suffer, once they have solved for themselves the bread and butter problem of alimentation, . . .'.[2] Once Gerald has gained mastery over material aspects of life, he begins to find life empty. His will turns to destruction and, at the end, even moves towards self-destruction.

The West African statuette is perhaps the most important symbol of the novel, and it points to another process of destruction in European civilisation. It stands in sharp contrast to the equivocal murkiness of

Bohemia, but they are at one in representing degeneracy. Rupert Birkin is critically aware of the primitive, as symbolised by the statuette, and this suggests Lawrence's own critical awareness, particularly as Birkin is the character in the novel closest to a projection of the author. Birkin is attracted to the statuette. At the same time, he is conscious both of a gap between himself and the statuette and of a dreadful decline in African life from creativeness to dissolution. It is a deterioration that the statuette represents, and to pay homage to it is to follow the African process of dissolution, the path that Gudrun, Minette and Herr Loerke are inclined to tread. Birkin goes on to refer to a different process associated with the 'white' men: 'The white races, having the Arctic north behind them, the vast abstraction of ice and snow, would fulfil a mystery of ice-destructive knowledge, snow-abstract annihilation'. This is the process followed by Gerald with his emphasis on will. Still, though different, the Arctic process converges with the African process in the desire to 'lapse into sheer unrestraint, brutal and licentious', as shown by Gerald's visit to Gudrun in 'Death and Love' (Chapter 24).

Gerald's relationship with Gudrun contains within it the seeds of its own failure. It demands the submergence of the individuality of one in the other, and both are unyielding. Gudrun feels that 'he made the burden for her greater', and on the Continent she drifts towards Herr Loerke. She feels a natural affinity with Loerke; both like primitive art, 'achieved perfections of the past', indulgence in sensation, and prefer Art to Life. Gudrun's recognition of the futility of life under Gerald's will leads to a view, a characteristically Lawrentian view, that modern mechanical civilisation distorts man's nature. Gudrun rejects industrial civilisation to live with Loerke in the Dresden Bohemia. She has no illusions about the kind of life there but she is unable to build a better way of living.

Thus, in *Women in Love*, contemporary personal relations and European civilisation are considered in interrelation. The evils of destructive relationships and destructive society are most searchingly analysed, and most powerfully dramatised. It is the positive side of the novel that is rather weak, and this indicates an aspect of Lawrence's sensibility which leads to primitivism. Lawrence sees the course of European history too simply as a decline from 'the organic community'. He does not recognise sufficiently the positive gains of industrialism; for example, it makes possible for the majority of people a longer and more comfortable life and opens up much wider horizons for more people. Lawrence, however, does not present a despairing or wholly one-sided view of personal and social evil. Through the relationship of

Birkin and Ursula Brangwen, he dramatises a positive alternative to the destructive relationships and destructive society.

Birkin tends to theorise about life, but he is sufficiently clear-sighted about himself and his aims to try to translate his ideals into reality. He rejects both the destructive love of moderns such as Gerald and Gudrun and the conventionally romantic kind of love which Ursula wants. 'Mutual unison in separateness' is what he desires as Ursula sees. He spells out this view to her in 'Mino' (Chapter 13): 'One must commit oneself to a conjunction with the other – for ever. But it is not selfless – it is a maintaining of the self in mystic balance and integrity – like a star balanced with another star'. In fact, he voices Lawrence's own view.[3] On the Continent Ursula reaches a state of being which accords with Birkin's. They affirm a kind of positive relationship which can help one to some extent to cope with modern life on a personal level. Its value on this level is limited because it is not sufficiently related to contemporary social problems which are linked with personal life. It has hardly any value on the social plane because the enormous, deep social problems which Lawrence raises in the novel can hardly be tackled by this kind of personal 'solution'.

The destructive tendencies of European civilisation seem to strike Lawrence more deeply than the sources of strength within Europe to combat them. It is significant that it is a foreign country, not England, that helps Ursula to repudiate finally the ice world; she is saved by her response to Italy. It is in Italy, once again, that the woman in Lawrence's tale, *Sun*, recovers her emotional being. He does not idealise Italy one-sidedly at the expense of England and other European countries. In *Twilight in Italy*, he explicitly recognises the potency of Italy,[4] but he can also see the narrowness and difficulties of Italian peasant life in San Gaudenzio.[5]

The emergence of primitivism in Lawrence is causally related to a complex of tendencies. It is linked with his belief that European civilisation was deteriorating, his critical awareness of the primitive in the case of the West African statuette in *Women in Love*, the weakness and element of foreignness in his positive standpoint. His primitivism also follows partly from the very nature of his positive values. Birkin and Ursula finally come to represent Lawrence's central view of wholesome living which he expounds in *Psychoanalysis and the Unconscious*: 'True, we must all develop into mental consciousness. But mental consciousness is not a goal; it is a cul-de-sac. It provides us only with endless appliances which we can use for the all-too-difficult business of coming to our spontaneous–creative fullness of being'.[6] His 'spontaneous–creative fullness of being' is close to an orthodox cultural primitivist's sense of nature as a norm of living which Arthur Lovejoy and George Boas explain: ' "Nature" is that in man which is not due to taking thought or to deliberate choice: hence, those modes of human desire, emotion, or behaviour which are instinctive or spontaneous, in contrast with those which are due to the labouring intellect, to premeditation, to self-consciousness, or to instruction'.[7] Lawrence gives naturalness first place, but favours a greater play of the mind than a cultural primitivist would concede.

Lawrence's transition from his European to his Mexican works is a perfectly logical and explicable development. When he locates an important part of his positive values in Mexico, a developing country more distant than Italy, he reveals a tendency which is almost that of a cultural primitivist: as Lovejoy and Boas state,

> The cultural primitivist has almost invariably believed that the simpler life of which he has dreamed has been somewhere, at some time, actually lived by human beings. He has not merely enunciated an ideal but has pointed to its exemplars. . . . But above all the cutural primitivist's model of human excellence and happiness is sought in the present, in the mode of life of existing primitive, or so-called 'savage' peoples. These contemporary embodiments of this ideal have usually been found among races not intimately known to, and existing at some considerable distance from, the people to whom the preacher of primitivism commends them as examples to be followed, or exhibits them as more fortunate branches of our species whose state is to be envied.[8]

The Mexicans whose life Lawrence commends to Europeans, are a distant, contemporary and primitive people. But he is not in this respect wholly a cultural primitivist. He does not seek a 'simpler life' as such, but a more vital life. For his balanced self, Mexico's vitality has to be linked with the civilised mind of Europe to form a wholly admirable totality.

St. Mawr finely illustrates Lawrence's sense of the radical deficiencies in a section of Western society and his quest for sources of strength in distant primitive lands. Vitality and depth in living have dried up in the world of Rico, the Witts and the Manbys, qualities which St. Mawr symbolises: 'But in his dark eye, that looked, with its cloudy brown pupil, a cloud within a dark fire, like a world beyond our world, there was a dark vitality glowing, and within the fire, another sort of wisdom'. St. Mawr and, to a lesser extent, Lewis and Phoenix compel Lou Carrington and Mrs Witt to recognise positive qualities which they possess and the sophisticated world lacks, to recognise the need to recover 'dark vitality' and 'another sort of wisdom'. F. R. Leavis argues that the tale is an equivalent in fiction of T. S. Eliot's *The Waste Land*, that it projects 'a representative view of the civilised world'.[9] But it seems to me that its social application is less wide. Lou represents, not European society as a whole, but the cosmopolitan 'smart set'. Mrs Witt and Rico are also representatives of the upper class. The tale has no representatives of the working class like the typist or the clerk in Eliot's poem; Lewis and Phoenix, as servants, are atypical.

Thus Lawrence's chronological primitivism, his sense of the deterioration of Western life, is intimately related only to a section of society. But it is critical and expressed well. When Lawrence presents St. Mawr, he is able to strike a delicate balance between the plane of everyday reality and the plane of symbolism, and he is able to pack a wealth of meaning into the episodes of the tale with perfect naturalness. In the episode when the horse rears away from a dead adder, St. Mawr represents instinctive sanity since his recoil from the snake though a dead one, is a natural reaction. Rico, however, without trying to understand the behaviour of the horse, attempts to force him down; his action indicates an uncomprehending cruelty of will. The actions of both are fully consistent on the realistic level, and this helps to make the symbolic extension of meaning unforced and convincing. St. Mawr is 'realised' with the inwardness and 'roundness' of a well-depicted human character. It is mainly through him that Lawrence expresses his positive values during the first movement of the tale, and it is partly in contrast to the kind of being he is that Lawrence conveys the deficiencies of upper-class Western society:

'No, mother [Mrs Witt]. We seem to be living off old fuel, like the camel when he lives off his hump. Life doesn't rush into us, as it does even into St. Mawr, and he's a dependent animal. I [Lou] can't live, mother. I just can't'.

'I don't see why not? *I'm* full of life'.

'I know you are, mother. But I'm not, and I'm your daughter. – And don't misunderstand me, mother. I don't want to be an animal like a horse or a cat or a lioness, though they all fascinate me, the way they get their life *straight*, not from a lot of old tanks, as we do. I don't admire the cave man, and that sort of thing. But think, mother, if we could get our lives straight from the source, as the animals do, and still be ourselves . . . .

It is mainly in terms of Lou's response to St. Mawr that Lawrence indicates the qualities of the horse. Lou sees a positive value in St. Mawr, in its unchoked vitality, and at the same time she is uneasily conscious that it is an animal. In trying to wriggle out of this *impasse*, she falls into wishful thinking: 'if we could get our lives straight from the source, as animals do, and still be ourselves'. Thus Lawrence, through Lou's dilemma, suggests the difficulty of expressing the positiveness he advocates as well as the difficulty of achieving it.

Lewis, the Welsh groom, and Phoenix, the half Indian, are less important as embodiments of positive values than St. Mawr, but they are presented with equal intelligence and skill. Lawrence is able to dramatise their unusualness brilliantly, as in the scene when Mrs Witt turns barber: the groom's kind of touchiness about his hair and, more so, about his beard suggests forcefully that he is different from ordinary men. Lewis and Phoenix get on with St. Mawr, and this suggests that they share the same kind of positiveness. Lou responds to the positiveness of Lewis and Phoenix just as she does to St. Mawr's: 'Nonsense, you're not dying'. 'I am, mother. And I should be dead if there weren't St. Mawr and Phoenix and Lewis in the world'. Even the nihilistic Mrs Witt finds herself getting attracted to Lewis and proposes marriage to him; Lewis has the strength to reject her. Both Lewis and Phoenix are presented critically as St. Mawr is and are not idealised: Lewis is a 'little, rather bow-legged, loosely-built fellow' and is isolated; Phoenix is rootless. It is important to understand the kind of positiveness which Lou seeks and Lawrence recommends:

> . . . 'I don't want intimacy, mother. I'm too tired of it all. I love St. Mawr because he isn't intimate. He stands where one can't get at him. And he burns with life. And where does his life come from, to him? That's the mystery. That great burning life in him, which never is dead. Most men have a deadness in them, that frightens me so, because of my own deadness . . .'.

Lou cannot find renewal of being in 'intimacy' or personal relationships. In this tale Lawrence finds that he cannot advocate a positive kind of relationship as the Ursula–Birkin relationship in *Women in Love* and his sense of the total failure of human relationships in the contemporary Western world generates a deep pessimism. Lou, the chief character in *St. Mawr*, cannot find regeneration on the Continent. She cannot find it in England and in Wales. She is driven still further west, to Mexico. Lawrence himself, in his personal life, was driven to this kind of 'search'.

Lawrence's chronological primitivism leads to cultural primitivism, an examination of the possibilities of regeneration offered to 'white' people by dark people and the possibilities of regeneration offered by distant primitive countries. When Lou goes with Phoenix to inspect a Mexican ranch that was for sale, an interesting situation arises:

> Nevertheless he was ready to trade his sex, which, in his opinion, every white woman was secretly pining for, for the white woman's money and social privileges. In the daytime, all the thrill and excitement of the white man's motor-cars and moving pictures and ice-cream sodas and so forth. In the night, the soft watery-soft warmth of an Indian or half-Indian woman. This was Phoenix's idea of life for himself.

Lawrence presents Phoenix perceptively and critically. Phoenix wants to consciously exploit the sexual attraction which primitive dark men hold for 'white' women. Lawrence does not merely suggest that Phoenix is cunning and sexually promiscuous. Phoenix appears a decadent primitive man, a primitive man who has been corrupted by modern 'white' society. Lou, however, is able to cope with him; she has a clear notion of both Phoenix and herself:

> . . . she knew more or less all that he felt. More or less she divined as a woman does.
> . . . . .
> He did not know what she was thinking. There was a certain physical sympathy between them. His obtuseness made him think it was also a sexual sympathy.

Lawrence thus rejects the primitivist tendency (in its decadent form) which regards dark people as potent and this potency as offering regeneration to 'white' people. He reveals another aspect of cultural primitivism when Lou sees the Mexican ranch: 'For me', she said, as she looked away at the mountains in shadow and the pale-warm desert beneath, with wings of shadow upon it: 'For me, this place is sacred. It is blessed'. Lawrence is being quite revolutionary in this tale: he usually finds positive value in personal relationships but here he finds it, not in people whether 'white' or dark, but in a place like Mexico. He does not idealise Mexico either; he rejects simple and traditional cultural primitivism. These are conditions on the ranch: 'And it all cost, cost, cost. And a man was always let down. At one time no water. At another a poison-weed. Then a sickness. Always some mysterious malevolence fighting, fighting against the will of man. A strange invisible influence . . .'. There are touches of vague rhetoric in Lawrence's language, but he is generally exact and unflinching; the evil in Mexico is precisely illustrated. He narrates the history of the Mexican ranch; this is thematically relevant and shows his kind of critical cultural primitivism. He underlines the 'beauty, beauty absolute, at any hour of the day' as well as 'a peculiar undercurrent of squalor, flowing under the curious tussle of wild life'. An American trader and his New England wife had lived on the ranch and their case parallels Lou's. They had tried to combine civilised human life (the wife had 'bright brass water-taps' and 'a little kitchen garden and nasturtiums') with the attractions of Mexico, while struggling valiantly against its crudeness and dangers. It is implied that Lou will have to make a similar attempt and thereby try to achieve 'spontaneous–creative fullness of being'. The final failure of the trader and his wife as well as the difficulties of Mexico suggest that even in Lou's case success is doubtful.

When Mrs Witt accompanies Lou to the ranch, Lou's feelings are unchanged; she feels that it is in primitive New Mexico that she could combine the worthy qualities Europe possesses with those she lacks.

'Very well, daughter. You will probably spend your life keeping to yourself'.

'Do you think I mind! There's something else for me, mother. There's something else even that loves me and wants me. I can't tell you what it is. It's a spirit. And it's here, on this ranch. It's here, in this landscape. It's something more real to me than men are, and it soothes me, and it holds me up. I don't know what it is, definitely. It's something wild, that will hurt me sometimes and will wear me down sometimes. . . . And to it, my sex is deep and sacred, deeper than I am, with a deep nature aware deep down of my sex. It saves me from cheapness, mother. And even you could never do that for me'.

Mrs Witt rose to her feet, and stood looking far, far away, at the turquoise ridge of mountains half sunk under the horizon.

'How much did you say you paid for Las Chivas?' she asked.

'Twelve hundred dollars' said Lou, surprised.

'Then I call it cheap, considering all there is to it: even the name'.

Lawrence's dialogue is trenchantly witty in this last scene of the tale as he plays off the characters of Lou and Mrs Witt. Lou is not uncritical in her response to Mexico: she feels a spirit there which is great as well as wild. But the tone of her speech suggests that she has lost her head somewhat. Mrs Witt sounds wry, rueful and seasoned. The last words of the tale are hers. Thus Lawrence is sceptical of the success of even the kind of primitivism to which he is finally driven.

St. Mawr, then, is a remarkable primitivist tale; Lawrence's primitivism is finely critical and sceptical. *The Princess* is set wholly in Mexico. The primitivism in it has the penetrating critical quality of that in *St. Mawr*, but here Lawrence concentrates on the interaction of the 'white' and dark races on the plane of individual relations.

> To her father she was The Princess. To her Boston aunts and uncles she was just *Dollie Urquhart, poor little thing.*
> Colin Urquhart was just a bit mad. He was of an old Scottish family, and he claimed royal blood. The blood of Scottish kings flowed in his veins. On this point, his American relatives said, he was just a bit 'off'.

The energy and sardonic tone of this striking opening of the tale are characteristic of the narrative in its first phase. The eponymous heroine had been brought up as 'a dignified, scentless flower' by her father. Lawrence's insight into her kind of character begins at the roots: he selects an aristocrat as his representative of coldness, suggesting that living has become super-refined at the expense of vitality; he places a part of her origins in Boston, a centre of devitalised life in Henry James's *The Europeans* and a part of that 'white' America whose people, James Baldwin suggests in *The Fire Next Time*, have lost the ability 'to renew themselves at the fountain of their own lives'.[10]

Long and varied contact with Europe and America have had no effect on the essential self of the Princess. But in Mexico a dark man is able to penetrate her barriers of isolation and coldness.

> It was curious no white man had ever showed her this capacity for subtle gentleness, this power to *help* her in silence across a distance, if she were fishing without success, or tired of her horse, or if Tansy suddenly got scared. It was as if Romero could send her *from his heart* a dark beam of succour and sustaining. She had never known

this before, and it was very thrilling.

The whole tale is placed in the past and this helps Lawrence to be consistently objective. The quality of his art varies in response to the changing situations to be presented. Here we see his tendency to put aside his early sardonic distance in relation to the tempo of the drama. The tempo quickens as the Princess ventures into the wilderness.

> The lifeless valleys were concaves of rock and spruce, the rounded summits, and the hog-backed summits of grey rock crowded one behind the other like some monstrous herd in arrest.
> It frightened the Princess, it was so inhuman. She had not thought it could be so inhuman, so, as it were, anti-life. . . .
> . . . . .
> The strange squalor of the primitive forest pervaded the place, the squalor of animals and their droppings, the squalor of the wild. The Princess knew the peculiar repulsiveness of it.

As in *St. Mawr*, touches of rather vague rhetoric constitute a minor flaw in Lawrence's rendering of the Mexican setting. On the whole, it is done with particularity and power; the image of petrified animality conveys both the physical shape of the highlands and their frighteningly inhuman quality. The wilderness, which Lou Carrington found bracing, appears 'anti-life' to the Princess.

It takes an arduous journey through this wilderness, complete isolation from society and the potency of a dark man to wring a slight change in her. She invites Romero to be intimate with her in the mountain cabin, yet her surrender is no more than an act of will. Her essential self is too hardened to change.

> 'Don't you like last night?' he asked.
> 'Not really', she said. 'Why? Do you?'
> He put down the frying pan and stood staring at the wall. She could see she had given him a cruel blow. But she did not relent. She was getting her own back. She wanted to regain possession of all herself, and in some mysterious way she felt that he possessed some part of her still.
> . . . . .
> Then a dark flame seemed to come from his face.
> 'I make you', he said, as if to himself.

Lawrence is closely engaged in this climactic scene of the tale. His psychological acuteness and breadth of outlook are put into fine dramatic form – the tense and changing interaction of two people, different in their cultural and racial affiliations, who lay bare different complexes of true feelings from incomprehension to vindictiveness.

Romero's attempt to force through a reciprocal relationship with the Princess is a failure. He appears to her 'some racking hot doom'. The *impasse* and the terrible hardships of secretive living in the wilderness kill the spirit of both and even unhinge them. With the Forest Service men, the pace of the action slows down, appropriately for a tale drawing to a close, and the drama becomes sardonic comedy:

> 'What'd this man start firing for?' he asked.
> She fumbled for words, with numb lips.
> 'He had gone out of his mind!' she said, with solemn, stammering conviction.
> 'Good Lord! You mean to say he'd gone out of his mind. Whew! That's pretty awful! That explains it then. H'm!'
> He accepted the explanation without more ado.

The kind of comedy here derives a part of its power from its ironies. The Forest Service men believe the Princess and thereby miss the truth. They look upon the incident as a part of their job and as something ordinary. The Princess sees Romero's madness but not her own. He dies, but she continues to live as a demented 'virgin intact'. This appears more dreadful.

The potency of the dark man is established as a positive value in terms of disturbing realistic drama which by its very fineness makes it acceptable. Lawrence's primitivism is more limited than in *St. Mawr*, but fully critical.

The Woman Who Rode Away is the most ambitious of the tales in this field. Lawrence begins by sketching in an incisive conversational prose the marital relation in Mexico between an American woman and her Dutch husband.

> She had thought that this marriage, of all marriages, would be an adventure. Not that the man himself was exactly magical to her. A little, wiry, twisted fellow, . . . it was obvious that the adventure lay in his circumstances rather than his person. But he was still a little dynamo of energy, . . .
> . . . . .
> He was a man of principles, and a good husband. In a way, he doted

on her. He never quite got over his dazzled admiration of her. But essentially, he was still a bachelor. He had been thrown out on the world, a little bachelor, at the age of ten. When he married he was over forty, and had enough money to marry on. But his capital was all a bachelor's. He was boss of his own works, and marriage was the last and most intimate bit of his own works.

. . . . .

Her husband had never become real to her, neither mentally nor physically. In spite of his late sort of passion for her, he never meant anything to her, physically. Only morally he swayed her, downed her, kept her in an invincible slavery.

The woman is evidently a romantic in her expectations. These are frustrated by the dead wilderness and the incompatible character of her husband. But her romanticism is incurable: 'At thirty-three she really was still the girl from Berkeley, in all but physique. Her conscious development had stopped mysteriously with her marriage, completely arrested'. The strain of frustration makes her all the more responsive to 'a young man's (a "white" man's) enthusiasm' for Indians as he converses with her husband during a short visit.

And this peculiar vague enthusiasm for unknown Indians found a full echo in the woman's heart. She was overcome by a foolish romanticism more unreal than a girl's. She felt it was her destiny to wander into the secret haunts of those timeless, mysterious, marvellous Indians of the mountains.

Lawrence's phrasing of the woman's notion of her 'destiny' catches beautifully the vague thoughtless yearning for the unknown of the typical romantic person. His own critical sense of the woman is explicit. Her romanticism makes her penetrate deep into Indian country, and he expands his thematic concerns to take in primitivism. The development from romanticism to primitivism seems perfectly natural and logical because in both are revealed a desire for life different from the usual.

Critics like F. R. Leavis and Julian Moynahan praise handsomely Lawrence's presentation of the Mexican landscape in this tale.[11] I wish to concentrate on the human side of the Indian phase. The woman's psychological states are rendered usually with remarkable acuteness and force from the pains and risks of travel to spiritual deadness. These psychological states are most striking when they are of an unusual and difficult kind – for instance, when the woman is stripped in the inner chamber of a house in the Indian village and undergoes the first rites accorded to a victim for sacrifice:

> Then the old man spoke again. The Indian led her to the bedside. The white-haired, glassy-dark old man moistened his fingertips at his mouth, and most delicately touched her on the breasts and on the body, then on the back. And she winced strangely each time, as the fingertips drew along her skin, as if Death itself were touching her.
>
> And she wondered, almost sadly, why she did not feel shamed in her nakedness. She only felt sad and lost. Because nobody felt ashamed. The elder men were all dark and tense with some other deep, gloomy, incomprehensible emotion, which suspended all her agitation, while the young Indian had a strange look of ecstasy on his face. And she, she was only utterly strange and beyond herself, as if her body were not her own.

Lawrence frankly and objectively renders the sacrificial rite as a rite. There is no narrow-minded condemnation of the Indians or excessive sympathy for the 'white' woman. Her state is rendered percipiently. He pinpoints her absence of shame, though her naked body was being touched in front of several unknown men. When he comes to subtler emotions, he employs vague epithets of unusualness. But these epithets act as a necessary preliminary to further elaboration which makes his points sufficiently specific. It is when he tries to plumb the emotions of the Indians that his psychological acumen is shown as having a limitation. He leaves vague the depths of their emotions.

The woman's stay in the Indian village as a victim for sacrifice forms the major and climactic phase of the tale, and it is seriously flawed. The ritual seems to drag on. It seems increasingly tame and static, dramatically. There is a certain intensity of suspense at the end, as the creeping rays of the setting sun mark the approaching hour of sacrifice. But it is not sufficient compensation. The significance of the sacrifice is the most important point of the tale, and, indeed, the whole action leads up to it: 'In absolute motionlessness he watched till the red sun should send his ray through the column of ice. Then the old man would strike, and strike home, accomplish the sacrifice and achieve the power. The mastery that man must hold, and passes from race to race'. The Indians are sacrificing the 'white' woman to the sun as an attempt to win back power from the 'white' men. Lawrence sees this in the light of the whole of human history. Unfortunately, not only is the Indian ritual presented rather dully, it is too often presented in itself. It is not closely related to the central ways of living of contemporary 'white' men. Moreover, Lawrence's portrayal of the Indians does not suggest that they offer a serious threat to 'white' supremacy, though they are meant to be regarded as such. They appear too backward and isolated. Their ideas, such as those expounded by the young Indian to the 'white' woman, confirm this impression:

> 'Because', he said, 'The Indian got weak, and lost his power with the sun, so the white men stole the sun. But they can't keep him – they don't know how. They got him, but they don't know what to do with him, like a boy who catch a big grizzly bear, and can't run away from him. The grizzly bear eats the boy that catch him, when he want to run away from him. White men don't know what they are doing with the sun, and white women don't know what they do with the moon. . . .'

Lawrence has fashioned skilfully an appropriate blunt folklore idiom for the Indian and conveys his confidence dramatically. But the ideas of the Indian are primitive. The key historical significance of the tale does not come off convincingly as art.

Lawrence's cyclical view of history is close to the Theory of Undulation of later chronological primitivists: as Lovejoy and Boas say, 'This theory sometimes takes the form, in later times, of the conception of a succession of empires or civilisations, each of which goes through a rise, decline, and fall, after the analogy of the life-history of an individual'.[12] Lawrence's view, however, has an important racial basis, which is not present in the orthodox primitivist conception and, probably, has been arrived at independently: he envisages the transfer of power and potency from the 'white' to the dark races. When he works it out in terms of correlatives in the real world, at times he is not sufficiently critical and his art suffers as a consequence.

Lawrence's primitivist thinking is expressed most comprehensively in *The Plumed Serpent*. The whole novel is conveyed through the consciousness of its most important character, Kate Leslie, and his own thoughts emerge partly through an exploration of hers. She finds herself in a very difficult predicament when her second husband dies.

She herself, what had she come to America for?

Because the flow of her life had been broken, and she knew she could not re-start it in Europe.

. . . . .

And all the efforts of the white men to bring the soul of the dark men of Mexico into a final clinched being has resulted in nothing but the collapse of the white man.

Kate sees her personal difficulty in large terms of civilisation and race. She affirms the individuality of the dark and 'white' races. To attempt 'to convert the dark man to the white man's way of life' is in her view to attempt a fatal and impossible task, as Lawrence himself underlined in *Mornings in Mexico*:

> The consciousness of one branch of humanity is the annihilation of the consciousness of another branch. That is, the life of the Indian, his stream of conscious being, is just death to the white man. And we can understand the consciousness of the Indian only in terms of the death of our consciousness.[13]

His view is that the Indians think and feel so differently from the 'white' men that they cannot become like the Indians without ceasing to be themselves.

Kate is analytically aware of her state of being; she is conscious of the qualities which she seeks in Mexico and which she considers Europe has exhausted – creativeness and 'wonder'. The cultural primitivism, which Lawrence expresses through her, is precisely motivated. She proceeds to see her position in even larger terms than civilisation and race, to see it as part of a comprehensive conception of human history:

> While the white man keeps the impetus of his own proud, onward march, the dark races will yield and serve, perforce. But let the white man once have a misgiving about his own leadership, and the dark races will at once attack him, to pull him down into the old gulfs. To engulf him again.
>
> Which is what is happening. For the white man, let him bluster as he may, is hollow with misgiving about his own supremacy.
>
> Full speed ahead, then, for the *debacle*.

Her cultural primitivism goes with chronological primitivism. She shares the latter with Richard Lovat Somers in *Kangaroo*:

In Europe, he had made up his mind that everything was done for, played out, finished, and he must go to a new country. The newest country: young Australia. Now he had tried Western Australia, and had looked at Adelaide and Melbourne. And the vast, uninhabited land frightened him. It seemed so hoary and lost. The sky was pure, crystal pure and blue, of a lovely pale blue colour: the air was wonderful, new and unbreathed: and there were great distances. But the bush, the grey, charred bush. It scared him.[14]

These mixed feelings are similar to the responses of Lou Carrington and the Princess to Mexico and New Mexico.

The reasons and feelings behind Kate's cultural and chronological primitivism are acceptable. Unfortunately, the way her decision to remain in Mexico is arrived at is not put quite convincingly. She has to make up her mind shortly after her arrival, and an exceptional power in Lawrence's presentation of character and situation within that short period is necessary to make her quick decision credible. Does Lawrence's presentation have exceptional power? Here Kate debates whether 'to stay or not to stay' (Chapter 4):

The country gave her a strange feeling of hopelessness and of daunt-lessness. Unbroken, eternally resistant, it was a people that lived without hope, and without care. Gay even, and laughing with indifferent carelessness.

They were something like her own Irish, but gone to a much greater length. And also, they did what the self-conscious and pretentious Irish rarely do, they touched her bowels with a strange fire of compassion.

At the same time, she feared them. They would pull her down, pull her down, to the dark depths of nothingness.

She reveals a complex and balanced awareness of Mexico. She is conscious of conflicting feelings in the Mexicans and in herself. But Lawrence employs the staple language of the novel at this moment when particularly forceful prose is needed. And this language is weak. Kate's ruminations are couched in a thin and feeble rhetoric. There is the weakly emphatic repetition, balance and rhythm, the wordiness and the over-use of imprecise phrasing for the unfamiliar as in the case of 'strange' and 'depths of nothingness' ('dark', however, is generally a peculiarly rich word for Lawrence). This is the kind of prose Lawrence uses as he strains to express the alien quality of Mexico and Mexican experiences.

Kate's primitivism is rewarded. Lawrence tries to show how Mexico enables her to achieve a new vitality and profundity of living, as during 'the move down the lake' (Chapter 6):

> So in her soul she cried aloud to the greater mystery, the higher power that hovered in the interstices of the hot air, rich and potent. It was as if she could lift her hands and clutch the silent, stormless potency that roved everywhere, waiting. 'Come then!' she said, drawing a long slow breath, and addressing the silent life-breath which hung unrevealed in the atmosphere, waiting.

Lawrence strains rather unsuccessfully to convey Kate's extraordinary experience. 'Greater mystery', 'higher power', 'the silent, stormless potency' and 'the silent life-breath' are key expressions of it, but their elevatedness is undercut by their woolliness. Kate herself cuts a theatrical figure especially because this kind of experience seems inconsistent with her kind of character. In the novel she is realised only as an attractive middle-aged widow, though Lawrence also tries to make her a woman with extraordinary potentialities.

The primitivism in this novel differs from that in *The Woman Who Rode Away*. Don Ramon and Don Cipriano are neither backward Indians, like those in the tale, nor civilised Europeans. They have the powers which belong to the dark inhabitants of Mexico, and they begin a religious revolution to save their people. This is the inspiring and original core of Lawrence's conception of salvation. Whereas an orthodox primitivist would conceive of regeneration as coming with a return to the life of primitive people in a secular way, Lawrence advocates a religious transformation of the primitive people themselves. Lawrence does not see this transformation as one of a series of historical cycles as the Theory of Undulation would have it. The religious revolution is regarded as a solution to the present ills of Mexico and the world, as a means by which civilisation may move forward out of its present *impasse*. No time limit is placed on the future it is intended to invigorate.

Not all in Mexico understand the nature of the revolution. Certainly, the German manager of the hotel in Orilla does not, and he seems a true representative of 'average' thinking. He suspects a religious movement to be a political 'dodge' (for 'national-socialism'). He betrays a conservative prejudice against the socialistic principle of the equality of men. He simplifies Don Ramon's motives to a selfish hunger for power. Don Ramon himself defends his cause against his passionately Catholic wife, Carlota, at Sayula:

'But believe me, if the real Christ has not been able to save Mexico – and he hasn't – then I am sure the white Anti-Christ of charity, and socialism, and politics and reform, will only succeed in finally destroying her. That, and that alone, makes me take my stand. – You, Carlota, with your charity works and your *pity*: and men like Benito Juarez, with their Reform and their Liberty: and the rest of the benevolent people, politicians and socialists and so forth, surcharged with pity for living men, in their mouths, but really with hate – the hate of the materialist *have-nots* for the materialist *haves*: they are the Anti-Christ. The old world, that's just the world. But the new world, that wants to save the People, this is the Anti-Christ. This is Christ with real poison in the communion cup. – And for this reason I step out of my ordinary privacy and individuality. I don't want everybody poisoned. About the great mass I don't care. But I don't want everybody poisoned'.

'How can you be so sure that you yourself are not a poisoner of the people? – I think you are'.

'Think it then. I think of you, Carlota, merely that you have not been able to come to your complete, final womanhood: which is a different thing from the old womanhoods'.

'Womanhood is always the same'.

'Ah, no, it isn't! Neither is manhood'.

'But what do you think you can do? What do you think this Quetzalcoatl nonsense amounts to?'

'Quetzalcoatl is just a living word, for these people, no more. All I want them to do is to find the beginnings of the way to their own manhood, their own womanhood. Men are not yet men in full, and women are not yet women. . . .'

Ramon defines the goal of his religious movement. In one way, he sees his movement as replacing unsuccessful and moribund Christianity. But one does not think that it will be a more effective force. Ramon, Cipriano and their movement seem puny and absurdly ambitious beside Christ, the patriarchs and the very influential Christian tradition with its enormous organisation. Moreover, Ramon's conception of the state as a whole seems theocratic. Quetzalcoatl is to provide the state not only with a religion but also with its secular organisation. His rejection of politics which is inevitable and necessary in the working of a modern state, is sweeping, ill-considered and very narrowly conservative. He lumps together carelessly and puts on the same plane 'charity, and socialism, and politics, and reform'. He does not pause to distinguish between them, or note that 'socialism' and 'reform' are 'politics'. He proceeds to ascribe the altruistic motive of reformist 'politicians and socialists and so forth' to merely personal spite. This kind of platitudinous conservatism also manifests itself in his choice of a flimsy pietistic term, 'Anti-Christ', for all secular attempts at social amelioration. It lies behind his uneasy compromise between scorn for the mass of the people and a certain altruism. Ramon's insistence on his own opinions and his self-posturing suggest the rather heady self-confidence with which he undertakes a self-chosen messianic role. The kind of mind he brings to it becomes clearer as he reaches his Fourth Hymn.

'I would like', he said, smiling, 'to be one of the Initiates of the Earth. One of the Initiators. Every country its own Saviour, Cipriano: or every people its own Saviour. And the First Men of every people, forming a Natural Aristocracy of the World. One must have aristocrats, that we know. But natural ones, not artificial. And in some way the world must be organically united: the world of man. But in the concrete, not in the abstract. Leagues and Covenants and International Programmes. Ah! Cipriano! it's like an international pestilence. The leaves of one great tree can't hang on the boughs of another great tree. The races of the earth are like trees; in the end they neither mix nor mingle. . . . And a new Hermes should come back to the Mediterranean, and a new Ashtaroth to Tunis; and Mithras again to Persia, and Brahma unbroken to India, and the oldest of dragons to China. Then I, Cipriano, I, First Man of Quetzalcoatl, with you, First Man of Huitzilopochtli, and perhaps your wife, First Woman of Itzpapalotl, could we not meet, with sure souls, the other great aristocrats of the world, the First Man of Wotan and the First Woman of Freya, First Lord of Hermes, and the Lady of Astarte, the Best-Born of Brahma, and the Son of the Greatest Dragon? . . .'

Ramon's projection of himself as 'one of the Initiates of the Earth' forms a part of an extended grandiose vision which embraces the whole world. His aristocratic bent accords fully with his disdain for the ordinary mass of the people. He condemns 'Leagues and Covenants and International Programmes' as 'abstract', but his own lofty conceptions are not more concrete. He elaborates freshly the traditional image of the tree of life, but it seems romantically flimsy. The religiose elevatedness derived from the mythological and religious references and the sermonising run of the rhetoric, goes with an impracticality and a vagueness in the relation of these references to everyday realities. Ramon is selfless and deluded.

The explanation and enactment of the rites of Quetzalcoatl and Huitzilopochtli occupy a disproportionately large place in the novel. The newness of the religion makes exposition necessary if it is to be understood, but Lawrence seems to have been carried away to grave excess in this vein. The elaborate rituals become increasingly tiresome, partly because they are usually dramatically tame and rather static. They involve long interruptions in the close contact between the action of the novel and its central consciousness, Kate Leslie, between the reader and Kate. Ramon and Cipriano have key roles in the religious episodes, whereas Kate plays a very minor part in them. Ramon is realised as a man with an exceptional physique, but with an essentially ordinary mind:

'. . . Senora, I [Ramon] have not a very great respect for myself. Woman and I have failed with one another, and it is a bad failure to have in the middle of oneself'.

Kate looked at him in wonder, with a little fear. Why was he confessing to her. Was he going to love her? She almost suspended her breathing. He looked at her with a sort of sorrow on his brow, and in his dark eyes, anger, vexation, wisdom, and a dull pain.

'I am sorry', he went on, 'that Carlota and I are as we are with one another. Who am I, even to talk about Quetzalcoatl, when my heart is hollow with anger against the woman I have married and the children she bore me? – We never met in our souls, she and I . . .'.

He experiences the failure and doubt of an ordinary human being. Because he seems so ordinary, the extraordinary religious hymns ascribed to him and his extraordinary role as a saviour seem inappropriate and unconvincing. Just as Don Ramon is too ordinary to be 'First Man of Quetzalcoatl' and is not realised as such, so is Don Cipriano too ordinary to be 'First Man of Huitzilopochtli' and not realised as such, Kate too ordinary to be 'First Woman of Itzpapalotl' and not realised as such.

Lawrence's terms for the new religion are taken from Mexican history. Quetzalcoatl was the name of 'the benign deity and cultural hero' of the Aztecs, and Huitzilopochtli was the name of the central cult of the Aztec religion.[15] Lawrence is right, historically, in making Don Ramon claim the failure of Christianity in Mexico. During the whole of its colonial period, from the defeat of the Aztecs by the Spaniards in 1519 to independence in 1821, Mexico had to concede a high position to the Christian church. Because of the proselytising zeal of the Spanish imperialists, the Church gained enormous powers, which it did not put to good use. It amassed so much wealth for itself that, by 1821, it possessed half the wealth of the country. It was almost completely in charge of education, but by 1821 only thirty thousand were literate out of a total population of about six hundred thousand. After independence the Mexican state became much more secular, and the federal constitution of 1857 marks a key stage in its evolution. This constitution specifically gave greater authority to the central government, and incorporated certain clauses against the Church. In 1859, Benito Juarez, the most capable politician during the period of Reform in Mexican history (1855–61), crippled the economic power of the Church by taking over its properties, suppressing clerical privileges, instituting civil marriages and making cemeteries public places. Thereafter the general tendencies of Mexican history are unmistakably towards secularisation and reform. They culminated in the constitution of 1917, which followed the revolution of 1910. This constitution confirmed the tendencies of the 1859 effort, and is the basis of Mexican political organisation even today. Lawrence's advocacy of a religious salvation for Mexico has no grounds in past history; secularisation and reform actually succeeded in rescuing Mexico from a rapacious and inept Church; there are no grounds for supposing that another religion would do better than Christianity or ordinary politics. He has no grounds in history around 1926, when *The Plumed Serpent* was written, to place faith in another religion. It was precisely at this time that the revolution of 1910 was bearing fruit. Under Obregon, another able leader, the Mexicans were moving towards a more broadly based prosperity, deriving from such moves as a re-distribution of land, organisation of labour, less unequal educational opportunities with an increase in the number of schools, and a fostering of Indian culture. With a wrong-headed notion of Mexico's past and present, it is virtually inevitable that Lawrence's view of Mexico's future would turn out to be false. He is right in noting the ferment among well-meaning people, socialists and other politicians. But he does not see that the future belongs to these sections of society, not to religion. In fact, in the 1930s, Mexico was markedly socialistic; there took place a further re-distribution of land, the nationalisation of railways and foreign oil companies. After 1940, Mexico followed more conservative policies partly because of the mismanagement of some of her nationalised projects; but she continued to maintain a certain progressiveness in her policies, a certain well-being and peace, unrivalled by Latin American countries generally. Ramon says, 'I am sure the white Anti-Christ of charity, and socialism, and politics, and reform, will only succeed in finally destroying her'. But the so-called 'Anti-Christ' proves to be Mexico's real saviour, as it had been in the past. Lawrence's view of Mexican history is for the most part at variance with fact. Besotted with the notion of a religious revolution, he blinded himself to the actual condition of Mexico and its historical likelihoods.

Towards the end of the novel, Lawrence reaffirms his chronological primitivist view of history through Kate: he sees 'the power of the world' passing from the 'white' men to the dark. But his presentation of the relationship of Kate and Cipriano suggests that he unconsciously resists this historical process. This relationship carries an important part of the novel's positive significance, and is intended to be significant for the whole world and its future history. It points to the 'new conception of human life', not to the mere acceptance of the transference of power from the 'white' men to the dark but to 'the fusion of the mental–spiritual life of the white people and the old blood-and-vertebrate consciousness'. To live out the new wholeness of life, Kate must stay back in Mexico: 'I must have both', she said to herself. 'I must not recoil against Cipriano and Ramon, they make my blood blossom in my body. I say they are limited. But then one must be limited. If one tries to be unlimited, one becomes horrible . . .'. The Mexicans would save Kate from becoming 'elderly and a bit grisly'. Unfortunately, the wide-ranging symbolic significance of her relationship with Cipriano is not realised adequately. The religious aspect of the novel pushes the relationship into a minor flickering strain. Furthermore, the unsatisfactoriness of the religious aspect infects the presentation of the personal relationship:

> The strange, heavy, positive passivity. For the first time in her life she felt absolutely at rest. And talk and thought, had become trivial, superficial to her: as the ripples on the surface of the lake are as nothing, to the creatures that live away below in the unwavering deeps.
> . . . . .
> Cipriano was happy, in his curious Indian way. His eyes kept that

flashing, black, dilated look of a boy looking newly on a strange, almost uncanny wonder of life. He did not look very definitely at Kate, or even take much definite notice of her. He did not like talking to her, in any serious way. When she wanted to talk seriously, he flashed a cautious, dark look at her, and went away.

In trying to define their happy married state, Lawrence hits upon an illuminating image of 'creatures' in a lake. But an occasional felicitous touch is swamped, as usual, by his staple rhetoric.

When one compares *The Plumed Serpent* and *The Woman Who Rode Away* with *St. Mawr* and *The Princess*, it turns out that the wider Lawrence ranges in the field of primitivism the more liable he is to uncritically surrender to one of its inherent dangers, unreality, and the more liable his art is to suffer as a consequence. It is in keeping with this tendency that *The Plumed Serpent* is his most flawed work in this field.

It is clear that primitivism in Lawrence the novelist is of radical importance. His sense of the ill-health of European civilisation may well have been sharpened by personal experiences. He found it difficult to get *The Rainbow* and *Women in Love* published. *The Rainbow* was suppressed soon after its publication in 1915, and was out of print in England from 1915 to 1926. He completed *Women in Love* in November 1916, but it was published only in November 1920 in an American private edition and in May 1921 in a British edition for the public. More importantly, his disillusionment with civilisation is related to the First World War, which he found extremely disturbing and dealt with in the digressive chapter, called 'The Nightmare', in *Kangaroo*. It is obviously no mere coincidence that it was around this time that he wrote *The Rainbow* and *Women in Love* and that he told Lady Cynthia Asquith in a letter:

> You asked me about the message of the *Rainbow*. I don't know myself what it is: except that the older world is done for, toppling on top of us: and that it's no use the men looking to the women for salvation, nor the women looking to sensuous satisfaction for their fulfilment. There must be a new world.[16]

His travels, after 1919, to Australia and New Mexico, brought him into contact with what he felt were vital cultures. His primitivist tendencies arise, then, from a serious contemplation of European and non-

European cultures, based on first-hand experience. I. A. Richards tries to explain and comment on Lawrence's primitivism with special reference to his poetry; his words implicitly extend to Lawrence's fiction.

> The central dominant change may be described as the *Neutralisation of Nature*, the transference from the Magical View of the world to the scientific, a change so great that it is perhaps only paralleled historically by the change, from whatever adumbration of a world-picture preceded the Magical View, to the Magical View itself. By the Magical View I mean, roughly, the belief in a world of Spirits and Powers which control events, and which can be evoked and, to some extent, controlled themselves by human practices.[17]

Richards puts his finger on the most important change in the world-picture from earlier ages to modern times. But he considers Lawrence's primitivism as a way of 'dodging those difficulties which come from being born into this generation rather than into some earlier age'.[18] The primitivism in Lawrence's fiction is very different. It is not a mere 'reversion to primitive mentality', to use Richards's words. Lawrence seizes upon a quality of the primitive Mexicans, their vitality, which, he thinks, Europe lacks. This is a valid point. His position is strong when he does not see salvation only in simple terms. His critical self advocates the fusion of the vitality of the primitive Mexicans with the civilised Mind of Europe. It is likely that the difficulties arising from the change in world-picture lie behind Lawrence's position, but there are certainly other factors, no less important and conscious, such as the evils of industrialism and social convention. Of course, in his sense of the evils of Western industrialism, he is a direct descendant of nineteenth century figures such as Carlyle, Dickens, Ruskin and Morris. Escapism is one of the potent and inherent lures of primitivism, but Lawrence's kind of primitivism seems to be a way of facing modern 'difficulties' and an attempt to solve them, rather than a way of 'dodging' them.

T. S. Eliot is guilty of much grosser misrepresentation and simplification of Lawrence's primitivism than Richards. He traces it to an alleged 'sexual morbidity' in Lawrence:

> But I cannot see much development in *Lady Chatterley's Lover*. Our old acquaintance, the game-keeper, turns up again: the social obsession which makes his well-born – or almost well-born – ladies offer themselves to – or make use of – plebeians springs from the same

morbidity which makes other of his female characters bestow their
favours upon savages. The author of that book seems to me to have
been a very sick man indeed.[19]

Lawrence's primitivism springs from a deep concern with large problems of history and civilisation, not from 'sexual morbidity'. Sexual
relationships are important, but they are only part of this concern.
When he focuses on them in his Mexican works, they are related to the
state of the wider cultures to which they belong. His primitivism does
not seem the reaction of 'a very sick man', but that of a man healthily
alive in the contemporary world and concerned about its well-being.
We saw that his primitivist thought is close, at points, to traditional
primitivist thinking. It is unlikely that he was, in any way, influenced
appreciably by traditional primitivist thought. He probably arrived at
his primitivist lines of thought independently. His closeness to the
tradition indicates how centrally and deeply he was in touch with the
world. His marked divergences from it clearly point to his originality.
His Mexican fiction extends his field of achievement in realising 'the
vast importance of the novel, properly handled. It can inform and lead
into new places the flow of our sympathetic consciousness, and it can
lead our sympathy away in recoil from things gone dead'.[20]
    Eliot welcomes Wyndham Lewis's attack on Lawrence's primiti-
vism in *Paleface: The Philosophy of the 'Melting-Pot'*. No doubt
Lewis's book is a landmark in Lawrence criticism, but not in the way
Eliot refers to it, a 'brilliant exposure' of Lawrence's 'incapacity for
what we ordinarily call thinking'.[21] Lewis is as wrong as Eliot. Lewis
takes Lawrence's *Mornings in Mexico* as his text in his attempt to
refute Lawrence's primitivism: 'In contrast to the White Overlord of
this world in which we live, Mr. Lawrence shows us a more primitive
type of 'consciousness', which has been physically defeated by the
white 'consciousness' and assures us that the defeated 'consciousness' is
the better of the two'.[22] Lawrence, certainly, does not simplemindedly
and unrealistically idealise primitive life at the expense of European
life. His critical sense emerges in the description of everyday happenings in *Mornings in Mexico*;[23] in his view, a 'crushed' spirit is a quality
that characterises the Mexicans. What he considers valuable in them is
suggested by his description of an Indian 'entertainment' in the same
book;[24] the song of the Indians manifests their creative vitality and
their oneness with the rhythms of nature. Lawrence's view of the Mexicans, then, is balanced. Yet the more important arguments of Lewis are
those relating to the wider social and historical implications of tradi-

tional and philosophical primitivism. Unlike Lawrence, Lewis does not believe in the decline of the 'white' race and thinks that the 'white' race can renew itself with its own resources, instead of regeneration coming with the help of the dark races.[25]

Lawrence's views cannot be conclusively proved to be true until our present phase of history is over, but it seems to me that his critical primitivism is likely to be accurate. Only in Lawrence among the selected writers is primitivism both prominent and philosophic. But the others do reveal primitivist awarenesses and tendencies. Kurtz's case in *Heart of Darkness* is, in a way, one of primitivism. Forster's pre-War novels reveal aspects of mind which have affinities with primitivism: he is discontented with his sophisticated society and a central positive value of his is 'natural' living whether embodied by Gino Carella or Stephen Wonham. Distinguished contemporaries of Lawrence in the 1920s shared and corroborate further his general primitivist tendencies. Among those who felt that Western civilisation had deteriorated were T. S. Eliot in *The Waste Land* (1922), W. B. Yeats in his vein of exalting the past at the expense of the present, F. R. Leavis in *Mass Civilisation and Minority Culture* (1930) and Oswald Spengler in *The Decline of the West* (Volume I in 1918, Volume II in 1922). They, too, tried to find ways of regeneration. Primitivism is important in modern painting and sculpture. Paul Gauguin turns to the primitive people of the South Seas in quest of the essentials of life for his painting and is stimulated to creativity. Picasso found inspiration in African masks for cubist innovations. In the 1920s Henry Moore 'became aware that in some examples of primitive art the sculptor had been bold enough to make three-dimensional form out of a solid block, and this gave him courage to do it in his own sculpture'. His sculptures of 'reclining figures with their very vigorous right-angled rhythm' have affinities with 'Mexican and particularly Aztec sculpture'.[26] Lawrence's view that the vitality of 'white' men is draining away implies that new insights and creativity will spring from dark people who, he thinks, have this quality. This is evident in the growing body of literature by such writers as James Baldwin, Ralph Ellison, Chinua Achebe, Wole Soyinka, Aimé Césaire, Mulk Raj Anand and R. K. Narayan. Some of Lawrence's primitivist points appear convincing partly because of the corroborating closeness of a long line of traditional primitivist thinking. Works of writers such as James Baldwin suggest that many of Lawrence's primitivist points are being proved by history to be penetrating and true insights. Baldwin can be regarded as convincingly showing the falsity of Lewis's views partly because his points are based on a deep knowledge and first-hand experience of America, Lewis's special concern, his 'Melting-pot' as he calls it. Moreover, Baldwin is part of the recent assertion of negro creativity which, as Marcus Cunliffe notes, contributed 'much' to American music and without which it would not have been possible for 'black idioms and the notion of the black life-style to represent the furthest advance towards literary truth for the white *avant-garde* in the United States'.[27]

In *The Fire Next Time* (1963), Baldwin contemplates the negro problem in the United States in an all-sided way. He is supremely realistic:

> But in order to change a situation one has first to see it for what it is: in the present case, to accept the fact, whatever one does with it thereafter, that the Negro has been formed by this nation, for better or for worse, and does not belong to any other – not to Africa, and certainly not to Islam. The paradox – and a fearful paradox it is – is that the American Negro can have no future anywhere, on any continent, as long as he is unwilling to accept his past.[28]

He is aware of the grave difficulty for a negro of arriving at a balanced view of his own problem: 'That sinners have always, for American Negroes, been white is a truth we needn't labour, and every American Negro, therefore, risks having the gates of paranoia close on him'.[29] With an awareness of these hazards, he can demonstrate the difficult kind of balance necessary for a sane discussion of emotionally charged subjects such as racial problems:

> In short, we, the black and the white, deeply need each other here if we are really to become a nation – if we are really, that is, to achieve our identity, our maturity, as men and women. To create one nation has proved to be a hideously difficult task; there is certainly no need now to create two, one black and one white.[30]

Points made with clarity and force by a mind such as Baldwin's, are convincing. He has a Lawrentian sense of the atrophy of the 'white' race[31] and goes on to spell out a Lawrentian path of regeneration for the 'white' man:

> ... The white man's unadmitted – and apparently, to him, unspeakable – private fears and longings are projected onto the Negro.

The only way he can be released from the Negro's tyrannical power over him is to consent, in effect, to become black himself, to become a part of that suffering and dancing country that he now watches wistfully from the heights of his lonely power and, armed with spiritual traveller's cheques, visits surreptitiously after dark.[32]

Baldwin is deeply analytical and positive. Like Lawrence, he points out the 'white' man's sense of the dark people as a menace to their supremacy: 'And black has become a beautiful colour – not because it is loved but because it is feared'.[33] His view of the passing of power from the 'white' to the dark people is close to Lawrence's view. It comes particularly close to Lawrence at the conclusion of his work when he considers history in terms of cycles, a view almost identical with the Theory of Undulation of the later chronological primitivists:

I could also see that the intransigence and ignorance of the white world might make that vengeance inevitable – a vengeance that does not really depend on, and cannot really be executed by, any person or organisation, and that cannot be prevented by any police force or army: historical vengeance, a cosmic vengeance, based on the law that we recognise when we say, 'Whatever goes up must come down'.[34]

9 Joyce Cary: the clash of cultures in Nigeria

> We cannot hope to leave this difficult question in a spirit of easy optimism. It is useless to pretend that there is not a conflict of principles in Africa today.
>
> Margery Perham, 'Future Relations of Black and White in Africa', in *The Listener*, 28 March 1934.

Joyce Cary's interests in Nigeria are very different from Lawrence's interests in Mexico, and his life was very different, too. Lawrence was never a colonial employee, but Cary entered the British Political Service and he served in Nigeria from 1913 to 1919. He published his first novel, *Aissa Saved*, only in 1932, about 13 years after he left Nigeria, but it was to Nigeria that he had turned for his themes. Indeed, his Nigerian experiences provided the stimulus for almost the entire first phase of his career as a novelist. *Aissa Saved* was quickly followed by *An American Visitor* (1933) and *The African Witch* (1936). In his next novel, *Castle Corner* (1938), he turns away from Africa for the most part, but *Mister Johnson* (1939) marks a complete return. His Nigerian novels and the Nigerian side of *Castle Corner* form a distinctive body of work.

Cary set his African works in Nigeria of the early twentieth century when it was still a colony and generally very backward in every way. During this period, Nigeria was under 'indirect rule'. 'The European magistrates, that is to say, did not govern the people directly, but through and by means of their own chiefs', as Cary notes in *Britain and West Africa*.[1] In his very first novel, Cary discovered the major preoccupation of all his African works and his true *métier*. He realised that *Aissa Saved* was about the 'impact of one culture on another'.[2] This impact of Western culture on African culture under 'indirect rule' became his central concern; this kind of clash of cultures is a key feature of all developing countries under imperialism. Each novel of his emphasises one aspect of this clash of cultures which may occupy a minor place, or be absent, in the others; yet a certain process of development is discernible through the novels. Thus, though all of them are characteristic of the writer, it is necessary to discuss each novel separately in chronological order and then come to an overall view of Cary's reaction to Nigeria.

In *Aissa Saved*, Cary's interest in the introduction of Western material progress into Nigeria is clear in the part played by Bradgate; the District Officer perseveres with his plans for roads, bridges, inns and markets despite opposition from conservative Nigerians such as Yerima and the inefficiency of his African workmen. But Cary's major preoccupation is with cultural impact in the sphere of moral values. He handles this in terms of the interplay of three implicitly contrasting groups of characters, the African pagans, the African converts to Christianity and the European Christians. The pagans are shown as primitive. Owule's view of the drought in Yanrin is shown as characteristic of them:

> Oke is the Kolua goddess of mountains and fertility, and every logical person in Yanrin saw at once that if Oke was indeed offended the bad harvest, the drought were easily explained. But why was she offended? Had they not besought her for good crops, and given her double the usual sacrifices?
> 'Yes', said Owule, 'but nevertheless she is offended. This is proved by the absence of good yams and early rains. Therefore your sacrifices are not good enough and you had better repent before her'.

Cary's irony exposes the superstitious, circular nature of primitive reasoning as he, a civilised critical observer, sees it, as well as its perfect logicality to primitive people. He presents another facet of the pagan mind during Obasa's inquiry into Aissa's escape from the pagan mob:

> Half a dozen witnesses pressed forward. An old woman, who had first noticed the yellow bitch, swore that Aissa had changed before her eyes, and caught up Abba in her teeth to gallop away with him. This evidence had great weight with Obasa, who had experience of legal enquiries and could tell when a witness was truthful and honest. But it was obvious to all that this old woman, known for her old-fashioned uprightness and integrity, was speaking the truth.
> The old lady for her part had no shadow of doubt that she had seen Aissa change because she knew already that the girl was a witch and able to change herself. As for her carrying off Abba in her

teeth, was it not obvious that she must have done so for how else could a dog carry a child?

Cary's understanding irony suggests the falsity of the old woman's views as well as her sincerity; her superstition has made her genuinely self-deluded. He conveys both his own critical view of reality and the primitive woman's view of it. He is able to maintain the same ironic balance when dealing with more disturbing pagan realities – for instance, the sacrifice of Numi, the small son of Ishe, to the goddess Oke:

> The boy now fully awake, and frightened to see his mother tied, and by the solemn looks of Owule and his two assistants, began to struggle and cry. Ishe also struggled and uttered a piercing scream. The assistant Gani put his hands to the side of her neck and compressed the veins until she was faint and almost unconscious. Ije then took Numi by the ears, and standing sidelong pulled his head forward and downwards towards the Oke mound. Owule struck off the boy's head with a matchet and the blood spurted upon the Oke mound.

The unflinching precision of the plain description suggests the unthinking cruelty of the sacrifice, in the eyes of a Cary, as well as the genuine, complete belief of the pagans in the necessity and rightness of human sacrifice which enables Gani, Ije and Owule to perform an atrocious deed in a business-like way. Thus, Cary's presentation of Owule's view of the drought in Yanrin, the old woman's view of Aissa's escape from the pagan mob and the sacrifice of Numi indicate that he presents a wide range of pagan life in a consistent characteristic way, both from his standpoint of a civilised, critical observer and from the viewpoint of the pagans themselves. The double vision is balanced and ironic.

African pagan realities were known to other contemporary British writers and were used by them in fiction – for instance, by Lord Baden-Powell in 'Jokilobovu' (1933), J. A. G. Elliot in 'The Ngoloko' (1933) and W. H. Adams in 'The Tail Girl of Krobo Hill' (1933). A comparison of these tales with Cary's African fiction shows how the same kind of realities may be used at different levels by writers of different talent. Lord Baden-Powell's presentation of the funeral of an African king is typical of them:

> Directly the King breathed his last one of the Royal oxen was slain

and the hide stripped off and wrapped round his body. A hole was cut in the back of the wall of the kraal and the corpse removed secretly during the night. Conveyed to the mountain, it was there bestowed in a cave. His widows accompanied it and took charge. And here they kept their painful watch until the hide became dry and hard, and that which was inside withered and dried up. From time to time the corpse was rocked by the attendant ladies, and when at last the rattling sound told of complete desiccation it was publicly proclaimed that the King was really and truly dead. ...

into it. The grave was large, because it had to accommodate something more than the Royal corpse. His widows had to enter, and kneeling round him, were buried with him. The great man could not be allowed to go alone into the next world. This was accountable for the somewhat natural hesitation on the part of the ladies to announce his death.[3]

This can be compared with Cary's presentation of the sacrifice of Numi. Cary's presentation comes alive as a dramatic scene with vivid specific actions performed by individualised characters. Baden-Powell's seems tame, generalised reportage. Far from Cary's double vision, Baden-Powell gives us a strong sense neither of a civilised critical view of these primitive funeral rites or of a pagan view of them as an integral part of a whole way of life. He describes the rites as if they were quaint customs of another world that have nothing seriously to do with his own kind of civilised life.

There are three European Christians in *Aissa Saved* – Bradgate, Harry and Hilda Carr – and they are realised as distinct individuals. The differences are particularly marked between Bradgate and the Carrs. Whereas Bradgate is an administrator in whose life religion is unimportant, the Carrs are missionaries by vocation. The Christianity of the Carrs and even of Bradgate emerges as superior to paganism. They are not savage, and are less superstitious than the pagans. The efforts of the missionaries are seen to have borne fruit in that some Africans have become more humane than they were because of their teaching and example. This claim of Cary in his 'Prefatory Essay' is true to the novel: 'Some correspondents took the book for an attack on the Missions. It is not so. African missions have done good work in bringing to Africa a far better faith than any native construction'.[4] Still, Cary's view of the Christianity even of the dedicated Carrs is not wholly favourable; it is characteristically critical and balanced. For instance, Christianity has a supernatural element and demands a certain blind faith from its adherents. These features, in both moderate and extreme forms, are presented dramatically, for example, during the Kolu episode. They appear in an extreme form in Ojo and Mrs Carr, in a moderate form in Harry Carr. Ojo, an African convert, thinks he has received 'a call' from Christ to hold a meeting of the Christians in the pagan stronghold of Kolu. Mrs Carr readily accompanies Ojo's followers because she believes in his call. Mr Carr, too, joins the expedition, but after a struggle with his conscience; he represses his sense of reason and human responsibility and adopts the attitude of his wife. The massacre at Kolu, from which the Carrs barely escape, underlines the wrongheadedness of Christian superstition and Christian blind faith, which are also implicitly criticised by their closeness to paganism. Thus, the Christian behaviour of the European Christians is seen from their point of view as well as from Cary's own balanced standpoint. They are presented through a double vision.

Cary portrays the African converts in the same way. Speaking of the Christianity of Aissa and other converts, he said: 'Actually her religion is a mixture of Christian and pagan ideas, and this is the case with all the converts'.[5] These words are true to the novel; it shows, as he says, 'what can happen to the religious ideas of one region when they are imported into another'.[6] The strength of paganism and the pagan-like element in the Christianity of the missionaries make the religion of the converts 'a mixture of Christian and pagan ideas'. They pray to one god, the Christian God, but they treat him very much as though he were a pagan deity. For instance, the converts are guilty of savagery in the name of Christ just as the pagans are in the name of Oke, during their conflict at Ketemfe:

Owule drooping with fear leant towards them and Aissa struck at the huge white face and glittering eyes, as big as plates, with her matchet, but could not reach it.

Owule tried to turn aside and avoid the blow, but the unwieldly dress swung and caught his feet. Aissa rolled off Ojo's shoulders and as she fell almost fainting against the white face she struck at it a second time with her matchet. It fell and she fell beside it. With yells of triumph the Christians who had watched the dual from the edges of the grove rushed forward. Someone with a torch lit the juju frame of plaited grass and the cloth and the whole burst into flames. Owule uttered loud screams within and kicked his legs through the grass, but Ladije and Makoto held him down with their spears.

This treatment of Owule by the converts, Aissa, Ladije and Makoto, is like the treatment of Numi by the unconverted Africans, Owule himself, Gani and Ije, and is presented in the same way. The language is both plain and forceful; the description is unflinchingly exact. The ironic double vision conveys both the brutality of the deeds of the converts as they strike a Cary, and their perfect normality, as the converts themselves see them. Aissa's inhumanity in the name of Christ goes with her pagan sacrifice of her child to Christ. In her the 'mixture of Christian and pagan ideas' is unmistakably prominent. This is natural and necessary because she is the heroine of the novel and because it is mainly through her that Cary presents the religion of the converts. The conflicts between the pagans and the converts, which form the body of the novel, end with the capture of Aissa by the pagans. They consider Aissa a witch and leave her on an ants' nest:

> Aissa soon grew weak; she could not remember where she was, the fire of the ants' tearing at her body did not scorch, it was like the warmth of flesh. Jesus had taken her, he was carrying her away in his arms, she was going to heaven at last to Abba and Gajere. Immediately the sky was rolled up like a door curtain and she saw before her the great hall of God with pillars of mud painted white and red. God in a white riga and a new indigo turban, his hands heavy with thick silver rings, stood in the middle and beside him the spirit like a goat with white horns. Abba was sitting on its back looking frightened and almost ready to cry. One of the angels was holding him and putting his cap straight. The others were laughing at him and clapping their hands.

This is the last scene of the novel and it is couched in a plain suggestive prose, characteristic of Cary. Aissa's mental collapse, brought about by her misfortunes (notably, the loss of Abba and Gajere, acute physical suffering), has led to delusion. In her vision of heaven, she conceives 'the great hall of God' as if it were a pagan temple, God himself and 'the spirit beside him' as if they were pagan deities. Thus, through his ironic double vision, Cary suggests that Aissa's vision is sincerely Christian to her but that to persons like himself it reflects the enduring, deep-seated 'mixture of Christian and pagan ideas' in her. The African converts, the pagans, the European Christians, in short, all the characters are treated with the same kind of art. Underlying Cary's double vision is a belief in the equality of all people as human beings and that all people, whether African or European, belong to a common humanity. He did not regard the negroes as forming a different and inferior species as Thackeray and even Conrad did.

The painful conclusion of the novel drives home Cary's kind of contemplation of a society in inner Nigeria. In his 'Prefatory Essay', he underlines the importance of moral values: 'Ethics are important enough, goodness knows, but the fundamental question for everybody is what they live by; what is their faith'.[7] He handles well this 'fundamental question'. He is mainly concerned with the moral condition of the Africans, as suggested by the dominant position occupied by the African characters and the emergence of Aissa as the heroine. He shows that the majority of the Africans remain pagans, uninfluenced by Christianity, and that the minority, who were converted, only partially change from paganism. The European Christians occupy a less important and smaller place in the novel than the Africans, and their values are more or less qualified. No character, African or European, is able to formulate a sound set of values or get close to one. Thus, Cary's moral outlook as it concerns both the Africans and Europeans, is pessimistic; at the same time, it represents a tough and realistic facing of the Nigerian situation.

In *Aissa Saved*, the very small number of isolated Europeans and the very large number of Africans truly reflect the distribution of races at a remote colonial outpost. Still, to have over fifty named Africans in one short novel is to make it too crowded. Because the main characters are clearly highlighted, the overcrowding is a minor flaw. The prominent Africans, such as Owule and Ali, are portrayed to much the same extent as the three Europeans. But Aissa is outstanding. We are first introduced to her in the Shibi mission. She is the 'star of the confirmation class', but she spits in the face of Frederick during the heated discussion about the venue of the next mission meeting. This suggests that, while she is in part religious, there are fires in her which are not dominated by Christianity. Cary reinforces these suggestions subtly when he presents Carr's view of her among the converts on their way to Kolu: 'Carr recognised Aissa laughing as usual with her whole body, her shoulders up to her ears and her hands clasped in ectasy. Then she threw her cloth over her face'. Aissa's full-blooded actions and the last movement suggest the submergence of the sensuous woman in the religious convert. This fundamental division within Aissa becomes clearer when the Carrs discuss her:

'Ojo seems to me a bit of a degenerate', said Carr. 'He enjoys work-ing himself up about things. And Aissa is nothing but a common or garden trollop'.

This was too much for Mrs Carr even in her tactfulness; she answered indignantly that Aissa was a very good girl.

'She has one of the most affectionate natures I've ever known in a native girl, truly affectionate, I mean, and she's sincere in her reli-gion too. I've seen her going into chapel by herself time and again. I really believe she goes every day; she never goes past without saying a prayer'.

'Yes, I've noticed that, there's no doubt she's been up to some-thing for some time. As for the affectionate nature, she's apparently run off to Kolu to find a man for herself – there's no doubt at least about her appetites'.

Cary is aware of the multiple ways of looking at a single character. Through his preceding portrayal of Aissa and the exaggeration in the language of the Carrs, Cary ironically suggests that the views of both are extremist, that they do not cancel out each other as the speakers think, that each contains a core of truth which belongs to different sides of Aissa.

Thus Cary, an educated Irishman, subtly and dramatically portrays a half-pagan, African woman of complex and changing character as the chief 'persona' of his very first novel. His ability to understand and to present uncivilised Africans, people so different from himself and other Europeans, is outstanding because it covers such a wide range of Afri-can life; and this includes their speech. He is aware that the English of the Africans is different from Standard English and so he captures their kind of English when they would probably use it:

Carr told him that Yanrin was also out of bounds.

'But, sah, if de spirit tell me to go, I hear de spirit, I no hear dat Bradgate'.

'Why, Ojo, you know you can't go. You'd only get yourself murdered like the others'.

But the boy was too excited to be frightened. 'Sah', he cried, 'you doan see, If de rain come now in Yanrin, dem priests say dey make it. De people no fit know we make it. Dey no give tanks to God. ah. Dey no come here to church'.

The African English has the flexibility and tones of living speech; Cary can use it to bring out character. In this instance, it conveys faultlessly slightly educated Ojo's religious enthusiasm and *naiveté*. But at moments when the more or less primitive Africans would probably speak in their native tongue, Cary employs Standard English as his equivalent for the vernacular:

> But Aissa cocked up her flat nose, struck a swaggering pose, and answered: 'I don't care for them, the bastards. We Christians are going to drive them all away'.
>   'Hold you tongue, you stupid girl'.
>   'Hold my tongue!' Aissa shouted. 'Why, I'm not afraid. I belong to Jesus now. It's the truth I tell you. We Christians are going to drive your Oke away. Then the rain will fall. Then all will be Christians. Then it will be the Kingdom of Heaven and Jesus will come. Then we'll all have plenty to eat and we'll have a good time always'.

Cary can use Standard English for Africans with the same skill as African English: in this case, to convey Aissa's naive confidence in Christianity.

Cary's characteristic method of organising his novels is not based on plot. He himself said: 'I do not write, and never have written, to an arranged plot. The book is composed over the whole surface at once like a picture, and may start anywhere, in the middle or at the end'.[8] The structure of a novel by him is characteristically determined by his informing interests and not by considerations such as symmetry or sequence. The need to express effectively his main interest, moral values, governs the fashioning of *Aissa Saved*. This novel has a central situation – the drought and the efforts of the Christians and pagans to bring about rain through the mediation of their respective deities. He brings out the conflicting values of the Europeans and the Africans mainly in terms of their thoughts and actions in relation to this unifying central situation. Golden L. Larsen thinks that 'there is a sort of mathematical predictability' about the ending of the novel;[9] this seems to be hardly possible given Aissa, a complex volatile 'protagonist', presented successfully from her first appearance to her last. Cary is a scrupulously objective narrator; he believes, 'An author has no more business in a book than a microphone on a screen. It is hard enough for him to give a clear coherent impression without unnecessary distractions'.[10] We have seen how Cary's themes and the critical 'placing' of his characters are conveyed by the skilful use of implication; how the oblique method works through points suggested by his language, the interplay of character and the course of the action.

Let us now consider his next novel, *An American Visitor*. In it he is mainly interested in the Western side of the cultural clash in Nigeria and he pays attention to Westerners more than to Africans; the introduction of Western material progress, which formed a minor concern of his in *Aissa Saved*, is here the major theme. The difference in emphasis between his first two novels is evident in that the most important character in *An American Visitor* is Marie Hasluck, an emancipated 'white' woman, whereas in *Aissa Saved* it was Aissa.

The meaning and achievement of *An American Visitor* hinges mainly on Cary's portrayal of its heroine. Marie is an American journalist and anthropologist. She is different from all the Englishmen around her in that she is against imperialism:

> Why couldn't she remember to keep quiet about the Empire. Yes, but it was because she liked these people so much that she hated to see them fixed in positions of domination and cruelty, in an artificial structure where even kind little Jukes and good-natured Frank were obliged to play the part of exploiters; and Mr Gore, who looked like a St. Francis, to be a tyrant over the conquered.

Marie's opposition to the Empire and the specific evils, which she rightly sees in it, are rendered here explicitly as a part of her thoughts. But her opposition is rarely, and the evils are never, dramatised. Because she does not see the good side of these 'exploiters', her anti-imperialism is shown implicitly to be unbalanced. It goes with a very sympathetic interest in the Africans and even an idealisation of them. Her attitude accords with District Officer Bewsher's. It is ironical that Marie and Bewsher come to love each other all the more strongly because of a mistaken view. The action of the novel is primarily about the future of the Birri, and Marie's love for Bewsher makes her participate all the more keenly in their struggles; she thinks:

> Whether Frank Cottee was right or wrong about the Birri, he was wrong in himself. What ever he might say about the blessings of civilisation he knew perfectly well that the kind he was going to introduce was not a civilisation at all. It was really and truly anarchy, a mess, a muddle. That was certain. Cottee was clever, but he was outside things. He didn't really feel them. He couldn't see that what he proposed to do was a crime which must be prevented.

And that was the most certain thing of all. For it was the most horrible kind of crime, to debauch and ruin a whole people for profit; it was like deliberately, just for one's own pleasure, infecting children with a filthy disease. Whatever Mr Bewsher said or did he would always be more right than Cottee, just because he did feel that, he did see that enormous fact, as big as a mountain. And he was prepared to ruin himself to prevent the Birri being degraded and exploited. That was why a man like Mr Bewsher, even if he was not very clever or well educated, was worth a million Frank Cottees, and that was why he must not be allowed to give way.

Marie takes sides passionately. Cary implies that her love for Bewsher and idealisation of the Birri make her reasoning somewhat biased and short-sighted; she compares Cottee and Bewsher as black against white. Bewsher is, certainly, a worthier man than Cottee, but Marie does not see that the stand of each has its respective virtues and weaknesses. To keep out external influence completely, as Bewsher wants to do, is to preserve economic, social and political stasis as well as the valuable aspects of indigenous culture. Moreover, the coming of Western civilisation is inevitable; Marie cannot see that Cottee is bound to beat Bewsher. Cary's double vision, which conveys both Marie's and his own view of realities, is couched in a vigorous prose with telling metaphors; for instance, the 'disease' and 'mountain' metaphors express both Marie's opinion and Cary's view of them. But Cary's portrayal of Marie would have been more effective if his double vision had shown itself less in terms of this kind of direct presentation of thoughts and more in terms of dramatic action.

Marie's love for Bewsher makes her even give up her opposition to imperialism. But her perceptiveness increases as the action unfolds itself. She gains an insight into the illusions, to her horrible, of primitive thinking as she contemplates Bewsher alone among the Birri; she tells Mrs Dobson: '... The chief that gets Monkey's brains to eat and Monkey's finger joints to hang round his neck will be a hero for the rest of his life, and every good Birri wants to be a hero'. Marie is shown as acting sensibly in crises. When the Birri threaten the Goshi mission, she does not share the complacency of the Dobsons or the optimism of Bewsher; she wisely sends for troops. Later on, when Bewsher is isolated among the Birri, she opposes the proposal to send troops against the tribe. She feels that Bewsher's safety lies in non-interference by soldiers, and her stand is justified by his escape. Still, Marie does not grow fully mature:

But she felt in her breast an intolerable longing – she wanted to cry – for the silly young woman who had seen in a little community of naked savages the pattern of an earthly paradise. The same silly young woman who at college had adored the Greeks and wished that she had been born two thousand four hundred years earlier.

Marie now has the clear-sightedness to see the silliness of her former idealisation of 'naked savages', but at the same time she is greatly attracted to that state. The persisting streak of unrealism in her becomes prominent, say, during the episode of Bewsher's death. When the Birri, led by Obai, attack the Goshi mission, Bewsher asks Marie for his gun to defend himself. Marie, however, 'had a hunch it was safer for him to trust in God' and conceals his gun. Bewsher, without any means of self-defence, is killed by Obai. Bewsher's death jolts Marie into the most realistic and perceptive stage of her life. She becomes aware of her own responsibility for his death and faces it squarely. She gains an insight into her own self, into the nature of her tragedy and into life in general.

Marie Hasluck is the first and only Westerner whom Cary attempts to portray in the proportions of a protagonist of a full-length African novel. She is a complex developing personality, like Aissa or Forster's Adela Quested; but though she is more articulate and self-aware than they, her character is rendered in terms too explicit and insufficiently dramatic, unlike theirs. Monkey Bewsher, another Westerner, is the character next in importance to Marie. He is much less complex and changes much less. His life as an administrator is characterised by a permanent desire 'to preserve and develop the rich kind of local life which is the essence and only justification of nationalism'. He thinks of plans to realise this:

> Federation, native courts, a code of law; in a year Birri would have a body as well as a soul. The tribe would be saved as people.
>
> And with federation accomplished he could afford to let the traders in. In fact, he would want them, . . . He would bar the missions altogether. . . .

He thinks of himself as the supreme guide of all the changes. The impracticality and futility of his paternalistic plans are brought out implicitly by the course of the action, and also presented as part of the immediate drama:

> Gore said nothing to this. Bewsher was one of the queerest of the

old gang who had ruled Nigeria like independent despots, but he wasn't a fool. He must know that he couldn't play fast and loose with the whole imperial government.

He looked thoughtfully at Gore. 'You'd rather fancy a mining camp in Birri – have you ever seen one?'

'No, sir, but I don't see how we can stop it now'.

'If the E.P.L. is invalid'.

'Don't you think that's rather unlikely? The new Nok boundary may be wrong in the Gazette of course, but the notice was drafted from your own map. It must have been. There isn't any other showing villages'.

. . . . .

But Gore, though he did not like his position any more than he cared for Bewsher's policy, which he thought impracticable, or his methods, which he thought undignified, stood where he was. He was just as obstinate as Bewsher in the pursuit of his different ends.

Bewsher's speech sounds more consistently authentic than Marie Hasluck's. Here it conveys the complete soundness of his ideas as they appear to him as well as their frailties and his unconscious sense of defeat as they strike a Cary. But Cary is not content to let his double vision speak for itself. He makes explicit what speech enacts – that Bewsher was like an 'independent despot', that his policy was 'impracticable', his methods 'undignified', that 'Gore was just as obstinate as Bewsher in the pursuit of his different ends'.

It is generally true that Bewsher is presented more creatively than Marie Hasluck. Though Cary knew about American women through reading, he had far less personal familiarity with them than with British colonial administrators: he himself had been one of these officials. But even the treatment of Bewsher reveals, and confirms, Cary's tendency in the novel to be too explicit and not sufficiently dramatic. Thus this tendency is deep-going. On an intellectual plane, Cary appears to understand sufficiently an imperial situation and its central fact, 'exploitation': we noticed his balanced criticism of both Marie and Bewsher. But his intellectual understanding is not sufficiently digested into his artistic self, into his imagination.

The Birri tribes disintegrate. The well-meaning plans of Bewsher and Marie for the welfare of the Birri are not realised. Their happy personal relationship comes to an untimely end with Bewsher's death. Thus, Cary's vision of both the personal and public sides of life in inner Nigeria is sad. It goes with a tough realism. Bewsher's premature death is inevitable, given Marie's unrealistic action of hiding his gun when he cannot do without it. Their plans for the welfare of the Birri are, as we saw, impractical.

> Cottee as a successful man could smile at Gore's romanticism as he had been annoyed by Bewsher's. For Bewsher's attempt to keep the Birri out of the general flux had sprung from the same source; as Jukes used to say all these officials were playboys moved by some impractical notion or other. For even if civilisation meant for the Birri a meaner, shallower kind of life, how could any man hope to fight against it when it came with the whole drive of the world behind it, bringing every kind of gaudy toy and easy satisfaction?

The inevitability in the coming and triumph of civilisation is brought out here implicitly by Cottee and supported by the drift of the whole action. Our sympathies are with the idealists but the self-seeking prospectors are objectively right. Cary's basic ideas and attitudes in the novel are sound enough,[11] but his tendency to be unduly explicit and undramatic makes its drift appear rather a forced thesis.

The interests, outlook and art of *An American Visitor* are of a piece with those of *Aissa Saved*. Cary has wisely selected fewer characters without reducing the possibilities of greater richness of meaning. But, though his interests are wider and more complex, they are not translated into sufficiently satisfying fictional terms.

His next novel, *The African Witch*, follows naturally from the first two. In it he is concerned with the African more than the Western side of the clash of cultures in Nigeria. Thus his broad preoccupation is similar to that in *Aissa Saved*, but the central issues in the two novels are very different: Aissa is a primitive African half-converted to Christianity, while the hero of this novel, Louis Aladai, is an Oxford-educated African Christian. In this novel, as in *An American Visitor*, Cary is concerned with the future of an African tribe. But this tribe is not as remote as the Birri (or the African communities in *Aissa Saved*): they live around a provincial town. Moreover, the problem is viewed from a fresh angle: in *An American Visitor* Marie, a 'white'woman, wants to preserve tribal culture, while in this novel Aladai, an African male, wants to reform tribal ways; Judy Coote, who markedly resembles Marie, plays a secondary role.

The action of *The African Witch* is centrally concerned with the future of the Rimi tribe. Louis Aladai is mainly responsible for setting the action in motion by making a very strong challenge to the existing order in Rimi. His Oxford education raises him, culturally, above his fellow tribesmen and gives him a place on a par with, if not superior to, the Europeans. Indeed, Jerry Rackham, the leading 'white' character, though he calls Aladai 'a performing ape and a monkeyfied Bolshie', thinks that the African 'was worth an infinity of Honeywoods because Honeywood was a robot'. Aldai's qualities and attitudes emerge dramatically through his contact with other characters, notably the two Englishwomen, Judy Coote and Dryas Honeywood. One of his important discussions with Judy leads to the large question of what is civilisation:

'But, Louis, Rimi has a civilisation of its own'.
He made a quick gesture, only short of impatience by a little politeness. 'Rimi civilisation! You know that it is a joke. Can you compare it with yours? – and that means all Europe. Think of the richness of the European peoples – the poetry, the music, the – the' – he waved his hand in the air – 'the greatness of every kind'. He turned on her again. 'Rimi civilisation! Do you know what it is? – *juju*'.
'Not all of it, Louis'.
But he was not in a mood for argument. 'It is soaked with *juju*. You may say a body is not blood – but if you took the blood out, what would be left? The blood of what you call Rimi civilisation is *juju* – so crude and stupid – you do not know what they can do. . . .'

Aladai has an educated mind capable of adding force to his views by means of analogies. His rejection of Rimi culture is founded partly on his understanding of it. Cary shows that Aladai sincerely believes that his notion of his own culture has been comprehensively reasoned. At the same time, he ironically suggests through Aladai's brusqueness and passionateness that Aladai has not sufficiently examined the nature of his view. His repudiation of his culture is also based partly on his estimate of Western civilisation. It has to him an obvious 'greatness'. But through his faltering at the height of his enthusiasm for it, through the vague extravagance of his speech, Cary also ironically suggests an emotionality in him which he cannot ground in actuality, a view of the West which is really a one-sided idealisation. Judy's views are shown as rational, in her own eyes, but as reflecting a person toppling over on the other side, from the standpoint of a Cary. Thus, Cary implicitly conveys his double vision in dramatic terms. As the conversation continues, he reveals with the same art more of their characters and his own remarkable understanding of Africans and Europeans in their colonial connections:

> 'It's too absurd – a million without schools – and Rimi civilisation! Rimi! No, I love Rimi, and it is because I love it that I want to give it something worth calling a civilisation'.
>
> 'But why not do it in Rimi's own language, Louis? You can always translate from English – and then your people can say that they understand Shakespeare better than we do'.

Cary shows both that Judy is sincerely progressive in advocating the use of Rimi language and, at the same time, that she is blind to the enormous difficulties of this undeveloped language achieving the capacity of English and the difficulties of achieving a satisfactory output of books in this language, difficulties connected with the condition of Rimi society. Judy emerges, with dramatic convincingness, as a vaporous English liberal in a colonial race-relations context, like Forster's Helen or Margaret Schlegel in an English class-relations context. In fact, Judy thinks in terms of mere translations from English, of understanding Shakespeare as a touchstone of civilisation, and, at the same time, she considers Rimi culture a 'civilisation': this reveals a kind of confused inverted racialism. Aladai's rather unbalanced view of Rimi culture and Western civilisation goes with an active, patriotic desire to improve his society. The need for improvement seems urgent in the light of the African realities Cary presents. Thus, both Aladai and Judy are shown to have their respective weaknesses as well as merits. On the whole, Aladai is sounder and he attempts to translate his ideas into action. He comes alive dramatically as a Westernised African reformer. He has the soundest claim to be the next Emir, and his high social position is an asset to his reforming zeal.

Though Aladai is as civilised as the Europeans and as able as the best of them, Rackham, he is not accepted as an equal by them, much less admitted into their society, because he is a black African. Judy Coote is boldly friendly with him, but she is the only European to be so. This state of affairs is depicted by the very first scene of the novel at the Rimi races; Judy is the only 'white' spectator to talk to Aladai, let alone be friendly towards him; the other Europeans are offended at what they considered his unpardonable intrusion. Aladai's second important experience of racial prejudice is at the exclusive Scotch club of the Europeans. He tries to admit himself into 'white' society by entering the club:

> He was for the moment blind with panic. The chairs at the fire
> wavered in front of him. But he did not stop walking calmly
> forward, because he found it impossible to do so. He was the prince
> among his people. He was with his own servants, and under the eyes
> of townspeople. He could not turn back and acknowledge to them,
> 'I am a conceited fool, and not even a brave one'. He could not have
> made his muscles and his nerves accept such a humiliation; for they
> were prouder than his mind.

Aladai has far greater self-awareness and depth than Aissa. Cary can
probe this African's mind with inwardness and sympathy: he can grasp
well Aladai's rapidly changing tense thoughts arising from his acute
doubt as to the wisdom of his decision to enter the club. These
thoughts are rendered effectively in an economical, almost wholly
plain prose, which has an immediacy of impact. Though Cary is not a
psychological novelist, he does explore the minds of his characters
when appropriate and to the necessary extent. He proceeds to present
the situation at the club when Aldai enters it:

> Suddenly Carphew and Sangster got up, and Carphew said, 'Come
> over to my place'.
> Miss Coote exclaimed in surprise, 'Where are you off to?' and in
> the same moment, glancing in the direction of Carphew's parting
> glance, saw Aladai. She turned red, and stared at him in plain
> dismay. Aladai with an uncertain smile, said, 'Good evening, Miss
> Judy. The Resident's not here yet'.
> 'No, not yet'. There was a slight pause. She looked round her
> with rather a wild expression, and then exclaimed, 'What a sky? I
> never saw it so black'.
> 'It is a black sky', Aladai agreed. 'The air must be unusually
> clear'. . . .
> . . . He [Honeywood] twisted slowly round to glare at Aladai.
> 'Be careful, Mr Burwash asked him', Judy murmured, inventing
> the lie most likely to have influence with Honeywood.
> 'I don't care who asked him', shouted Honeywood. 'It's not
> Burwash's club – it's the station club'.
> 'Then go quietly', murmured Judy in agony. 'That's the best
> thing'.
> 'I am going', said Dick solemnly. . . .

This can be compared with the scene at Fielding's College in *A Passage to India*:

> 'Your mother will return shortly, sir', said Professor Godbole, who had risen with deference. 'There is but little to see at our poor college'.
>
> Ronny took no notice, but continued to address his remarks to Adela; he had hurried away from his work to take her to see the polo, because he thought it would give her pleasure.
> . . . . .
> 'Don't trouble to come, mother', Ronny called; 'we're just starting'. Then he hurried to Fielding, drew him aside and said with pseudo-heartiness, 'I say, old man, do excuse me, but I think perhaps you oughtn't to have left Miss Quested alone'.
>
> 'I'm sorry, what's up?' replied Fielding, also trying to be genial.
>
> 'Well . . . I'm the sun-dried bureaucrat, no doubt; still, I don't like to see an English girl left smoking with two Indians'.
>
> 'She stopped, as she smokes, by her own wish, old man'.
>
> 'Yes, that's all right in England'.
>
> 'I really can't see the harm'.

The considerable similarity between these two scenes in Nigeria and India respectively conveys in dramatic terms the fact that colonial situations in different countries have much in common. The racially prejudiced Englishmen snub the educated 'natives' by ignoring them. The former unashamedly articulate their prejudices to their fellow 'white' people, Judy Coote and Fielding. They feel close to these people, even though they can see that their attitudes are different. The liberal-minded Judy and Fielding are embarrassed and try unsuccessfully to bring about harmony. It is true that Forster presents the dramatic interaction of more diverse characters in greater depth with more delicately telling art than Cary, but Cary is sufficiently alert to a recurring feature of social life in the colonies.

All the Englishmen quit the Scotch club sooner or later, after Aladai arrives; Judy is left alone to talk to Aladai. She herself, however, is soon called away by Jerry Rackham, who had departed from the club not long after Aladai entered. The African, then, has no company till Dryas Honeywood comes. She suffers from racial prejudice, but is polite to Aladai. Her mere politeness evokes a sense of gratitude in him; through his double vision, Cary shows Aladai's gratitude as sincerely proportionate to Aladai and as understandably excessive from the author's point of view; it is reflected in his letter of thanks. The excess is shown as understandable because of the strain he underwent as a consequence of being ostracised by the male members of the Scotch club. This whole episode points to Cary's adequate sense of the psychology of race relations. Aladai's third important experience of racial prejudice is when Rackham assaults him for merely being polite to Miss Honeywood. Aladai loses the fight and his defeat suggests the realism of Cary's characterisation. He is not idealised as an all-conquering, perfect man. The balanced realism in Cary's treatment of Aladai – it is like Forster's portrayal of Aziz – was also evident in the appraisal of his views, which we noticed above. The temptation to idealise the alien would have been greater in Cary's case than in Forster's because Aladai is the hero of the entire novel whereas Aziz, though an important character, is not a hero.

After three solid rebuffs at the hands of the 'white' people, Aladai decides to attach himself more closely to his own people. He discards his European clothes, and this action symbolises his changed attitude. Still, he does succeed in the difficult task of maintaining a certain balance of mind in these circumstances. He does not throw away the enlightened ideas derived from his Western education and experience; he continues to oppose ju-ju resolutely. His deepened nationalism becomes militant, but his militancy leads to no positive results. The Rimi forces are split between himself and Salé, a Mohammedan. Salé also puts forward a claim to be the next Emir and, though his claim is less sound than Aladai's, he is favoured by the ruling Emir. Unscrupulous Salé murders the Emir after a while, and his succession is recognised by the British Resident, Burwash. Thus, when Aladai takes up arms against Salé, he has to face British soldiers. He is killed during the unequal battle. His complex and developing character is brought out dramatically by Cary. His plans to improve Rimi society come to nothing and he makes no lasting impact on it. It is partly through his fate that Cary suggests how difficult it is for tribes to emerge from a primitive state and throw aside their colonial yoke.

This difficulty is also suggested partly through the roles of Doctor Schlemm and Coker. Schlemm is a humane missionary. Coker's Christianity is racialist in an anti-'white' way and primitive, but superior to the local religion. Yet Schlemm comes into conflict with Coker and his head is cut off by Coker's followers. Even Coker does not live much longer than Schlemm. He is killed in the same battle as Aladai. Thus, both Christian leaders come to an untimely end and are not able to change appreciably the primitiveness of the Rimi. The primitiveness itself is bodied forth concretely in the novel mainly through Elizabeth Aladai, the sister of Louis, but a ju-ju priestess. She is not portrayed with the fullness of Louis, but is sufficiently realised as a secondary character to fulfil all the demands of her role. She has an impressive personality, and Cary is able to present her in her key role as priestess at witch-trials:

> She was not conscious of her direction. Yet the girls felt her turn them this way and that, by a slow pressure, as she glided through the rigid, breathless crowd.
>
> For half an hour she sought. Then, as she was passing close by the plaintiff's group, her hand jerked suddenly out, as if worked by a string, and gripped Osi by the wrist.
>
> She continued to hold the girl, who stood staring at her with an expression of foolish wonder. Her husband, father-in-law, the whole of her family, had already shrunk back from her. Osi's tongue appeared between her trembling lips; she looked around and smiled, as if to say, 'This is silly'.
>
> But in looking round she found herself alone, and the smile disappeared. She licked her lips again, and murmured something.
>
> Elizabeth, meanwhile, stood still in her trance. She shivered and uttered a deep sigh; her eyes opened slowly. She looked at Osi, and appeared as much surprised as the girl herself.
>
> 'You, Osi', she cried.

The trial of Osi comes alive as a full-length scene. The precision and comprehensive detail of the dramatisation, notably of Elizabeth, and the absolute sureness of the author's touch reveal Cary's knowledge of primitive life. His double vision is implicit in his objective, unblinking treatment of primitive realities: he shows the genuineness and depth of the belief in ju-ju of Elizabeth and her audience as well as their unconsciousness of the cruel irrationality (to us) of the procedure, underlined by the pathos of Osi's plight as the victim; we see the drama of Osi trying to maintain a friendliness which is crushed by witchcraft. This state of the participants in ju-ju evokes both shock and compassion in the civilised reader. Thus, Cary presents the backwardness of the Rimi with remarkable art. Aladai had vowed to wipe out ju-ju from Rimi, but at the end of the action Elizabeth, still the ju-ju priestess, is as strong in her power as at the beginning. Of course, her husband, Akande Tom, does break with her and embrace Christianity. But he is soon back in her fold and the final scene of the novel shows him cringing before her. The success of Elizabeth Aladai also suggests the immense difficulty for civilising tendencies to overcome primitive tendencies.

Cary presents not only characters such as Louis Aladai, Schlemm, Coker, Elizabeth, who are much involved in the life of the Rimi, but also characters such as Rackham, Judy Coote, Dryas Honeywood, who are less involved in indigenous life but are not unimportant in the presentation of relations between and within races in this colonial environment. Rackham does not have the simple instinctive prejudice against the Africans of Mrs Pratt:

> Rackham suddenly made a little speech, neatly phrased and spaced, in which he declared that he had no irrational dislike, or, if Rubin chose to use the word, complex, about coloured people. It was obviously absurd to divide people by colour. He objected to exactly the same things in whites as blacks, and he liked the same things. No doubt in the future world-state, which Judy liked to talk about, there would be no distinction by colour.
>
> 'I shouldn't think there'll be much inter-marriage', Judy put in; but Rackham paid no attention to her, and went on, 'But at present I think you've got to consider the political situation. The blacks out here are not fit to run their own show, and it will be a long time before they learn. Meanwhile we've got to keep the machine running, and the only peaceful way of doing that is to support white prestige'.

Rackham tries to maintain a front of non-prejudice: the absurdity of colour distinction and the temporary incapacity of the Africans for self-government are objective truths. But his real self is racialist. It is betrayed by his use of the term 'blacks' for Africans and by his superior tone. As Michael Banton notes, 'a ruling minority often needs a mystique of being different',[12] but Rackham's advocacy of racialism as the sole, absolute necessity of peaceful government accords with apartheid. He can privately be objective about an African as an individual, as in the case of Aladai. But his response to an African as a member of his race is different: when Aladai treats Dryas Honeywood as an equal, he assaults him. He hates Nigeria.

We saw that Judy Coote is a rather confused liberal, much like Forster's Adela Quested. Dryas Honeywood is different from Judy. She instinctively hates coloured men and frankly confesses her hatred to Rackham. Her conscience, however, tells her that her hatred is wrong. This duality of attitude is exemplified by her conduct towards Aladai in the African bush: 'It was not only because she felt a nervous disgust of his black skin that she was particularly careful to be polite to him – she sympathised with him for being black'. Unlike Judy, Dryas is not concerned about the Rimi.

The varied and more or less complex attitudes of Jerry Rackham, Judy Coote and Dryas Honeywood towards the Africans reveal diverse aspects of race relations in Nigeria. Personal relations between individuals of the same race form a secondary interest of Cary and help to give his presentation of a colonial environment a realistic, comprehensive totality; his novel is no quasi-documentary essay on colonialism. Among the Africans, he deals briefly with, for instance, the relationships between Aladai and Coker, between Elizabeth and Akande Tom; he dramatises Aladai's domination of Coker and Elizabeth's domination of Tom. Cary presents relationships within the European community with a fullness absent in his depiction of personal relations among Africans; this is because the importance of the roles of the Africans is predominantly of a public kind; they essentially matter in so far as they affect the future of their society. Among the Europeans, the most important and prominent relationships are those between Rackham and Judy Coote, between Rackham and Dryas Honeywood. The former is introduced at the very beginning of the action:

> Rackham was attractive to women because of his good looks, gaiety, and his love of women; because, too, of something feminine in his neatness, his fastidious dress. He had plenty of love-affairs, and it was generally agreed that at thirty-three he was inoculated against marriage. But on the voyage home, seven months before, he had found at the captain's table a little brown woman, with short-sighted brown eyes and a lame leg, who was introduced to him as Miss Judith Coote. She had been an Oxford don. Rackham who liked pretty amusing women, found himself condemned to sit beside this creature for a fortnight. He at once planned to remove from the table. He failed to do so on the first night; and a week later he was engaged.
> . . . . .
> Mrs Pratt said, 'He's fallen in love with her *brains*', as if the man who did that must be a fool. But Rackham had not fallen in love with a mere brain, but with a whole woman just as passionate as himself, and perhaps rather more intelligent – certainly better

trained. He had liked her at first because of her clear quick mind. Its judgment pleased all that was fastidious in his own. But he had soon loved the woman for the nature of the judgment, for her capacity to love him, and, at last, for her looks too. . . .

In describing the coming together of Rackham and Judy, Cary hastens over whole tracks of emotional development. His analysis of the sources of their love is undistinguished; it is rendered in bald abstractions. Their first important rupture takes place when Judy leaves the Rimi races in the company of two Africans, Aladai and Coker. Rackham regards her action as unseemly behaviour for a 'white' woman and feels 'as if he had suffered a misfortune'. Her friendliness towards and respect for Aladai bring about friction between herself and Rackham on two more occasions – when she converses with Aladai at the Scotch club and when she leaves Dryas with Aladai in the African bush. These differences between Rackham and Judy indicate that Cary is aware of the influence of race relations in colonial society, the influence on relationships between individuals of the same race; but he is not sufficiently skilled to bring this point to life artistically.

While Rackham is in love with Judy, he strikes up a relationship with Dryas Honeywood. His association with her grows closer, while his feelings towards Judy become less warm. Judy has the intelligence to notice the change and to break off her engagement to him. Finally, all three, Rackham, Judy and Dryas, suffer misfortune. After the Kifi battle, Dryas cannot be found, and Judy is a mental wreck. Rackham leaves Nigeria and reaches England safely. But though he is materially well-off in England, he lacks life-giving interests. Thus, not only do both love relationships come to nothing but also all three individuals involved in them have no hope of fulfilment in later life.

This fate of Rackham, Judy and Dryas, on the one hand, and, on the other, the failure of the Rimi reformers, Aladai, Schlemm and Coker, make the total outlook of *The African Witch* deeply pessimistic. But Cary's pessimism characteristically goes with a tough realism which enables him to face squarely the grave difficulties of achieving satisfactory personal relationships or securing individual fulfilment particularly in a colony, on the one hand, and, on the other, the enormous difficulties attending African advancement. This novel has a greater scope than *An American Visitor* and is far more successful. The artistically unrealised intimacies form only a minor side of the novel. Louis Aladai is a character in much the same proportions as Marie Hasluck, but his character is fully realised.

After the achievement of *The African Witch*, Cary turns away from
Nigeria for the most part in his next novel, *Castle Corner*. This seems to
have been a grave mistake because the novel is, on the whole, a failure;
it has no central and unifying thematic concerns. However, its Nigerian experiences are of interest. Cary is mainly concerned with the
Western side of the cultural clash in Nigeria as in *An American Visitor*,
but here the aspects are different: Marie Hasluck was an idealistic
anthropologist–journalist, whereas Felix Corner is a profit-seeking
businessman. The presentation of characters like Felix Corner, Pepper,
Pooley, Kentish and Hatto reveals art and attitudes typical of Cary:
these characters are individualised Europeans who 'go native' under
different circumstances, and the author never suggests that they are
lowering themselves; he does not view this recurring feature of colonial
life as 'denationalisation' in the manner of Sir Hugh Clifford or as 'the
white man sinking slowly to the level around him' in the manner of
Benjamin Kidd. Cary's portrayal of the British in their own country
also provides an insight into his breadth of vision. Here is an episode in
the life of Bridget Foy which is important to her:

> She pulled up her dress and shift to her neck and held out the locket.
> She looked at it with awe, not feeling the cold rain which drifted
> against her bare body. In the cold grey light, the diamonds had no
> sparkle, the gold was less bright than the gilt tinsel on the holy
> picture. But Bridget knew that the little stones were diamonds, the
> pale yellow metal dimmed with her sweat, was gold. Her eyes were
> full of wonder while she gazed at the mysterious treasure. She knew
> what a halfpenny could do; but she could not imagine the power of
> gold except as a vague glory. All this power and the glory of it was
> in her hand.

To the simple-minded Irish peasant, Bridget, gold is not merely a
source of excitement but a symbol of inspiration; what matters is not
its ordinary intrinsic value but its emotional value for her. Gold to her
is like shoes to Mister Johnson, the simple-minded Nigerian clerk. The
simple-minded, whether in Britain or Africa, have qualities in
common. Porfit is a hetorical local politician in South-West England:

> He thought how she [Lucy] had coloured when he had said, 'The
> battle for human freedom is a true work of the spirit', and he felt the
> complex thrill of the preacher, the artist who creates and forms
> emotion. . . . He saw again her look, like that of any of the girls who

sat beneath him at meeting, and turned up their startled eyes towards him when he shouted and thumped the desk. 'Freedom under God – that is a word greater than Empire'.

He smiled as he picked his way along the kennel of the muddy lane. He was in a slum. . . .

But Porfit's smile was not the hearty grin of the curate; it was absent-minded; as free of motive as the expression of the lane itself; its cracks, its dirt, its grey walls, which looked like the under vaults of a tropical jungle, dark, dirty, cut off from the sun, the old battlefields and corpse ground of a forest whose upper branches, far above, were engaged in another battle for life in the free air. He, for whom the slum was a kind of local hell for the improvident and the godless, noticed the looks as little as the children. He was absorbed in the quickening of his life, the expansion of his dream, a release like the opening of leaves in the air.

Cary can justly compare an English lane and 'a tropical jungle' because for him tropical nature has its own place in the scheme of things. His analysis of Porfit brings out the general human tendency which he put theoretically in *Power in Men*: 'Nationalist feeling increases by compound interest. The man who feels at the beginning that his own tribe is the greatest and grandest in the world delights in the idea of that greatness and grandeur when it is presented to him; and then he loves the idea too and all its symbols'.[13] As David Craig suggests, here Cary sees Western man and tribal man as part of a universal human situation.[14] He sees human beings in developed countries, his own fellow countrymen, and those in developing countries as part of common humanity; the Africans are not in a category by themselves.

Cary's conception of the *Castle Corner* project is stated in his 'Prefatory Essay' to the novel: '*Castle Corner* was to have been the beginning of a vast work in three or four volumes showing not only the lives of all characters in the first volume, but the revolutions of history during the period 1880–1935'.[15] After struggling for some time with this enormous scheme, it was correct artistic instinct which made him turn wholly to Nigeria once again in *Mister Johnson*, to one full-length novel on a congenial subject.

In *Mister Johnson*, Cary is chiefly concerned with the African side of the cultural clash in Nigeria as in *Aissa Saved* and *The African Witch*, but from a fresh angle. It is set in a more urbanised provincial area than the locale of *The African Witch*, and presented mainly in terms of the character and life of Mister Johnson. Johnson is a young African who has received some education at a mission school. He had been called up from school in an emergency to serve as a third-class government clerk at Fada. His Western education and experience of Western civilisation are more than those of Aissa in *Aissa Saved* but less than those of Louis Aladai in *The African Witch*. Aladai's education and experience make him national-minded, whereas Johnson's lesser education and experience make him biased towards the West. His job as a clerk pleases, and deepens, his pro-Western slant:

> Besides, he thoroughly enjoys opening a mail – that is, tearing open large, expensive envelopes and throwing them on the floor. This gives him a sense of the wealth and glory of the Empire and he becomes part of it. Reading official letters is a pleasure to him, for it makes him feel like part of His Majesty's Government, . . .

This slant becomes so dominant that he discards his own nationality and feels superior to other Africans. He asserts this feeling even in such adverse circumstances as when he is being led to prison for the murder of Gollup:

> The native *dogarai*, always rough with prisoners, threaten him with their spear butts. 'Get up'.
> He shouts at them, 'But I must put on my shoes'.
> 'Get up, son of a dog'.
> Johnson shouts furiously, 'I am not the son of a dog, but an English gentleman. If you were not rubbish, you would not propose to take a gentleman barefoot through your disgusting town'.

His shoes are a recurring symbol of his Westernisation. In declaring his Westernisation in these circumstances, he appears both comic and pathetic. He seems comic in clinging incongruously to the superficialities of civilisation in so serious a situation, while he is pathetic in being reduced to the level of a criminal. Cary's simultaneous presentation of the humorous and pathetic sides of a single situation forms a characteristic part of his skill in portraying Johnson and in creating the tragi-comic world of the novel as a whole. Johnson woos Bamu thus:

> He comes again to the yam field and asks her to marry him. He tells her that he is a government clerk, rich and powerful. He will make

her a great lady. She shall be loaded with bangles; wear white women's dress, sit in a chair at table with him, and eat off a plate.

'Oh, Bamu, you are only a savage girl here – you do not know how happy I will make you. I will teach you to be a civilised lady and you shall do no work at all'.

Johnson's feeling of superiority is not offensive and appears a pardonable human weakness. For one thing, it is characteristically expressed, as here, with an engaging *naiveté*. For another, its causes have some real justification. His occupation is important as far as the Africans are concerned; it was among the highest posts open to them under the colonial system of 'indirect rule' in Nigeria in the early twentieth century. His Westernisation, though shallow, gives him an element of civilisation, while most members of his society are primitive.

Johnson has other important qualities which contribute to make him very much an individual; he is not a mere type, the superficially Westernised African. He has an essential good-heartedness which helps to redeem his frailties. It emerges in a simple form when he invites Bamu to be his wife partly for her own good. It appears in a complex light when he invites Benjamin and Ajali to a party:

Johnson is suddenly angry. The truth is that his debt to Moma, the station headman, is of a peculiar kind. It is his duty each week to pay the gang of station labourers and gardeners; Blore gives him a lump sum of thirty-six shillings, and he distributes it, six shillings to Moma and five shillings to each man. But for the last weeks he has paid five shillings to Moma and four to each man, promising to make up the rest at the weekend with sixpence interest. He is not troubled much by this debt, which can be wiped off by a single advance, but by a dim fear that he may have infringed some law or regulation of the service by taking forced loans from the labourers. He therefore hates even to think of Moma and now he makes a vigorous gesture as if to knock him out of the air and cries, 'What you talking about? I don't care for dat ole Moma now. Mister Rudbeck my frien'. You come dis evening, Mister Benjamin, we drink to Missus Johnson, and you, Mister Ajali, for a happy evening'.

Johnson wishes to share his 'happy evening' with two others. His good-heartedness goes with a zest for life which is manifested in his very desire for a party. But these qualities are not firmly grounded in reality: he refuses to pause over serious practical problems such as indebtedness, a chronic malady in his case, and the possible infringement of 'some law or regulation of the service'. Cary analyses well how Johnson gets rid of irksome obligations. Here Johnson is aware of moral sanctions, but at times he is amoral. As he wants to enjoy life despite falling into debt, at a certain point the need to placate his creditors makes him divulge without compunction Blore's confidential remarks on the Emir, the Chief Justice, the Treasurer, the Waziri and the chiefs to the Waziri himself. He reveals the same qualities when he levies a toll on Rudbeck's new road without the District Officer's knowledge. He uses the illegal money to provide his labourers with beer so that they work harder, while he feels a sense of satisfaction when the road-making progresses well. Thus, he is morally confused; his shallow Westernisation has cut him off from native norms, but has not implanted in him an alternative moral sense. From these instances, it is also clear that his moral lapses are usually not very serious. His murder of Gollup, however, is a grave crime indeed. But because of his unawareness of its seriousness, its unpremeditated nature and Gollup's unpleasantness, it wins our sympathy rather than excites our horror. His moral confusion is an important and necessary concomitant of his zest for life. So is his peculiar imaginativeness. Characteristically, he recovers from disappointing situations by transforming them through his imagination into circumstances that favour him: Bamu had been completely indifferent to him at their first meeting, but he tells Benjamin:

> 'Oh, but, Mister Benjamin, my Bamu is mos' beautiful, clever girl you can tink. First time she sees me, she says, "Mister Johnson, I 'gree for you, I don't like dese savage men – I like civilised man. Mister Johnson", she says, "You good nice government man, me government lady. I love you with all my heart – we live happy, loving couple all time everyday"'.

The irony in this speech, which springs from Cary's playing off of Johnson's imaginary scene against reality, suggests sharply how Johnson deceives both others and himself. His imaginative dissimulation takes as its subjects only his personal setbacks and is quite harmless. His African English is flexible living speech in both the words spoken in his own right and in the words ascribed to Bamu. This quality in the supposed words of Bamu and their perfect appropriateness for deceiving, point to his inventiveness. We respond to him as both a very fallible and very engaging personality.

Johnson comes alive as a complex character, but he does not undergo any development during the whole course of the action. Indeed, his tragedy springs from his kind of ebullient unchangeableness, which reflects his skin-deep Westernisation; and he is prone to be half-uprooted in this tragi-comic way because he is a feckless wishful-thinking man. Charles G. Hoffman is wrong in thinking that 'Johnson himself disintegrates as his world crumbles about him'.[16] Johnson continues to be his irrepressible self, even though dismissed three times from his job. After his third dismissal, without a pang of conscience, he can steal money from Gollup and even murder the trader when he is in danger of being caught in the act of stealing. His absolute unchangeableness even in the face of the most acute crisis emerges clearly in the execution scene:

> . . . But he remains gloomy and depressed. 'That report of mine – I don't know if I was quite fair to you'.
>
> 'Oh, yes, sah'. Johnson shakes his head while he quickly seeks a means of restoring Rudbeck's opinion of himself, and also, of course, his own idea of Rudbeck. 'Oh, no, sah – I much more bad den ever you tink – I do plenty of tings behin' you back – I steal plenty times out of de cash drawer – I sell you paper to Waziri – I too bad – I damn bad low trash, good for damn nutting tall'.
>
> 'An when I sacked you from the road –'
>
> 'Oh, sah, I never mean to stay at dem road. I tink I get more money for trade'.
>
> 'Oh, you had another job in your mind?'
>
> 'Yes, sah. I tink dis work for road don' finish – I tink I go make plenty more money, go tief Sergeant Gollup's money'.
>
> 'What, you mean to go thieving even then, did you?'
>
> Johnson has no recollection of what he meant to do, but his imagination has never failed him in a pinch, whether to glorify a story, his own deeds, or a friend's opinion of himself. 'Oh, yes, sah', he cried. 'I always say so – I always say, I go tief Sergeant Gollup's money – if he stop me – den I go kill him. Oh, Mister Rudbeck, you report quite true – I very bad man'.
>
> 'So you don't think this trouble of yours is partly my fault, perhaps'.
>
> 'You fault, sah? Why, if you didn't be so good frien' to dis Johnson, he tief all every place in Fada, he murder plenty people, all kinds, he most wicked, bad-hearted kind of man you ever see. If I

tell you how I tink every night, I go tief, I go murder, you tink I too bad'.

Rudbeck sits hunched in his chair. He is still dissatisfied, not with Johnson's explanation, for he knows that Johnson is actually a thief and a murderer, but with everything. He feels more and more disgusted and oppressed, like a man who finds himself walking down a narrow, dark channel in unknown country, which goes on getting darker and narrower; while he cannot decide whether he is on the right road or not.

The same kind of scene is an important part of the anonymous story, 'My First Execution', which appeared in *Blackwood's Magazine*:

> Everything was in order. I saw the condemned man. A *padre* was already with him. He was quiet, apparently callous, but he looked most horribly alive. His eyes gleamed with unnatural intensity, and every muscle of his magnificent physique seemed strained and tense. I asked if he wanted anything, and he curtly demanded something to drink. There was still no sign of the doctor, under whose advice alone I was strictly allowed to supply him with alcohol, but I disregarded that point and promised to send him what he wanted. . . .[17]

The average writer describes his situation, whereas Cary dramatises his. Both the Standard English, spoken by Rudbeck, and the African English, spoken by Johnson, are alive, flexible and perfectly in character at every point. The difference in the quality of their English underlines the ironic contrasts between them; unlike the average writer, Cary goes deep into the minds of both the condemned African and the European judge–executioner. Even the imminence of death fails to change Johnson's buoyant nature; he is characteristically indifferent to the true moral import of his deeds and words. The condemned man is not affected by this critical moment, but his judge–executioner, certainly, is. Rudbeck becomes conscience-stricken; he questions Johnson about his own past treatment of him in an effort to find out whether he himself is partly responsible for Johnson's 'trouble'. The judge–executioner needs, and gets, moral reassurance from the condemned man, whereas the latter does not need, and does not get, moral help from Rudbeck or anyone else. Even at this last moment Johnson does not give Rudbeck a true account of himself and his actions, when it is that alone which could save him from death; even at this point he gains no knowledge of his nature or Rudbeck's; his main interest lies in maintaining 'Rudbeck's opinion of himself and also, of course, his own idea of Rudbeck'. On the other hand, Rudbeck is sufficiently disturbed to probe Johnson's plight and his own conduct, but his unease remains vague and he believes Johnson's false 'explanation'. These multiple ironies indicate the richness and subtlety of Cary's dramatic art. The tensions in the scene of the average writer suggest that it contains much the same potentialities as Cary's, but these remain latent in rather bald reportage. Cary's ironies generate the blend of humour and pathos which is characteristic of this tragi-comic novel. Through them, he critically 'places' his characters. Arnold Kettle thinks that 'there is about these final pages an incomplete disassociation of the writer from Rudbeck's own sentimental attitudes'.[18] But it seems to me, in the first place, that Rudbeck's attitudes are not 'sentimental'; they reflect genu-ine, deep stirrings of conscience of a fundamentally decent man. In the second place, I regard Cary's consistently sound ironic–critical treat-ment of Rudbeck's attitudes as based on a sufficiently detached con-templation of them. Rudbeck's execution of Johnson makes the conclusion of the novel sad, but it also reflects a characteristic tough realism of Cary in facing squarely the kind of ill-fated end all too likely to befall a superficially Westernised character such as Johnson.

Clearly, *Mister Johnson* is an unusual novel. The art of its important scenes, such as the execution scene, is remarkable. Even the art of its ordinary scenes, such as this presentation of Johnson soon after his first meeting with Bamu, is not undistinguished:

> Johnson, with his morocco bag of letters under his arm and his patent-leather shoes in his hand, travels at high speed, at a pace between a trot and a lope. In his loose-jointed action, it resembles a dance. He jumps over roots and holes like a ballet dancer, as if he enjoyed the exercise. But, in fact, his mind is full of marriage and the ferry girl. He imagines her in a blouse and skirt, shoes and silk stockings, with a little felt hat full of feathers, and makes a jump of two yards. All the advertisements of stays, camisoles, nightgowns in the store catalogues pass through his imagination, and he dresses up the brown girl first in one and then in another. Then he sees himself introducing her to his friends: 'Missus Johnson – Mister Ajali'.

The prose is generally plain and, at the same time, exact as it renders both Johnson's movements and changing thoughts. The touches of metaphor are unobtrusively illuminating. As in this instance, Cary uses the present tense throughout his novel. He chose it because, as he said, 'Johnson lives in the present, from hour to hour'.[19] This is most appropriate and it does help him to succeed in the difficult task of conveying a sense of Johnson blithely living in the present, a sense of the rhythm of his kind of mind. But a use of the present tense alone cannot ensure this kind of success; the energy of the prose and the liveliness of the pace of the action, which is helped in a small way by the division of the novel into chapters without headings or even numbers, make an essential contribution. Of course, Cary uses the same tense in respect of the other characters, too. This helps to make us respond to the whole action as if it were contemporaneous with our own lives and makes for homogeneity without reducing the marked differences in character and importance between Johnson and the rest, established in other ways.

Johnson as hero dominates the novel. There are varied other characters, both African and European, who add richness and significance to the novel. Indeed, to present concretely the impact of Western civilisation on primitive African culture, Cary *has* to portray in all his African novels representatives of this impact, representatives of primitive African culture and representatives of Western civilisation.

There are characters who embody aspects of this impact different from those represented by Johnson. Benjamin's deeper Westernisation goes with a moral sense and social concern. Ajali is also a Westernised person, but he is different from both Benjamin and Johnson. His Westernisation is superficial, like Johnson's, but it does not go to form an attractive character, like Johnson's. He is disgustingly crooked. Unlike Benjamin, he harbours malice towards Johnson and covers it under a coating of friendliness: he warmly supports Johnson's proposal to rob Gollup, though he knows that Johnson will be running a grave risk of getting caught.

Primitive African culture is represented by a number of varied, minor characters such as the conservative shrewd Waziri, the diffident Aliu, the affectionate inefficient servant Sozy and the lazy, greedy mistress Matumbi. The most important among them is Bamu. She marries Johnson, and the failure of their marriage is rendered well. It reflects the unevenness of the impact of Western civilisation on African culture and the personal problems created by this kind of impact. While Johnson is a half-uprooted man, Bamu belongs to Nigerian society and is uninfluenced by the West. Thus, their characters are so different that they are unable to strike a reciprocal relationship: at their wedding, she follows her own inclinations despite his requests to her to follow Western ways. After several months of married life, she is unmoved by his dismissals from jobs, and can look upon him 'as if he were a strange dog or an unusual and possibly dangerous beast'. She coldly leaves him when he can no longer support her and rejoins her family. When he seeks refuge in her family home after he has murdered Gollup, she helps her brother to betray him to the police.

Varied aspects of Western civilisation are embodied by a variety of Europeans. The most important of them is Rudbeck, the District Officer of Fada. He betrays a sense of racial superiority. He refers to the Africans as 'apes'. When he discovers that Johnson has levied a toll on his new road without his knowledge, he conventionally condemns all Africans in a rage: 'They all do it – you can't trust any of 'em anywhere any time'. But his sense of racial superiority goes with a paternal concern for the Africans, a combination of attitudes whose political expression is the concept of 'indirect rule'. When he advocates road-building, he is not wholly wrapped up in trade:

> 'We're obviously breaking up the old native tribal organisation or it's breaking by itself. The people are bored with it'.
> 'Yes, yes, and I'm not surprised', Bulteel says. Rudbeck is greatly surprised, 'Don't you believe in the native civilisation?'
> 'Well, how would you like it yourself?' Bulteel smiles at him sideways with a kind of twinkle.

This has the pointedness and dramatic vivacity characteristic of all the scenes in the novel: Rudbeck is anxious about the consequences of the impact of civilisation on African society, whereas Bulteel the Resident is blithely unconcerned about them. Cary is realistically aware of British officials such as Bulteel who fall more or less short of the ideals of 'indirect rule'. Tring is different from Bulteel and Rudbeck. He is new to his job and, partly because of this, he is a stickler. He is shocked that Rudbeck had wangled government financial votes even though for the purpose of completing a road. He reports the irregularity to Bulteel and cannot share the Resident's tolerant attitude towards Rudbeck's kind of action. Thus, Rudbeck, Bulteel and Tring come alive as different kinds of colonial officials, though the last two play very minor roles in the novel.

Characteristically for his African novels, in *Mister Johnson* Cary is interested not only in the varied kinds of people in Nigeria but also in the varied connections between them, as we have seen. He pays little attention to relationships between primitive Africans. He is concerned a little more with those among Westernised Africans: we notice the friendship of Johnson, Benjamin and Ajali. The greater detail and importance of the primitive Bamu's relationship with the Westernised Johnson indicate Cary's greater interest in connections between primitive and Westernised Africans. He, however, concentrates most on the relationships between Europeans and the Africans. Gollup's unsatisfactory relationship with Matumbi and Celia's superficial association with Johnson are minor instances. The major one is Rudbeck's association with Johnson. From the beginning of the action until his death, Johnson adores Rudbeck. His only real connection with Rudbeck is the slight official one between a third-class clerk and his District Officer, though he boasts to his friends of a close friendship. Still, Cary shows that they have certain temperamental affinities. They have in common 'the power of refusing to notice unpleasant things until they force themselves' upon them. Rudbeck has in him an element of Johnson's easy-going nature: both of them do not mind wangling government financial votes to ensure the completion of Rudbeck's road project. The likenesses do not serve to bring them together on a personal level. But after a long time, constant official association kindles in Rudbeck a spark of affection for Johnson. Yet he can curtly dismiss him when he learns that he has been levying a toll on his new road without his knowledge. Still, this little friendliness affects him during a far more important matter, Johnson's trial for the murder of Gollup; partly because of this, it is with reluctance that he executes him. Thus, all the personal relationships between Westernised Africans and primitive Africans, between Europeans and Africans, are more or less unsatisfactory; indeed, there is very little contact between people in these different categories. This state of affairs is part of the colonial world of the novel. As Nigeria early in this century was less developed that India during the same period, there were no equivalents in that country for a Dr Aziz and the Aziz–Fielding relationship. Mister Johnson is an index of its level of development.

AN OVERALL VIEW

As a novelist, Cary is partly traditional and partly modernistic. Like Defoe, Fielding and Dickens, he sees man mainly as a social animal and presents his characters mainly in terms of their interaction with each other. Thus he has his roots in the old tradition of the social novel. Of course, he is interested in the working of the individual mind, but he does not probe the deeper levels of consciousness as James Joyce, Virginia Woolf and D. H. Lawrence do. Still, Cary also has qualities which are early twentieth-century innovations of form – a scrupulous objectivity, an organic structure independent of plot, a strict economy of material. These qualities are characteristic of Conrad, too, and it is not for nothing that Cary considers Conrad one of his 'masters'.[20] In successfully fusing the traditional and the new in fiction, Cary makes an important contribution to the development of the English novel in the mid-twentieth century.

Cary's African fiction reveals certain lines of development. He tends to make his chief characters increasingly important. The importance of Aissa in *Aissa Saved* is surpassed by that of Marie Hasluck in *An American Visitor*, the importance of Marie by that of Louis Aladai in *The African Witch* and the importance of Louis by Mister Johnson's. Cary's artistic development is not from an unsatisfactory to a rewarding novelist: his very first novel is a worthy one. But it is unfair to expect any writer to compose a series of novels showing unfailingly steady progress in every way. *An American Visitor* is a more ambitious novel than *Aissa Saved*, but it seriously lacks dramatic vitality. When Cary comes to *The African Witch*, his interests have grown a little wider and more complex; but he has improved so much that the unsatisfactoriness in the novel is minor. Its strength makes it as valuable as his last African novel. *Mister Johnson* is a more homogeneous and more evenly successful novel than *The African Witch*, but it is smaller in scale and less complicated. *Mister Johnson*, however, has a special importance by virtue of the genre to which it belongs. As a remarkable tragi-comedy, it opens up a rarely-trodden avenue in twentieth-century fiction.

Cary's African novels are unified, in a way, by a common central concern – the impact of European civilisation on African culture. His major characters change from novel to novel, the Westerners representing different facets of the Western mind, the Africans representing different facets of the African and the Westernised African mind. The novels dramatise convincingly a great many sides of that impact. Cary can do so partly because of his remarkable wide understanding of Western and African life in colonial Nigeria, ranging from the most ordinary (for example, bridge-building in *Aissa Saved*) to the very remote. He is lucid, concrete and assured even when presenting African realities most unfamiliar to civilised men such as the human sacrifices in *Aissa Saved* and *Castle Corner* or the ju-ju in *The African Witch*. Robert Bloom is wrong when he says:

As readers of Cary we are always saddled with the responsibility of making judgments which he has himself been unwilling to make. Wherever we turn, we encounter his mystifying liberality. The novels, though, are able to live by letting live, for we almost never have the sense that a character is being deprived of his nature or his autonomy in order to serve thematic or structural ends. Having submitted himself to the indeterminate flavour of reality, Cary is in a position to profit from an attendant vitality.

. . . . .

Cary's suspended, unresolved fictional world derives in large measure from a deft management of place and time. When he begins to write novels, he turns instinctively to a remote, unfamiliar setting – Africa. The four African novels, *Aissa Saved, An American Visitor, The African Witch* and *Mister Johnson*, owe much of their flavour to their location in a kind of indeterminate country.[21]

Bloom has responded inadequately to Cary's objective art in the African novels. Cary does try to refrain from direct comment, but his views are clearly implied, if not made explicit. His objectivity does not preclude unambiguous implication. So 'we encounter' no 'mystifying liberality'. When he fails to write sufficiently objective drama, we do have 'the sense that a character is being deprived of his (her) nature or his (her) autonomy in order to serve thematic or structural ends', as in the case of Bewsher and Marie Hasluck. Yet Cary's successful African fiction has 'vitality', and it is not an 'indeterminate flavour' that his fictional world has. The novels really 'owe much of their flavour' to their location in a country portrayed with specificity and sureness. Africa is 'a remote, unfamiliar setting' to the ordinary Westerner, but, certainly, not to Cary. Moreover, he presents it with immediacy and realism. His art is less intense and less rich than that of Conrad's *Heart of Darkness*, but it has nothing similar to the woolly rhetoric of the Kurtz phase. Cary never lacks knowledge of African realities in the way Conrad does in this key phase of the tale.

The number of 'white' people in Cary's African novels remains steadily around five and consists of a few kinds (colonial officials, their wives, missionaries, businessmen, visitors). This reflects the paucity and range of Westerners in Nigerian colonial outposts. But within this small range, Cary makes varied fine distinctions: we saw in *Mister Johnson* that Rudbeck, Bulteel and Tring are all colonial administrators and that they are different from each other. In each novel, only two or three 'white' people appear important characters. This kind of selective stressing is necessary partly because of the normal proportions of the novels. From the beginning Cary can portray successfully his fellow Westerners in an alien colonial context when they are important secondary characters: the Carrs in *Aissa Saved* come alive as effectively as Rudbeck in *Mister Johnson*. But when, after his first novel, he tries to present them in larger roles, he falls more or less short of success for a variety of reasons, as shown by the discussions of Bewsher, Marie Hasluck and Rackham's love life.

Cary's portrayal of Africans reveals certain lines of development. In his first novel itself he is able to present successfully Aissa as his chief character. In *An American Visitor*, however, the most prominent of the Africans, Uli and Obai, are minor characters. But in *The African Witch*, Cary's abilities in this field reach a peak in his presentation of Louis Aladai. Mister Johnson is different from the others, but his portrayal is no less an achievement than Aladai's.

It is partly the necessity for selective stressing in his novels that makes Cary select only two or three Africans as important characters in each. But the enormous range and large number of minor African characters in all his novels help to suggest the presence of whole African societies. The impression of overcrowdedness, which is inescapable in *Aissa Saved*, is reduced as Cary moves on to *An American Visitor* and *The African Witch* and it disappears in *Mister Johnson*. Cary's tendency to lessen the number of minor Africans and his increasingly careful selection of them reflect a sensible self-disciplining of his artistic powers. That he could bring to life whole African societies and successfully present three very different African protagonists point to a fertile capacity to depict these alien people with their alien speech in their alien context. In these novels he achieves a much greater measure of consistent success in portraying the Africans rather than his fellow Westerners; the difference reflects, not so much a difference in knowledge, as a more consistent ability to keep to his strength in characterisation – to contemplate characters from the outside – probably because of their 'alienness'.

It appears that there is a relation in Cary between the artist and the theorist on colonial affairs. In *Britain and West Africa* (1946), he wrote:

Talk of the white man's burden is now a joke. Probably it is good that it should be a joke, for it was too easily used to cover a mean complacence and to breed that hypocrisy which of all vices most quickly corrupts a nation. But the responsibility of Britain towards her dependents was not a joke to the Whigs who impeached Hastings; to the men who fought the slave trade; to the church people who have always supported the missions; nor to the thousand humble officials in the British service, whose duty, as they were taught, was to the African people.

And behind this official policy there was a vast public opinion at home which from imperial pride, or vanity, if you like, demanded from those Empire servants the highest standards of justice and sympathy. We can call that public romantic. It made heroes of the pioneers in Africa. But it made them romantic heroes, and asked much of them; it made a policy of exploitation impossible for any British Government.[22]

Cary's advantage over Kipling in point of time helps him to regard the imperial banner, 'the white man's burden', less simple-mindedly than Kipling. His detachment also derives partly from an Anglo-Irish family tradition; as Malcolm Foster notes, 'he loved Ireland in a way that he never had England, however English he might feel at times'.[23] Yet he does subscribe to the Kiplingesque notion of 'the responsibility of Britain towards her dependents'. He is like Kipling in his blindness to 'exploitation', which is one permanent and necessary side of all imperialism, the British variety included. His view is paternal whereas Kipling's is imperial. In his fiction Kipling is critical of the administrative superstructure. It is the superstructure that during a famine sent wheat to rice-eaters in 'William the Conqueror', that formulated a faulty bill for the Sub-Montane Tracts before the Legal Member learnt of the error in it from Tods in 'Tods' Amendment', that 'at the last moment added two feet to the width of the bridge, under the impression that bridges were cut out of paper, and so brought to ruin at least half an acre of calculations' in 'The Bridge-Builders'. But the predominant impression in Kipling of the imperial system at work is produced by his presentation of the administrative infrastructure. In 'William the Conqueror', Jim Hawkins, Scott and Martyn do their utmost under difficult conditions to overcome a famine in South India. Even when Scott and William come to love each other, they subordinate their personal relationship to the task of famine-relief. In 'The Head of the District', Yardley-Orde had found it difficult to maintain his wife on his salary and she has to depend on charity to return to England at his death. He regards his fate as not uncommon:

It's not nice to think of sending round the hat; but, good Lord! how

many men I lie here and remember that had to do it! Norton's dead
– he was of my year. Shaughnessy is dead, and he had children; I
remember he used to read us their school-letters; what a bore we
thought him! Evans is dead – Kot-Kumharsen killed him! Rickets
of Myndonic is dead – and I'm going too.

His concern for the Indians is so deep that he thinks of them even on
his death-bed:

> . . . That reminds me, Dick; the four Khusru Kheyl villages in our
> border want a one-third remittance this spring. That's fair; their
> crops are bad. See that they get it, and speak to Ferris about the
> canal. I should like to have lived till that was finished; it means
> so much for the North-Indus villages – but Ferris is an idle beggar –
> wake him up.

It is Tallantire who quells the 'uprising' of the Khusru Kheyl when an
Indian replaces Orde. A leader of the Khusru Kheyl tells the dying
Orde: '"And thou art our father and our mother", broke in Khoda
Dad Khan with an oath. "What shall we do, now there is no one to
speak for us, or to teach us to go wisely!"' It is likely that among the
colonial officials there were some who toiled selflessly in a tropical
developing country alien to them. But Kipling has exaggerated these
facts and has played down others such as their recreations and luxuries
as members of the 'ruling race'[24] to create a general imperial myth of
colonial officials altruistically working to death (quite literally) on
poor pay in virtually lethal conditions. This myth is the whole theme of
'At the End of the Passage' and the impression of melodrama produced
by it in this story is obvious and pervasive. Devotion to duty in India
kills the chief character, Hummil the assistant engineer, and Jevins the
sub-contractor. It is also going to kill (so the story has it) all the other
characters – Lowndes of the Civil Service, Mottram of the Indian
Survey and Spurstow, the doctor of the line. A central irony in that
myth derives from the contrast between the altruism of the officials and
the thanklessness, even malignancy, of the country, between the
benefits they confer on such a country by their actions and their own
sufferings, even deaths, as a consequence of these very actions.

In Cary the paternalistic theorist and the artist are not exactly one.
Indeed, 'exploitation' is central to the subject of *An American Visitor* as
it never is in Kipling. Judy Coote in *The African Witch* is a liberal
among imperial-minded Europeans. Still the main motives of imperia-

lism, self-interested economic and political considerations (the imperialism in Nigeria is no exception, as will be shown below), enter less into Cary's Nigerian fiction than they could have and should have. His typical mixture of support for and criticism of the British Empire in Nigeria appears in his treatment of key British officials such as Bradgate in *Aissa Saved* and Rudbeck in *Mister Johnson*. The well-meaning efforts of these officials to improve the lot of the Africans take the major stress. Their deficiencies are presented as minor even though they include such qualities as Rudbeck's racialism. Cary does not show how such officials, apart from those in *An American Visitor*, are consciously or unconsciously serving and are a part of an 'exploiting' system. To say that he writes so much fiction about Nigeria, that he renders a great many aspects of it and yet frequently does not convey a sense of the main motives of imperialism which permeate life in an imperial environment, is to indicate a limitation in his imagination. The presence of colonial officials as important characters in all his novels raises the question of these motives and makes them important for the reader, but he hardly takes them into account except in *An American Visitor*. His idealistic liberal paternalism (discussed in detail below) makes his presentation of the Western side of Nigerian realities too glowing. We have noticed that in *An American Visitor* his radicalness is not sufficiently digested into his imagination. M. M. Mahood and William Van O'Connor consider *The African Witch* as an attempt by Cary 'to match *Nostromo*' and they think that it achieves a considerable measure of success on similar lines.[25] It seems to me that *An American Visitor* is closer to *Nostromo*, whatever the intention of the author, because 'exploitation' is central to both but not to *The African Witch*, though the impression of social life in *An American Visitor* is less dense than in *The African Witch*. But the more important point is that neither in *An American Visitor* nor in *The African Witch* nor in any other African novel does Cary write fiction of the order of *Nostromo*: his imagination works successfully within the more or less limiting framework of his paternalism, whereas Conrad's deep scepticism is of the essence of his imagination and this enables him to get far beyond the thinking of the majority of enlightened British people in artistic terms. We have noticed that in *Nostromo* Conrad sees that 'material interests' and the life related to them are central to a region subject to imperialism and that he presents them magnificently as such. In this respect, one can take away from all Cary's novels hardly anything more than the feeble impression produced by the interaction of Marie, Bewsher and the prospectors in *An American Visitor*. He could not have written that luncheon scene on board the *Juno* in *Nostromo* in which Conrad dramatises the multiplicity of ironies in the roles of the imperialists. Cary, the lesser artist, is by the same token less able to penetrate to the centre of imperialism in imaginative terms. Indeed, his sense of the evils of imperialism, as it runs through his successful fiction, is less acute than that of prominent British colonial experts of his period such as Frederick (later Lord) Lugard, the architect of 'indirect rule', and Margery Perham.

> Let it be admitted at the outset that European brains, capital, and energy have not been, and never will be, expended in developing the resources of Africa from motives of pure philanthropy; that Europe is in Africa for the mutual benefit of her own industrial classes, and of the native races in their progress to a higher plane; that the benefit can be made reciprocal, and that it is the aim and desire of civilised administration to fulfil this dual mandate.[26]

This is Lugard in 1922. Over twenty years later, Margery Perham's position is the same: 'Britain is not in doubt or in retreat about this question. She is resolute to show that the imperial bond can be made of equal service to herself and to the dependent peoples'.[27] Cary conveys a strong sense of how the so-called 'dual mandate' or 'the imperial bond' serves 'the native races' or 'the dependent peoples' without an adequate sense of how it helps Britain. This means, not that Cary was less honest than Lord Lugard and Margery Perham, but that he was genuinely more idealistic. He was, probably, influenced too much by his own role in Nigeria; he had developed beyond his early racialism and had helped the Africans for a great part of his life; he paid insufficient attention to the nature of the system which he was serving. It took a socialist, experienced *and* well informed in imperial matters, such as Leonard Woolf, to see that imperialism in Africa meant, not 'reciprocal benefit' (Lugard) or 'equal service' (Perham), but much gain to Britain and little to the Africans. British imperialism was not as brutal as Belgian imperialism in the Congo. The Africans in British colonies on the West coast were treated much better than those else-where. But even in Nigeria, self-interested economic and political inter-ests were the chief motives of British imperialism. Therefore the State grossly neglected education. The first British consul to Nigeria was appointed in 1849 and the Berlin Conference of 1885 recognised the supremacy of British interests in the Niger districts. But as late as 1942, the school-going population was small and very few proceeded beyond secondary education. Higher education began only in 1930 with the opening of a medical school; only 18 students entered this school in 1934 and during the next ten years the highest entry for a year was 36.

Cary, then, as a successful artist is an idealistic paternalistic liberal. Though he is, in a way, less aware than Lord Lugard of Britain's gains from its Empire, he is, in another way, more forward-looking. In *The Case for African Freedom* (1941), probably partly because Cary is writing it almost twenty years after Lugard's classic *The Dual Mandate in British Tropical Africa*, he can conceive African autonomy in a way Lugard does not. The latter's views on the future of Nigeria are much the same as Sir Hugh Clifford's:

> Assuming . . . that the impossible were feasible – that this collection of self-contained and mutually independent Native States, separated from one another, as many of them are, by great distances, by differences of history and traditions, and by ethnological, racial, tribal, political, social and religious barriers, were indeed capable of being welded into a single homogeneous nation – a deadly blow would thereby be struck at the very root of national self-government in Nigeria, which secures to each separate people the right to maintain its identity, its individuality and its nationality, its own chosen form of government; and the peculiar political and social institutions which have been evolved for it by the wisdom and by the accumulated experience of generations of its forebears.[28]

Clifford is accurate in noticing the deep differences between the 'Natice States', and these differences are partly responsible for Nigeria's present problems. But Nigeria is finding it difficult to become a nation partly because of the British system of 'indirect rule' which Clifford endorses; the system itself was divisive. The official policy was that 'national self-government' should apply only to 'self-contained and mutually independent Native States', and most of these states, if not almost all, could hardly become viable modern nation-states. In addition, Clifford never considers the question of who should finally control the superstructure of these 'Native States'. Thus Lugard and Clifford are liberal imperialists; they represent the majority of enlightened British people in the 1920s. But W. B. Crocker, who had been an administrative officer in Nigeria like Cary and pondered colonial rule more deeply than is usual with such officers, is not more far-seeing in the 1930s than Clifford or Lugard:

> Though while necessary to emphasise the mistakenness of the

notion that we derive great material advantages from Empire, it is, of course, academic to argue for its retention or its abandonment on this ground. If the Empire was not ours, some other Power or Powers would possess themselves of it. It will be ours for as long as colonial empires continue to exist. We may as well, then, concern ourselves with the question how best to run it.[29]

Crocker's views are not put to shame by Lord Hailey, though his *An African Survey* is the most comprehensive and authoritative British study of Africa in the 1930s. Hailey cannot face the rightness of a development towards 'the political supremacy of the native majority'; so much so that the British ideals of 'responsible self-government' and 'trusteeship' seem half-mockery. He cannot see the obvious wrongness of minority 'white' rule in South Africa and Southern Rhodesia.[30] Imperialist thinking is prominent in the 1930s. Still, barely three years later, Cary could argue this thesis in *The Case for African Freedom*: 'I suggest that though the ideal of self-government is necessary and good, the latter and more modern object, to protect the masses, to free them from ignorance, misery, and dependence should come first'.[31] Cary's deep liberal-mindedness is revealed by his thoughtful and concrete proposals for 'social education and economic development to protect the masses, to free them from ignorance, misery, and dependence'. His basic position – self-government after improvement – is characteristic of the liberal paternalist. His views and interests are not exceptional; they are in line with those of Margery Perham, expressed four years earlier in *Native Administration in Nigeria*.[32] Indeed, as Margery Perham indicates, liberal paternalism was becoming the declared policy of the British government. Colonel Oliver Stanley, the Secretary of State for the Colonies, was making a statement of policy when he said on 13 July 1943: '. . . we are pledged to guide Colonial people along the road to self-government within the framework of the British Empire. We are pledged to build up their social and economic institutions, and we are pledged to develop their natural resources . . .'.[33] Cary reflects the prominent changes in post-War British colonial thinking. In the 1920's liberal imperialism was dominant; in the 1930s it was important, but not dominant; in the 1930s and 1940s liberal paternalism represented enlightened majority opinion among the British. The post-1930 liberal paternalism of Cary and Margery Perham is not remarkable; it merges with the enlightened majority opinion in Britain at this time.

Liberal paternalism is a middling, rather unrealistic standpoint.

The primary motive of imperial agencies, profit, would not permit the loss involved in a balanced, all-sided development of a colony, and at a reasonable pace, too. Moreover, subject people do not usually wait till the ruling power thinks the country is sufficiently developed to be granted independence. But Cary's position is, in fact, the most advanced in his day as far as it concerns Africa outside views of the Left argued, say, by Leonard Woolf and H. Rathbone,[34] which were in a minority. Moreover, though Cary's successful art falls within the more or less limiting framework of an idealistic and paternalistic liberalism, no British author at this time wrote novels about Africa with a wider framework and of comparably high quality.

Thus Cary's outlook as a novelist and the novels themselves are, in a way, unique in his period. When one nears the end of an overall estimate of Cary's African novels, one may be worried by two basic questions, as Arnold Kettle is towards the close of his appraisal of *Mister Johnson*: 'Is this an entirely just appreciation of the African situation? Does it not leave out something essential, that rising tide of African national consciousness and effectiveness which today one knows to be a vital element in the cultural and political issues of West Africa?'.[35] Kettle is asking too much of a single novel of normal proportions. He would be asking too much even if he is referring to the whole series of novels. He seems to be confusing the tasks of a historian with the ways of an artist: one can demand comprehensive and just treatment of all major facts only from a Margery Perham when her announced aim is to write on *Native Administration in Nigeria*. Still, Cary does provide a 'just appreciation of the African situation' in a way a talented artist does. He does not intend to present all the important aspects of 'the African situation', but a proper contemplation of it has enabled him to choose a pervasive major social phenomenon, the clash of Western civilisation and African culture, as his central subject. He portrays a great many facets of this clash, but not all: he does not bring in Lagos and Calabar, the only two towns of importance in early twentieth-century Nigeria, where this clash of cultures was most complicated and intense. Still, Lagos and Calabar are exceptional places. The two different settings in the interior of Nigeria (Yanrin and Birri) and the two different urbanised settings (Rimi and Fada), selected by Cary, are truly representative of the country as a whole. The question whether Cary left out 'something essential, the rising tide of African national consciousness and effectiveness' does not arise: this 'rising tide' did not exist before 1937. There had been strong criticism of British rule in the *Lagos Weekly Record* from 1891 to the early 1930s;

there were organisations which tried to obtain 'concessions' from the British, notably the National Congress of British West Africa (from 1920 to 1930) and the Nigerian National Democratic Party (from 1923 to 1938). But these organisations were not very active and their limited activity was confined to Lagos and Calabar, though their declared policies frequently referred to 'Nigeria'. Moreover, there was no 'national consciousness and effectiveness' as such during this period, only abortive efforts to modify British rule. 'National consciousness', as reflected in a widespread sense of corporate identity and in opposition to foreign rule, was born in Nigeria in 1938, with the return of Nnamdi Azikwe and H. O. Davies after their education and experience in the West. Nationalism had no important effect on alien rule till 1947, when the Nigerian constitution was somewhat radically changed. Thus, in his novels which were set in Nigeria before 1937 and in places outside Lagos and Calabar, Cary does not leave out 'something essential'. Indeed, Louis Aladai, a tribal reformer on his return from the West, is a prevision of Nnamdi Azikwe and H. O. Davies.

Cary's kind of 'appreciation of the African situation' is revealed most remarkably in his selection of realities for his novels and his manner of presentation. He is aware that, though the 'white' men in Nigeria form an extremely small number of the total population, they are important because they are the rulers; so in each of his novels there are two or three important 'white' characters. At the same time, he is aware that in Nigeria not only do the Nigerians vastly outnumber the Westerners but that they matter most; so not only are most of his characters Africans but three out of his four protagonists are African. No British writer – not Conrad, Kipling, Forster or Lawrence – has brought into fiction the culture of a developing country so substantially, understandingly and skilfully. His double vision covers a considerable range of both Western and African aspects of realities in Nigeria. His outlook is sombre. He faces the difficulties produced by the clash of Western civilisation and African culture – the difficulties of achieving satisfactory personal and race relations, the difficulties of fulfilment for individuals and the difficulties of African advancement. His sombreness is justified by his tough realism. He is never despairing. His liberal paternalism is a positive, though limited, framework for his successful fiction. Still, his sense of the difficulties in Africa is much greater than his sense of its potentialities for development, and this is validated by the troubled course of Nigerian history till today.

Because it is his liberal paternalism rather than his radicalism that has been well digested by his imagination, he does not present Nigerian realities as fully and profoundly as Conrad does South American realities through a deeply sceptical vision in *Nostromo* and Forster does Indian realities through a radical vision in *A Passage to India*. But his African novels and the African side of *Castle Corner* do have distinction. They form a body of work more valuable than Conrad's Malayan novels and Kipling's Indian fiction, and as valuable as Forster's pre-War novels.

10 Between cultures

> In elephants and the east are two devils, in all men maybe.
> The mystery of the dark mountain of blood, reeking in homage, in
> lust, in rage,
> And passive with everlasting patience, . . .
>
> D. H. Lawrence, 'Elephant' (April 1923).

These are lines from Lawrence's only poem about Ceylon. They suggest that, though his stay there was brief and he got to know little about it, he responded to it with the extraordinary perception of a great artist. In the first line he suggests that there are qualities common to all men – a point which relates to traditional wisdom but is worth saying in the context of contacts between different cultures and races. This has emerged from this study, too. There are qualities common to people in different developing countries, even though they may be at different stages of development: Cary's Africans, Aissa and Mister Johnson, are caught between Western and indigenous cultures, as are Conrad's Malayan, Nina, Forster's Indians, Aziz and Hamidullah. There are qualities common to people from different Western countries who go to developing countries: in Conrad, it is greed that takes the Belgians, Kayerts and Carlier, to an outpost in the Congo, as well as the Dutchmen, Almayer and Willems, to Sambir. There are qualities common to people in pre-industrial societies of the developing world and those in such societies in the West: in Cary, shoes to Mister Johnson, the Nigerian clerk, are as gold is to Bridget Foy, the Irish peasant; in Forster, Aziz's emotional capacity is similar to that of Gino Carella, the Italian peasant. There are qualities common to people in developing countries and those in developed countries; this matters most in this study because we are dealing with writers from the latter presenting the former. In *Heart of Darkness*, Marlow as a civilised Englishman is gravely disturbed on his journey to Kurtz's station when he perceives an affinity between the primitive Congolese and himself. In *The Secret Agent*, 'Chief Inspector Heat's appearance recalled a certain native chief to the memory of his superior',[1] and the Assistant Commissioner later finds in Heat much the same kind of self-interest and unreliability as in the 'native chief': he has to force out of Heat his discovery of an identifying label on Stevie's dead body and his use of Verloc as an informer. The qualities people of different cultures have in common help writers from one culture to write about another. Incidentally, this suggests the stupidity of conventional Western views of 'coloured' peoples as 'inscrutable' or as anonymous inferior masses or as animal-like as well as the stupidity of the inverse conventional Westerners' views of themselves. This also suggests the fallacies in similar views of 'coloured' peoples: for example, their tendency to see only Westerners as fiendishly cunning and two-faced, a reaction of colonised people to qualities which they share with the colonisers but which they are generally unable to employ with the finesse and on the scale of the Westerners because they belong to less developed and less powerful cultures.

Lawrence says that there are 'maybe two devils in all men'. He is tentative and presumably also senses the differences between men. Indeed, when he goes on to present Eastern culture, he does so in terms of contraries – 'homage' and 'patience', on the one hand, 'lust' and 'rage', on the other. This illustrates the struggle of a European writer trying to come to terms with a culture alien to him and at a different stage of development from his own. All the writers in this field of study are faced with this struggle. At a simple level, the struggle is for a European writer to apprehend an external nature alien to him. That the struggle is not easy is evident in the strains in the prose of Conrad's *Almayer's Folly* and *Outcast of the Islands* and even in Lawrence's *St. Mawr*. But it is not an impossible one: Conrad triumphed in *Nostromo*, Forster in *A Passage to India* and Lawrence in *The Princess*. Still the more difficult struggle is for a European writer to come to terms with peoples alien to him in cultures alien to him, speaking languages alien to him. The selected major writers are consistently able to see the lives of people alien to them from the point of view of these people as well as from their own; they develop a double vision, unlike a writer such as Clifford who, however conscientious, cannot see beyond the assumptions of his own culture. Kipling is not blind to Indian ways, but he does not go deep into them: even the Lama in *Kim* is a rather idealised priest. To render the speech of alien people is not an easy problem: Clifford fails to find a satisfactory equivalent for the Malayan vernacular. But the selected writers solve it, though Kipling is even at best a little crude. It is not at its most difficult when the focus is on the Westernised sections among these people and the Westernised are portrayed in situations in which they speak varied forms of English. Then the standard technique is for the writers to apprehend these varieties: for instance, Indian English in the case of Forster's Aziz and

Hamidullah, African English in the case of Conrad's Makola and Cary's Mister Johnson. The problem is complicated when it becomes necessary for European writers to portray people alien to them both in contexts in which they speak varieties of English and in contexts in which they speak their own vernaculars. The standard techniques for rendering vernaculars have been to fashion an equivalent in English suited to the cultural contexts in which they are spoken or to employ the varieties of English spoken in those parts of the world as substitutes or to blend the two methods. Cary is faced with a particularly difficult task because it is he, among the selected writers, who penetrates most deeply into a culture very different from the British and brings very many Africans into the centre of his novels. He uses Standard English as an equivalent for the vernacular in certain contexts to distinguish it from African English spoken in other contexts, sometimes by the same characters when they are meagrely educated.

Are writers reluctant to take on such alien matters? Forster, certainly, was:

> I had a great deal of difficulty with the novel [*A Passage to India*], and thought I would never finish it. I began it in 1912, and then came the war. I took it with me when I returned to India in 1921, but found what I had written wasn't India at all. It was like sticking a photograph on a picture. However, I couldn't *write* it when I was in India. When I got away, I could get on with it.[2]

Still, Forster is characteristically very tentative and was about to dry up anyway. Cary took a little time to use Africa, but that was because he was self-exacting as a learner-writer.[3] Lawrence is famous for writing readily about each new experience, and even on occasion treats his Mexican and New Mexican work as a sort of imaginative report to his friends.[4] Conrad was willing to base his most massive novel, *Nostromo*, on a part of the world where he had spent only a very short time and to gather material from second-hand sources. Generally speaking, Kipling wrote his early and less interesting work in India; his most substantial work had to wait for his return to England.

Developing countries are subject to imperial interests and this was particularly so when the selected writers were at work. Thus they portray countries in which the Western presence is important and thereby reveal aspects of their own civilisation. Lawrence is exceptional in that he was not concerned at all with foreign economic activity in the Mexico he depicted. Yet his primitivism is impelled by a sense that Western civilisation had declined and by a desire to find a way of regeneration. The art of the writers in this field of study is relevant to people in developed countries as well as developing ones, since the interests of the two kinds of country interlock and since either may serve as an example of civilisation or of decadence.

Kipling, Forster and Cary were themselves members of the race which ruled the developing countries they present; Conrad was a European who settled in Britain, the country with the largest empire during his day. Thus they wrote from privileged positions. How did these positions affect their art? Kipling suffers most from weaknesses to which writers in his kind of position are prone partly because he is the least talented; he is at times imperial-minded and, at best, a liberal imperialist. Cary constantly shows a fine open-minded interest in African culture, a culture very different from the British and at an earlier stage of development, rather like the openness we feel in Forster's account of the Hindu festivities in the last part of *A Passage to India*. But Cary's awareness of the ironies of his position, evident in *An American Visitor* and suggested by his treatment of the predicaments of Africans such as Aissa and Johnson, is not quite sufficiently absorbed into his creative process. On the other hand, Conrad and Forster are keenly conscious of the ironies of their positions: this is suggested by the former's portrayal of Marlow in *Heart of Darkness* and the latter's portrayal of Fielding. Forster's radical vision is achieved with the help of contemporary liberal and socialist thought. Conrad's sceptical vision derives in part from his multinational experience and also probably from his Polish origins which we discussed above: Poland had no Empire and was, in fact, subject to Russian imperialism; as a Pole, he had been at the receiving end of imperialism and had seen it kill his parents; he was a member of a ruling class which itself was a suppressed class and was national-minded; his family tradition, on both his father's and mother's side, had a nationalist aspect. But he suffers from an artistically not unimportant weakness deriving from his privileged position: he has something of the conventional 'white'-ruling-race view of negroes.

All the selected writers have first-hand experience of the developing countries which they depict. Indeed, it is difficult to imagine a person who could write a work of serious interest set in a developing country without any first-hand experience of such environments. Immense first-hand experience helps even average writers such as Hugh Clifford and Frank Swettenham to produce fiction which is not without interest. Experience makes a difference to the quality of the art: Forster in *A*

Passage to India penetrates much deeper into Indian life than Kipling usually does, partly because he, as an employee of a 'native', experienced more of it than the latter as a journalist. But this is not to take the stand of a 'factualist', Saul Bellow's term for 'one sort of realist who would require a writer to spend several years on location before daring to place his characters there'.[5] The extraordinary perceptiveness of an artist could compensate for the lack of sheer informedness, of first-hand knowledge. Conrad was far more of a European outsider in the Far East than Clifford and Swettenham, but his Malayan fiction is considerably more interesting than theirs. Of course, the degree of first-hand knowledge which an artist needs, depends on the kind of imagination he has, on his powers and interests at the time of writing and on the congeniality of his material. Conrad had a kind of imagination that fed mainly on his personal experiences and contacts. He had, more or less, meagre first-hand experience of the Malay Archipelago, the Congo and South America. But *Heart of Darkness* is better as art than any of his Malayan novels partly because he wrote it at a stage in his career when he could write better, partly because he had more first-hand experience of the Congo than of the Malay Archipelago and partly because his Congo experience was more disturbingly enlightening than his Malayan experience. *Nostromo* is even better as art than *Heart of Darkness* partly because he wrote it at a stage in his career when he could write a great novel and also partly because his material was, it seems to me, more congenial. He would have felt more akin to more of the leading characters in this novel than to those in the African tales and the Malayan novels: the Goulds are more English than Costaguanan; Holroyd is an American; the leading Blancos are Europeanised; they are national-minded but not radical, like the Polish 'appeasers' (the Bobrowskis were among them) and 'Whites'; Decoud as a sceptical Europeanised *deraciné* appears partly a projection of Conrad himself; Nostromo and Viola have European (Italian) origins.[6]

We have noticed certain instances of how the qualities of each developing country, its level and pace of development have contributed to the shaping of the kind of fiction written about it. Forster said: 'There are a hundred Indias, but only two or three Egypts. Now and then one has the illusion that Egypt also is multiform and infinite, and that the Nile, like the Ganges, flows from the hair of God through men into Hell'.[7] Nigeria and the Niger could be taken as equivalents of Egypt and the Nile. The impression of social life in Cary is less complex than that in Forster partly because Nigeria appears a less complex country than India (though this may or may not seem so for a Chinua Achebe) and also partly because Cary's view of reality is simpler than Forster's: Cary's portrayal of Mister Johnson compares well with Forster's portrayal of Aziz, but his portrayal of Rudbeck is simpler than the latter's portrayal of Fielding. Conrad can see no points of growth in the Congo in *Heart of Darkness* because there were none to see; the country had been so ruined. On the other hand, because India was in a much better state and at a higher level of development, Forster can show national awakening among the Indians themselves.

Whether or not a writer, in presenting the country in his work, develops the perspectives proved (or being proved) right by history, is usually a sign of the degree of success or of failure of his art: compare the discussion above of *Nostromo* and *A Passage to India*, on the one hand, and of *The Plumed Serpent*, on the other. Kipling stressed what he called 'the white man's burden', what T. S. Eliot later termed 'responsibility',[8] as a justification of imperialism. This was widely accepted as sound, particularly in his period, and reveals Kipling's inability to rise above contemporary majority opinion in this respect. 'The Enlightenments of Pagett, M. P.' hardly seems a work of fiction. It virtually seems a documentary defence of imperialism in India,[9] but it is worth noticing because it makes plain Kipling's blindness to clear and plentiful signs of the British retreat from the subcontinent – for instance, Lord Ripon's proposals (Ripon was viceroy from 1880 to 1884) to give municipalities greater freedom from official control and to increase the measure of local autonomy permitted to Districts, and Lord Dufferin's proposals (1892) for the non-official Indians to participate more closely in the government, proposals which were implemented in part in the Indian Councils Act. It is certainly difficult to develop the right historical perspectives, especially when they are at variance with majority views. But this has been shown to be possible by Conrad, Forster, Lawrence and Cary. Kipling does not do so and is by the same token a lesser artist. It is not insignificant that Conrad and he wrote fiction set in developing countries in the same period.

Leslie Stephen thinks that literature is 'a kind of byproduct . . . far too small a part in the whole activity of a nation, even of its intellectual activity, to serve as a complete indication of the many forces which are at work, or as an adequate moral barometer of the general moral state'.[10] This view is not true of the literature in this field of study. The essential forces at work in the interaction of developed and developing countries from their marked beginnings in the Elizabethan age till today have entered British literature. Of course, this is not to claim,

say, that all the major events have got in: after all, the ways of literature are not the ways of history and journalism. Let us consider this
matter with reference to *A Passage to India*. On the one hand, Rose
Macaulay and K. Natwar-Singh argue that it has been set in pre-1914
India; on the other hand, Malcolm Bradbury argues that it has been
set in India in the 1920s.[11] It is likely that Forster's experiences in
India, both pre-1914 and post-1920, go into the novel and it seems to
me dubious whether it belongs to one or the other of these periods. It is
best approached as an impression of India under the British Empire in
the whole first quarter of this century. Notice how Indian nationalism
enters the novel. By 1914, the Indian Congress, very much a middle-
class movement, had a following in all parts of the country; it is the
Congress, again, that launched the mass 'progressive non-violent non-
cooperation' movement in the 1920s.[12] In the novel, Indians such as
Aziz and Hamidullah are not figures in the Congress movement, but
they represent a strong undercurrent of nationalist-inclined thoughts
and feelings, a reflection of the nationalist currents during this whole
period.

We have noticed that developing countries play a key role in the
careers of the selected writers who are among the major artists in
modern times. We have noticed the difficulties they encounter when
they depict these countries. Now let us discuss the advantages they
enjoy in presenting them. Let us compare a novel set in England and
one set in a developing country by a single writer, Forster's *Howards
End* and *A Passage to India*. When Forster wrote these novels, he
already had behind him *Where Angels Fear to Tread*, *The Longest
Journey* and *A Room with a View*. In *Howards End*, he wants different
sections in society to 'connect'. The Schlegels represent the world of
cultured personal relations, the Wilcoxes represent the world of
efficient practical business, and the Basts represent the working class.
One side of Forster's mind is shrewdly aware that the Schlegels, the
Wilcoxes and the Basts are different products of the same class and
property system and that personal relations cannot resolve deep social
differences. He points out, for instance, that the work of Wilcoxes and
Basts makes possible the income of Schlegels, that the income of Schlegels enables them to lead leisured cultured lives, and that Helen's
attempt to help the Basts through personal association is futile. Yet
Forster deteriorates into unrealism. The union of the world of personal
relations and the world of business, Forster's main concern in the
novel, is to be conveyed chiefly through the relationship of Margaret
Schlegel and Henry Wilcox, but Forster's presentation of their rela-

tionship is only partially successful. Margaret has no illusions about Henry and she wants to escape from spinsterhood. But she is severely shaken when she learns of Henry's liaison with Jacky and Henry's character, which is not compatible with hers, does not change. Forster has to do violence to character and plot to keep the Magaret–Henry marriage going: Henry breaks down after his son's imprisonment and Margaret looks after him; their final reconciliation is between a broken man and a woodenly-presented rather mystical woman. The novel closes with an almost idyllic scene which patriotically glorifies the English yeoman and soil, and has no place for the Basts. On the other hand, in *A Passage to India*, the Indian situation helps, if not compels, Forster to be consistently objective and realistic as well as deeply significant. This is exemplified in his presentation of Fielding's friendship with Aziz from its uneven beginning, through the crisis in the Caves, to their final recognition of the gulf between them. It is chiefly through the course of their friendship that Forster convincingly dramatises the immense difficulty of achieving harmonious race relations. He is not tempted into wishful thinking, though he desires races to live harmoniously; in *Howards End*, he desires classes to unite and falls into wishful thinking. Probably because realities in developing countries are more naked than those in developed countries and because they are distant, British writers find it easier to be more objective and realistic about them rather than about realities at home. This is, probably, one important reason why, after 1880, more good fiction by British writers has been set in developing countries rather than in Britain itself: works by major writers in the modern period – Conrad, Kipling, Forster, Lawrence, L. H. Myers, Cary, Graham Greene and Doris Lessing – have been set in these countries.

Notes and references

INTRODUCTION

1. *Encyclopaedia Britannica* (London, 1966 ed.) Vol. 18, p. 25; the *Encylopaedia* recognises Tylor's true position.
2. E. B. Tylor, *Primitive Culture* (London, 1929 ed.) p. 149.
3. John Holloway, 'The Literary Scene', in *The Modern Age*, ed. Boris Ford (London, 1961) p. 57.
4. Joyce Cary, 'Prefatory Essay': *The African Witch* (London, 1961 ed.) p. 9.
5. Ibid., p. 10.
6. William Wordsworth, 'Preface' to *The Lyrical Ballads* (1800). *Lyrical Ballads*, ed. R. L. Brett and A. R. Jones (London, 1965 ed.) pp. 244–5.
7. 'Graham Greene takes the Orient Express', in the *Listener*, 21 November 1968, p. 674. For a similar view expressed even more recently on the basis of experience of the Middle East, see P. H. Newby, 'Something to Celebrate', in the *Guardian*, 23 April 1969, p. 8.
8. Karl Marx, 'The Future Results of British Rule in India' (1853), in K. Marx and F. Engels, *On Colonialism* (Moscow, n.d.) p. 88.
9. Jean-Paul Sartre, 'Preface', in Frantz Fanon, *The Wretched of the Earth* (London, 1967 ed.) pp. 21, 7. For the same kind of view expressed more recently, see Stuart Hall, 'The New Revolutionaries', in *From Culture to Revolution*, ed. Terry Eagleton and Brian Wicker (London, 1969) p. 208.
10. J. A. Hobson, *Imperialism, A Study* (London, 1938 ed.) p. 5.
11. Professor Seeley, *Expansion of England*, quoted by Hobson, *Imperialism*, p. 6.
12. Hobson, *Imperialism*, p. 304.
13. V. I. Lenin, *Imperialism, The Highest Stage of Capitalism* (Moscow, 1966 ed.) p. 82.
14. D. K. Fieldhouse, 'Imperialism: An Historiographical Revision', in *The Economic History Review* (Cambridge, 1961), Second Series, **14**, 2, 197.
15. Ibid., p. 204.
16. Ibid., p. 207.
17. Ibid., p. 207.

18. Michael Barratt Brown, *After Imperialism* (London, 1963) p. 85.
19. Conor Cruise O'Brien, 'Author's Preface', in *Murderous Angels* (London, 1969) p. xxiii.
20. Leonard Woolf, *Imperialism and Civilisation* (London, 1928) p. 88.
21. Ibid., p. 89.
22. Marx, 'The British Rule in India' (1853), in K. Marx and F. Engels, *On Colonialism* (Moscow, n.d.) p. 39.
23. Ruth Benedict, *Race and Racism* (London, 1959 ed.) p. 6.
24. Joseph Conrad, *An Outcast of the Islands* (London, 1951 ed.) p. 74.
25. Gordon Childe, *Social Evolution* (London, 1963 ed.) p. 33.
26. Ibid., p. 34.
27. Woolf, *Imperialism and Civilisation*, p. 50; A. J. Hanna, *European Rule in Africa* (London, 1961) p. 15; Margery Perham, 'The British Problem in Africa', in *Foreign Affairs* (New York, 1951) **29**, 4, p. 638; Lord Lugard, *The Dual Mandate in British Tropical Africa* (London, 1965 ed.) pp. 1–2.
28. Melville J. Herskovits, *The Myth of the Negro Past* (New York, 1941) pp. 57, 61–2.

CHAPTER 1 – *Antecedents*

1. Quoted from Simone de Beauvoir, *Force of Circumstance* (trans. Richard Howard; London, 1968 ed.) p. 387.
2. Eldred Jones, *Othello's Countrymen: The African in English Renaissance Drama* (London, 1965) pp. 12–13.
3. Joseph Conrad, *Victory* (London, 1954 ed.) p. 145.
4. T. S. Eliot, 'Shakespeare and the Stoicism of Seneca', in *Selected Essays* (London, 1963 ed.) pp. 129–31; F. R. Leavis, 'Diabolic Intellect and the Noble Hero', in *The Common Pursuit* (London, 1962 ed.) p. 146.
5. Leavis, *The Common Pursuit*, p. 142.
6. G. M. Matthews, 'Othello and the Dignity of Man', in *Shakespeare in a Changing World*, ed. Arnold Kettle (London, 1964) p. 124.
7. Joseph Addison, *The Spectator*, No. 69 (19 May 1711), in *The Spectator*, ed. Gregory Smith (London, 1967 ed.) Vol. 1, p. 214.
8. Alexander Pope, *The Rape of the Lock*, Canto 1. Cf. 'Moral Essay' III, lines 361–2.
9. Benjamin Kidd, *The Control of the Tropics* (New York and London, 1898) p. 65.
10. William Roscoe, 'Preface', in *The Wrongs of Africa* (London,

1787) p. iv.

11. Angus Ross, 'Introduction', in Daniel Defoe, *The Life and Adventures of Robinson Crusoe* (London, 1965 ed.) p. 11.
12. Defoe, *The Life and Adventures of Robinson Crusoe*, pp. 212–13.
13. Ibid., p. 218.
14. Ibid., p. 222.
15. Quoted from Kenneth Ramchand (ed.) *West Indian Narrative* (London, 1960) pp. 10–11.
16. William Delafield Arnold, *Oakfield or Fellowship in the East* (London, 1853) Vol. 1, p. 16.
17. Ibid., Vol. 1, pp. 69–70.
18. Ibid., Vol. 2, p. 57.
19. Ibid., Vol. 2, p. 219.
20. Ibid., Vol. 2, p. 224.
21. E. M. Forster, 'William Arnold' (1944), in *Two Cheers for Democracy* (London, 1965 ed.) p. 204.
22. Fanon, *The Wretched of the Earth*, p. 48.
23. Arnold, *Oakfield*, p. 254.
24. Ibid., Vol. 2, p. 138.
25. Ibid., Vol. 2, p. 140.
26. Ibid., Vol. 2, p. 141.
27. Ibid., Vol. 2, p. 141.
28. Forster, *Two Cheers for Democracy*, p. 201.
29. Arnold, *Oakfield*, Vol. 1, p. 189.
30. Ibid., Vol. 1, pp. 168–9.
31. Ibid., Vol. 1, pp. 170–1.
32. Ibid., Vol. 1, p. 180.
33. For example, in his essay 'Equality' (*Mixed Essays*), Matthew Arnold responds delicately and humanely to 'the great inequality of classes and property'; but politics is to him mere machinery and turbulence.
34. David Craig, *The Real Foundations: Literature and Social Change* (London, 1973) p. 138.
35. William Knighton, *Forest Life in Ceylon* (London, 1854) Vol. 2, p. 361.
36. Ibid., Vol. 2, p. 69.
37. Ibid., Vol. 2, p. 249.
38. For a similar view, see Arnold, 'Preface' to *Oakfield*, p. ix.
39. Knighton, *Forest Life*, Vol. 1, pp. 7–8.
40. Ibid., Vol. 1, p. 20.
41. Winston S. Churchill, *India: Speeches* (London, 1931 ed.) p. 47.

42. Percival Spear, *A History of India* (London, 1968 ed.) Vol. 2, p. 155.

CHAPTER 2 – *Challenges and problems of the Far East*
(i): *Conrad's tales*

As the creative works of the major writers in my field of study are available in numerous, equally good editions and as they are well-known, I have not usually given the page references to quotations from the editions used by me. I have made clear the context of each quotation or the quotation itself indicates its context – so that reference will be easy, whatever the edition. If words quoted by me in my text are not assigned to a particular source, they come from the creative work under discussion.

1. F. R. Leavis, *The Great Tradition* (London, 1962 ed.) pp. 26–8, 32.
2. Long after he had settled in England, in a letter Dr Ernst Bendz of 7 March 1923, he suggests that he is different from Jack London mainly because he is 'a good European, not exactly in the superficial, cosmopolitan sense, but in the blood and bones as it were, and as the result of a long heredity' – G. Jean-Aubry, *Joseph Conrad: Life and Letters* (London, 1927) Vol. 2, p. 294.
3. Joseph Conrad, *A Personal Record*, in *The Mirror of the Sea and A Personal Record* (London, 1960 ed.) p. 87.
4. G. Jean-Aubry, *Joseph Conrad in the Congo* (Boston, 1926) p. 73.
5. V. S. Pritchett, 'A Pole in the Far East', in *The Living Novel* (London, 1960 ed.) p. 143.
6. Gordon N. Ray (ed.), *The Letters and Private Papers of William Makepeace Thackeray* (London, 1946) Vol. 3, p. 198.
7. A. J. Guerard, 'On the Nigger of the "Narcissus"', in *Conrad: A Collection of Critical Essays*, ed. Marvin Mudrick (New Jersey, 1966) p. 24; Cecil Scrimgeour, 'Jimmy Wait and the Dance of Death: Conrad's *Nigger of the Narcissus*', in *The Critical Quarterly* (London, 1965), 7, 4, 341.
8. Guerard, 'On the Nigger of the "Narcissus"', p. 22.
9. Guerard, 'On the Nigger of the "Narcissus"', p. 24. Scrimgeour holds a similar view; Guerard's 'something', which is 'larger than Death', is in his view 'death'; 'Jimmy Wait and the Dance of Death', p. 350.
10. Joseph Conrad, 'Author's Note' to *Typhoon and Other Stories*

(1919), in *The Nigger of the 'Narcissus', Typhoon and Other Stories* (London, 1963 ed.) p. 147.

11. V. G. Kiernan, *The Lords of Human Kind* (London, 1969) p. 163.
12. Ibid., p. 163.
13. Zdzislaw Najder, 'Introduction', in *Conrad's Polish Background* (London, 1964) p. 2.
14. Jerry Allen, *The Sea Years of Joseph Conrad* (New York, 1965) p. 46.
15. Conrad portrays Chinese again in *Victory* (1915) – the owner of Davidson's firm, Schomberg's 'boy' and Wang. But only Wang is not negligible. Conrad constantly refers to 'his peculiar manner' in terms which suggest 'vanishing out of existence rather than out of sight, a process of evaporation rather than of movement'; this way of describing him suggests that he, Heyst's self-effacing servant, is seen from an external standpoint of an employer; but the standpoint is fair-minded and realistic. Thus, *Victory* confirms Conrad's kind of ability to present Chinese in more or less minor roles and his novelistic tact in refraining from going beyond his knowledge and powers in this field.

CHAPTER 3 – *Challenges and problems of the Far East* (ii): *Conrad's Malayan novels*

1. Letter to R. B. Cunninghame Graham, April 1898, in *Joseph Conrad's Letters to R. B. Cunninghame Graham*, ed. C. T. Watts (Cambridge, 1969) p. 82.
2. Conrad, letter to Henry S. Canby, 7 April 1924, in Jean-Aubry, *Joseph Conrad: Life and Letters*, Vol. 2, p. 342.
3. See A. C. Haddon, *Head-Hunters, Black White and Brown* (London, 1932 ed.) p. 2.
4. Edward Crankshaw, *Joseph Conrad: Some Aspects of the Art of the Novel* (New York, 1963 ed.) pp. 118–19.
5. Hugh Clifford, 'Concerning Maurice Curzon', quoted from *A Freelance of Today* (1903), in *Stories by Sir Hugh Clifford*, ed. William R. Roff (Kuala Lumpur, 1966) p. 1.
6. Kidd, *The Control of the Tropics*, pp. 50–1.
7. Joseph Conrad, 'Author's Note to 1917 Edition', in *Lord Jim* (London, 1953 ed.) p. 2.
8. Anonymous, 'A White Rajah', in *Blackwood's Edinburgh Magazine* (Edinburgh and London, February 1880), **127**, DCCLXXII, 193,

199–200.

9. Charles Kingsley, letter to J. M. Ludlow, December 1849, in *Charles Kingsley: His Letters and Memories of his life*, ed. his wife (London, 1877) Vol. 1, p. 222.

10. Jocelyn Baines, *Joseph Conrad* (London, 1960 ed.) p. 253.

11. Baines, *Joseph Conrad*, pp. 253–4; Norman Sherry, *Conrad's Eastern World* (Cambridge, 1966) pp. 116–18, 135.

12. Alfred Russel Wallace, *The Malay Archipelago* (London and New York, 1890 ed.) p. 71.

13. Joseph Conrad, unpublished letter to T. Fisher Unwin, 14 April 1897 (Brotherton Collection, Leeds University Library).

14. Hugh Clifford, *The Quest of the Golden Fleece*, in '*Blackwood*' *Tales from the Outposts* (Edinburgh and London, 1933 ed.) Vol. 8, pp. 178–9.

15. Hugh Clifford, 'Concerning Conrad and his Work', in *The Empire Review* (London, May 1928) **47**, 328, 288.

CHAPTER 4 – *Conrad's Malayan novels: problems of authenticity*

1. For instance, compare Old Singleton in Conrad's *The Nigger of the 'Narcissus'* 'who in the last forty-five years had lived no more than forty months ashore'.

2. Norman Sherry, *Conrad's Eastern World*, p. 139.

3. The epigraph to this chapter is characteristic of Hugh Clifford's criticism of Conrad. Leavis, *The Great Tradition*, p. 210.

4. Joseph Conrad, *Almayer's Folly*, in *Almayer's Folly and Tales of Unrest* (London, 1947 ed.) pp. 166–7. Cf. *An Outcast of the Islands* (London, 1951 ed.) p. 49; *The Rescue* (London, 1949 ed.) p. 5.

5. Hugh Clifford, 'The East Coast', from *In Court and Kampong* (1897), in *Stories by Sir Hugh Clifford*, p. 16.

6. Leavis, *The Great Tradition*, p. 210.

7. Hugh Clifford 'The Art of Mr Joseph Conrad', in *The Spectator*, 29 November 1902, pp. 827–8.

8. Conrad, *Lord Jim*, pp. 161–2. Cf. *Victory* (London, 1954 ed.) pp. 2–3.

9. J. I. M. Stewart, *Joseph Conrad* (London, 1968) p. 39.

10. Ibid., p. 40.

11. Leavis, *The Great Tradition*, p. 229.

12. Conrad speaks of originals in life for his desperadoes in his 'Auth-

or's Note' (1920), in *Victory* (London, 1960 ed.) pp. xi–xv.

13. M. C. Bradbrook, *Joseph Conrad: Poland's English Genius* (New York, 1965 ed.) p. 65.

14. Sherard Osborn, *My Journal in Malayan Waters* (London, 1861 ed.) p. 69.

15. For instance, compare E. M. Forster's account of an Indian 'public wedding' in which Islamic prayer and Western music mix – Forster, 'Adrift in India', in *Abinger Harvest* (London, 1967 ed.) p. 330.

16. Arnold Kettle, *An Introduction to the English Novel* (London, 1962 ed.) Vol. 2, p. 71.

17. Pritchett, *The Living Novel*, p. 145.

18. Najder, *Conrad's Polish Background*, pp. 3–4.

19. J. D. Legge, *Indonesia* (New Jersey, 1964) p. 112.

20. George McTurnan Kahin, *Nationalism and Revolution in Indonesia* (New York, 1963 ed.) p. 2.

21. Kettle, *Introduction to the English Novel*, p. 71.

22. Wallace, *The Malay Archipelago*, p. 168.

23. Osborn, *My Journal in Malayan Waters*, pp. 175–6.

24. Frank S. Marryat writes: '. . . the Malays who inhabit the coast of Borneo are a cruel, treacherous, and disgusting race of men, with scarcely one good quality to recommend them. . . . In their physiognomy these Malays are inferior to the Dyaks: they have a strong resemblance to the monkey in face, with an air of low cunning and rascality most unprepossessing'. – Marryat, *Borneo and the Indian Archipelago* (London, 1848) pp. 99–100.

25. Wallace, *The Malay Archipelago*, p. 448.

26. Frank Swettenham, 'The Real Malay', in *Malay Sketches* (London, 1895) pp. 2, 8.

27. Quoted from Sherry, *Conrad's Eastern World*, p. 142. Conrad refers to 'Alfred Wallace's famous book on the Malay Archipelago' in *The Secret Agent* (London, 1961 ed.) p. 118.

28. Osborn, *My Journal in Malayan Waters*, pp. 133–4, 175–6.

29. Fred McNair, *Perak and the Malays: 'Sarong and Kris'* (London, 1878) pp. 207–8.

30. 'Indo-China was the first country I fell in love with after West Africa. It was partly the beauty of the women – it's extraordinary – . . .' – 'Graham Greene takes the Orient Express', *The Listener*, 21 November 1968, p. 674.

31. Osborn, *My Journal in Malayan Waters*, pp. 225, 360.

32. Bradbrook, *Joseph Conrad*, p. 14.

33. I do not propose to discuss the nature of these influences or attempt to find out the years when they operated appreciably. I shall briefly suggest the difficulty of these tasks: in 1918 he told Hugh Walpole that he had not read Flaubert till *Almayer's Folly* was finished (Stewart, *Joseph Conrad*, p. 38), but 'the novel was begun on the margins of a copy of *Madame Bovary*' (Bradbrook, *Joseph Conrad*, p. 14); and Conrad's memory was extraordinarily retentive.

34. Letter to Clifford, 17 May 1898, in Jean-Aubry, *Life and Letters*, Vol. 1, p. 237. See also Conrad, 'Author's Note' to *A Personal Record*, pp. iv, v.

35. William Blackburn (ed.), *Joseph Conrad: Letters to William Blackwood and David S. Meldrum* (North Carolina, 1958) p. 34.

36. Letter to Clifford, 17 May 1898, in Jean-Aubry, *Life and Letters*, p. 237.

37. Joseph Conrad, 'An Observer in Malaya' (1898), in *Notes on Life and Letters* (London, 1949 ed.) p. 58.

38. Joseph Conrad, 'Author's Note' to *A Personal Record*, p. iv. He inscribed *Chance* 'to Sir Hugh Clifford whose steadfast friendship is responsible for the existence of these pages'. See also *Letters to Blackwood and Meldrum*, p. 64.

39. Quoted from Jessie Conrad, *Joseph Conrad and his Circle* (London, 1935) pp. 76–7.

40. Conrad, 'An Observer in Malaya', in *Notes on Life and Letters*, p. 60.

41. Hugh Clifford, *A Talk on Joseph Conrad and his Work* (Colombo, 1927) pp. 4–5.

42. Joseph Conrad, letter to the 'Ranee' Brooke, 15 July 1920, in *Letters to Cunninghame Graham*, p. 210.

43. E. M. Forster, 'Notes on the English Character' (1920), in *Abinger Harvest*, p. 22.

44. Conrad, 'Author's Note' to *A Personal Record*, pp. vi–vii.

45. Ibid., p. vii.

46. Joseph Conrad, 'Prince Roman', in *Tales of Hearsay and Last Essays* (London, 1955 ed.) p. 29.

47. Pritchett, *The Living Novel*, p. 145.

CHAPTER 5 – *Conrad's African tales: ironies of progress*

1. Conrad, 'Author's Note' to *Tales of Unrest*, in *Almayer's Folly and Tales of Unrest*, p. vii.

2. A. J. Guerard, *Conrad the Novelist* (Massachusetts, 1966) pp. 64–5; J. I. M. Stewart, *Joseph Conrad*, pp. 75–7.

3. Joseph Conrad, letter to William Blackwood, 31 December 1898, in *Letters to William Blackwood and David S. Meldrum*, p. 37.

4. Najder, *Conrad's Polish Background*, pp. 16–17.

5. Joseph Conrad, *Heart of Darkness*, in *Youth, Heart of Darkness, End of the Tether* (London, 1956 ed.) p. 48.

6. See, for example, Sir Hugh Clifford, 'The Quest of the Golden Fleece', in *'Blackwood' Tales from the Outposts* (Edinburgh and London, 1933 ed.) Vol. 8; Lord Baden-Powell, 'Jokilobovu', ibid., Vol. 9; J. A. G. Elliot, 'The Ngoloko', ibid., Vol. 9; Lieut-Colonel R. L. Kennion, 'A Country Postman', ibid., Vol. 1; Lieut-Colonel F. M. Bailey, 'A Quiet Day in Tibet', ibid., Vol. 1.

7. These works first appeared in *Blackwood's Edinburgh Magazine*, Vol. 162, 1897; Vol. 164, 1898; Vol. 166, 1899; and Vol. 165, 1899, respectively.

8. Conrad, *Heart of Darkness*, p. 48.

9. Thomas Sprat, *The History of the Royal Society* (1667), in *Critical Essays of the 17th Century*, ed. J. E. Spingarn (Oxford, 1908) Vol. 2, pp. 112–13.

10. René Maunier, *The Sociology of Colonies*, in *British Imperialism*, ed. Robin W. Winks (New York, 1966) p. 69.

11. D. H. Lawrence, *Etruscan Places*, in *Mornings in Mexico and Etruscan Places* (London, 1956) p. 1.

12. Walter Allen, *The English Novel* (London, 1962 ed.) p. 306.

13. Kettle, *An Introduction to the English Novel*, Vol. 2, p. 81.

14. Knighton, *Forest Life in Ceylon*, Vol. 1, pp. 281–3.

15. T. S. Eliot, *Notes towards the Definition of Culture* (London, 1959) pp. 90–1; Orwell, 'Shooting an Elephant' (1936), in *Collected Essays* (London, 1968 ed.) p. 16.

16. Roger Casement, 'The Congo Report' (11 December 1903), in *Roger Casement: The Black Diaries*, ed. P. Singleton-Gates and Maurice Girodias (London, n.d.) pp. 98–100.

17. Joseph Conrad, 'The Congo Diary', in *Tales of Hearsay and Last Essays* (London, 1955 ed.) p. 162.

18. Virginia Woolf, 'Joseph Conrad' (1924), in *Collected Essays* (London, 1966) Vol. 1, p. 304.

19. Douglas Hewitt, *Conrad: A Reassessment* (Cambridge, 1952) p. 18; Guerard, *Conrad the Novelist*, p. 37.

20. See Richard Curle's notes to 'The Congo Diary' in Conrad's *Tales of Hearsay and Last Essays*.

21. Baines, *Joseph Conrad*, p. 117.
22. Norman Sherry, *Conrad's Western World* (Cambridge, 1971) p. 95.
23. Stephen A. Reid, 'The "Unspeakable Rites" in *Heart of Darkness*', in *Conrad, A Collection of Critical Essays*, ed. Marvin Mudrick (New Jersey, 1966) p. 45.
24. Joseph Conrad, letter to R. B. Cunninghame Graham, 26 December 1903: Jean-Aubry, *Life and Letters*, Vol. 1, p. 326.
25. Stewart, *Joseph Conrad*, p. 79.
26. Hugh Clifford, 'The Art of Mr. Joseph Conrad', in *The Spectator*, 29 November 1902, p. 828; F. R. Leavis, *The Great Tradition*, p. 200; M. C. Bradbrook, *Joseph Conrad*, p. 28; J. I. M. Stewart, *Joseph Conrad*, p. 77; Norman Sherry, *Conrad's Western World*, p. 92.

CHAPTER 6 – *Conrad's* Nostromo: *the morality of 'material interests'*

1. Joseph Conrad, letter to Edward Garnett, 3 September 1904, in Jean-Aubry, *Life and Letters*, Vol. 1, p. 335.
2. Allen, *The Sea Years of Joseph Conrad*, p. 31.
3. Joseph Conrad, letter to Cunninghame Graham, 31 October 1904, in *Letters to Cunninghame Graham*, p. 157.
4. Joseph Conrad, 'Author's Note' (1917), in *Nostromo* (London, 1963 ed.) p. 13.
5. Joseph Conrad, letter to Dr Ernst Bendz, 7 March 1923, in Jean-Aubry, *Life and Letters*, Vol. 2, p. 296.
6. Kettle, *An Introduction to the English Novel*, Vol. 2, p. 80.
7. Michael Wilding, 'The Politics of *Nostromo*', in *Essays in Criticism* (Oxford, 1966) **16**, 4, 448.
8. Walter Allen, *The English Novel*, p. 309; Hewitt, *Conrad*, p. 47; Robert Penn Warren, '*Nostromo*', in *The Sewanee Review* (Tennessee, 1951), **59**, 3, 381. The words quoted are from Allen's book.
9. Irving Howe, *Politics and the Novel* (Cleveland and New York, 1962 ed.) p. 105.
10. David Craig, 'The Defeatism of *The Waste Land*', in *The Critical Quarterly* (London, 1960), **2**, 3, 248; Craig, *The Real Foundations*, pp. 206–7.
11. Wilding, 'The Politics of *Nostromo*', p. 445.
12. Conrad, 'Author's Note' (1917), in *Nostromo*, p. 12.
13. Ibid., p. 13.

14. Ibid., p. 12.
15. Wilding, 'The Politics of *Nostromo*', p. 447.
16. Ibid., p. 444.
17. Compare, on the one hand, Kettle ('their depths and complexities are well established'; Kettle, *Introduction to the English Novel*, Vol. 2, p. 73) and, falling over in the opposite direction, Baines ('their psychology is on the whole crude, blurred or even unconvincing'; Baines, *Joseph Conrad*, p. 299); Mudrick goes even further along Baines's line (*Nostromo* is 'a prodigiously ingenious waxworks museum, which in certain lights and to certain innocent minds appears to be an assemblage of live human beings'; Marvin Mudrick, 'Introduction', in *Conrad, A Collection of Critical Essays*, p. 10).

CHAPTER 7 – *Difficulties of connection in India:*
Kipling and Forster

1. Margery Perham, 'African Dreams', in *The Listener*, 12 March 1970, p. 336.
2. Louis L. Cornell, *Kipling in India* (New York, 1966) p. 108.
3. W. W. Robson, 'Kipling's Later Stories', in *Kipling's Mind and Art*, ed. Andrew Rutherford (Edinburgh and London, 1965 ed.) p. 258.
4. Rudyard Kipling, *Something of Myself* (London, 1964 ed.) p. 207.
5. For instance, 'thirty-two of the *Plain Tales* had been printed in the *Civil and Military*; the remaining eight made their first appearance when the book was published, in January 1888'; Charles Carrington, *Rudyard Kipling: His Life and Work* (London, 1955) p. 91.
6. The observation about the diction is that of the secondary narrator who introduces Pansay's account. – Kipling, 'The Phantom Rickshaw', in *Wee Willie Winkie* (London, 1964 ed.) p. 102.
7. James Baldwin, *The Fire Next Time* (London, 1967 ed.) p. 63.
8. Walt Whitman, 'Passage to India', in *Walt Whitman: Complete Poetry and Selected Prose and Letters*, ed. Emory Holloway (London, 1964 ed.) p. 380.
9. Joseph Chamberlain, 'A Young Nation' (11 November 1895), in *Foreign and Colonial Speeches* (London, 1897) p. 89.
10. Cecil Rhodes, letter to W. T. Stead, quoted from C. E. Carrington, *The British Overseas* (London, 1950) p. 681.
11. All extracts from Kipling's poetry are from *Rudyard Kipling's Verse, Definitive Edition* (London, 1960 ed.).

12. Jack Dunman, 'Rudyard Kipling Re-estimated', in *Marxism Today* (London, 1965) **9**, 8, 243; M. Tarinayya, 'East–West Encounter: Kipling', in *The Literary Criterion* (Mysore, 1966) **7**, 3, 28. For similar attempts to play down Kipling's racialism and other imperial prejudices, see, for instance, T. S. Eliot, 'Rudyard Kipling', in *A Choice of Kipling's Verse*, ed. T. S. Eliot (London, 1963 ed.) p. 29; Bonamy Dobrée, *Rudyard Kipling: Realist and Fabulist* (London, New York and Toronto, 1967), pp. 81, 84.

13. Charles Carrington, *Rudyard Kipling*, p. 258.

14. A. E. Rodway, 'The Last Phase', in *From Dickens to Hardy*, ed. Boris Ford (London, 1958) p. 389.

15. George Orwell, 'Rudyard Kipling', in *Kipling's Mind and Art*, ed. Andrew Rutherford p. 71; Michael Edwardes, ' "Oh to meet an Army Man": Kipling and the Soldiers', in *Rudyard Kipling, the man, his work and his world*, ed. John Gross (London, 1972) p. 44.

16. A. E. Rodway, 'The Last Phase', p. 392.

17. Alan Sandison, 'Kipling: The Artist and the Empire', in *Kipling's Mind and Art*, ed. Andrew Rutherford p. 155.

18. Louis L. Cornell, *Kipling in India*, pp. 47–50.

19. Our Indian Correspondent [E. M. Forster], 'Reflections in India' I, in *The Nation & The Athenaeum*, 21 January 1922, p. 614; notice also Ramsay MacDonald, *The Government of India* (London, 1919) p. 272, quoted later in the chapter.

20. Frederick C. Crews, *E. M. Forster: The Perils of Humanism* (New Jersey and London, 1962) pp. 153, 162; John Colmer, *E. M. Forster: A Passage to India* (London, 1967) p. 11.

21. For example, the stories 'The Road from Colonus', 'The Other Side of the Hedge' and 'The Eternal Moment' appeared in Vol. 3, No. 9, June 1904; Vol. 4, No. 14, November 1904; and Vol. 6, No. 21, June 1905, respectively. 'Rostock and Wismar', a creative description of two towns, appears in Vol. 9, No. 33, June 1906, and 'Literary Eccentrics', a review of John Fyvie's *Some Literary Eccentrics* (1906), appeared in Vol. 11, No. 37, October 1906.

22. E. M. Forster, *Goldsworthy Lowes Dickinson* (London, 1953 ed.) p. 115.

23. Ibid., p. 116.

24. E. M. Forster, 'Preface' (1953), in *The Hill of Devi* (London, 1953 ed.) p. 10.

25. Leonard Woolf, *Growing: An Autobiography of the Years 1904–1911* (London, 1964 ed.) p. 135; Kipling, *Something of Myself*, pp. 42–3.

26. Virginia Woolf, 'The Novels of E. M. Forster' (n.d.), in *Collected Essays*, Vol. 1, p. 344; F. R. Leavis, 'E. M. Forster', in *The Common Pursuit*, pp. 261–2. Cf. 'I learned the possibilities of domestic humour' [from Jane Austen] – E. M. Forster in 'The Art of Fiction', in *The Paris Review* (Paris, 1953) 1, 1, 39.
27. E. M. Forster, 'What I believe' (1939), in *Two Cheers for Democracy* (London, 1965 ed.) pp. 75–6.
28. Leonard Woolf, *The Village in the Jungle* (London, 1961 ed.) p. 27.
29. Forster, 'Notes on the English Character', in *Abinger Harvest*, p. 18.
30. Ibid., pp. 15–16.
31. Forster, *The Hill of Devi*, p. 43.
32. Compare the contrast between English frigidity and inhibition, on the one hand, and Italian impulsiveness, on the other, in *Where Angels Fear to Tread* and *A Room with a View*.
33. Nirad C. Chaudhuri, 'On Understanding the Hindus', in *Encounter* (1965) 24, 6, 24. Michael Edwardes thinks on much the same lines: 'E. M. Forster's *A Passage to India*, though hailed by Indians for its attack on "Anglo-Indian" society and its prejudices, is just as offensive in its drawing of Indian character as its predecessors'. – Edwardes, *Raj: The Story of British India* (London, 1967 ed.) p. 202.
34. Forster, *The Hill of Devi*, p. 160. Compare Q. D. Leavis who thinks that it has been 'the fashion in intellectual circles centring on Bloomsbury and radiating to India to deny the virtues of English governing-class character' and she cites *A Passage to India* as an example. – Q. D. Leavis, 'English Character', in *Scrutiny* (1943) 12, 1, 69.
35. Chaudhuri, 'Passage to and from India', in *Encounter* (1954) 2, 6, 21.
36. George Orwell, 'Shooting an Elephant', in *Collected Essays*, p. 16.
37. Churchill, *India: Speeches*, p. 94.
38. Chaudhuri, 'Passage to and from India', p. 21. Compare K. Natwar-Singh who thinks that Forster 'was harder on his own people' — Natwar-Singh, 'Only Connect ... : Forester and India', in *Aspects of E. M. Forster*, ed. Oliver Stallybrass (London, 1969) p. 44.
39. Churchill, *India: Speeches*, p. 69.
40. R. Palme Dutt, *World Politics 1918–1936* (London, 1936) p. 46.
41. For instance, in *The Hill of Devi*, Forster writes: '. . . it is even more difficult here than in England to get at the rights of a matter.

Everything that happens is said to be one thing and proves to be another' – *The Hill of Devi* (London, 1965 ed.) pp. 59–60.

42. E. M. Forster, *A Passage to India* (London, 1959 ed.) pp. 83–4. Cf. 'there is something esoteric in India about all animals' – Forster, 'The Art of Fiction', p. 39.
43. Forster, *A Passage to India*, p. 135.
44. Churchill, *India: Speeches*, pp. 46–7.
45. J. Ramsay MacDonald, *The Government of India* (London, 1919) p. 272.
46. Annie Besant, 'India's Demand for Freedom', in *The Socialist Review* (1924) **24**, 130, 41.
47. Our Indian Correspondent [E. M. Forster], 'Reflections in India' I, in *The Nation & The Athenaeum*, 21 January 1922, p. 615.

CHAPTER 8 – *D. H. Lawrence: Primitivism?*

1. D. H. Lawrence, *Lady Chatterley's Lover* (New York, 1959 ed.) p. 146.
2. D. H. Lawrence, *Psychoanalysis and the Unconscious* (London, 1961 ed.) p. 244.
3. Ibid., p. 245.
4. D. H. Lawrence, *Twilight in Italy* (London, 1956 ed.) pp. 44–5.
5. Ibid., p. 87.
6. Lawrence, *Psychoanalysis and the Unconscious*, p. 248.
7. Arthur O. Lovejoy and George Boas, *Primitivism and Related Ideas in Antiquity* (Baltimore, 1935) p. 13.
8. Ibid., p. 8.
9. F. R. Leavis, *D. H. Lawrence: Novelist* (London, 1964 ed.) p. 235.
10. James Baldwin, *The Fire Next Time*, p. 39.
11. F. R. Leavis, *D. H. Lawrence*, p. 285; Julian Moynahan, *The Deed of Life: The Novels and Tales of D. H. Lawrence* (Princeton, 1966) p. 178.
12. Lovejoy and Boas, *Primitivism*, p. 2.
13. D. H. Lawrence, *Mornings in Mexico* (London, 1956 ed.) p. 46.
14. D. H. Lawrence, *Kangaroo* (London, 1954 ed.) p. 18.
15. *Encyclopaedia Britannica* (London, 1966 ed.) Vol. 2, p. 938.
16. Lawrence, letter to Lady Cynthia Asquith, 7 February 1916, in *The Letters of D. H. Lawrence*, ed. Aldous Huxley (London, 1956 ed.) p. 316.
17. I. A. Richards, *Science and Poetry* (London, 1935) p. 52.

18. Ibid., p. 79.
19. T. S. Eliot, *After Strange Gods* (New York, 1934) p. 68.
20. Lawrence, *Lady Chatterley's Lover*, p. 94. I have quoted Lawrence's own classic formulation because of its suggestive appropriateness in this context, though it has been invoked rather too often.
21. Eliot, *After Strange Gods*, p. 63.
22. Wyndham Lewis, *Paleface: The Philosophy of the 'Melting-Pot'* (London, 1929) p. 193.
23. For example, Lawrence, *Mornings in Mexico*, p. 11.
24. Ibid., p. 48.
25. Lewis, *Paleface*, pp. 147-8.
26. Henry Moore (text) and John Hedgecoe (editor and photographer), *Henry Moore* (New York, 1968) pp. 45, 52-5.
27. Marcus Cunliffe, 'Black Culture and White America', in *Encounter* (January 1970) **34**, 1, 35.
28. James Baldwin, *The Fire Next Time*, p. 75.
29. Ibid., p. 63.
30. Ibid., p. 90.
31. Ibid., p. 39.
32. Ibid., pp. 88-9.
33. Ibid., p. 72.
34. Ibid., p. 98.

CHAPTER 9 – *Joyce Cary: the clash of cultures in Nigeria*

1. Joyce Cary, *Britain and West Africa* (London, 1946) p. 53.
2. Joyce Cary, 'My First Novel', in the *Listener*, 16 April 1953, p. 638.
3. Lord Baden-Powell, 'Jokilobovu', in *'Blackwood' Tales from the Outposts* (Edinburgh and London, 1953), Vol. 9, pp. 2-3.
4. Joyce Cary, 'Prefatory Essay', in *Aissa Saved* (London, 1960 ed.) p. 8.
5. Cary, 'My First Novel' p. 637.
6. Cary, 'Prefatory Essay', in *Aissa Saved*, p. 8.
7. Ibid., p. 8.
8. Cary, 'My First Novel', p. 637.
9. Golden L. Larsen, *The Dark Descent: Social Change and Moral Responsibility in the Novels of Joyce Cary* (London, 1965) p. 23.
10. Joyce Cary, 'The Way a Novel Gets Written', in *Adam International Review* (London, November–December 1950) **18**, 212-13, 5.

11. Cary's abiding interest in these problems is shown in his later political work, *The Case for African Freedom*; in it he demonstrates the practicality of his view; see Joyce Cary, *The Case for African Freedom* (London, 1941) pp. 45, 46; ibid. (revised and enlarged edition, London, 1944) pp. 42, 43. Cary's ideas are corroborated by Margery Perham's, which were expressed around the time when Cary was writing the final draft of *An American Visitor* and when he first published it; see Margery Perham, 'Nigeria Today', in *Colonial Sequence 1930–1949* (London, 1967) p. 64. This article first appeared in *The Times*, 30 December 1932. See also Margery Perham, 'Problems of Indirect Rule in Africa', in *Colonial Sequence 1930–1949*, p. 106. This was an address to the Royal Society of Arts, 24 March 1934; it was published in the Journal of the Society for 8 May 1934.

12. Michael Banton, *Race Relations* (London, 1967) p. 225.

13. Joyce Cary, *Power in Men* (Seattle, 1963 ed.) p. 165.

14. David Craig, 'Idea and Imagination: A Study of Joyce Cary', in *Fox* (Aberdeen, 1954) p. 4.

15. Joyce Cary, 'Prefatory Essay', in *Castle Corner* (London, 1960 ed.) p. 5.

16. Charles G. Hoffman: 'Joyce Cary's African Novels', in *The South Atlantic Quarterly* (North Carolina, 1963) **62**, 2, 242.

17. Anonymous, 'My First Execution', in *'Blackwood' Tales from the Outposts* (Edinburgh and London, 1933) Vol. 9, pp. 115–16.

18. Arnold Kettle, 'Joyce Cary: *Mister Johnson*', in *An Introduction to the English Novel*, Vol. 2, p. 193.

19. Joyce Cary, 'Preface', in *Mister Johnson* (London, 1965 ed.) p. 9.

20. Cary, 'Prefatory Essay', in *Aissa Saved*, p. 10.

21. Robert Bloom, *The Indeterminate World: A Study of the Novels of Joyce Cary* (Philadelphia, 1962) pp. 44–5.

22. Cary, *Britain and West Africa*, p. 48.

23. Malcolm Foster, *Joyce Cary: A Biography* (London, 1969) p. 298.

24. Their recreations included polo and hunting. Kipling as a journalist was of 'low' social status in Anglo-India, but he wrote: 'Personally I'm in the lap of luxury. My bedroom even at midnight which I consider the hottest time of the twenty four hours never goes beyond 86° but that means six men are working night and day in relays to keep it cool'; Kipling, letter to Miss Margaret Burne-Jones, 17 June 1886, in Carrington, *Rudyard Kipling*, p. 75.

25. M. M. Mahood, *Joyce Cary's Africa* (London, 1964) p. 146ff; William Van O'Connor, *Joyce Cary* (New York and London, 1966)

p. 19.

26. Lord Lugard, *The Dual Mandate in British Tropical Africa* (London, 1965 ed.) p. 617.

27. Margery Perham, 'Education for Self-Government', in *Colonial Sequence 1930 to 1949*, p. 275. This article first appeared in *Foreign Affairs*, October 1945.

28. Sir Hugh Clifford, address to the Nigerian Council, 29 December 1920, quoted from James S. Coleman, *Nigeria: Background to Nationalism* (Los Angeles, 1963) p. 194.

29. W. R. Crocker, *Nigeria: A Critique of British Colonial Administration* (London, 1936) p. 270.

30. Lord Hailey, *An African Survey* (London, 1938) pp. 1639–40.

31. Joyce Cary, *The Case for African Freedom* (London, 1944 ed.) p. 60.

32. See Margery Perham, *Native Administration in Nigeria* (London, 1937) p. 360.

33. *Parliamentary Debates*, House of Commons (London, 1943) 5th Series, Vol. 391, column 48.

34. '. . . As we have shown, the extreme exploitation of the Africans is the very essence of imperialism. . . . independence is the primary condition for the improvement of the Africans' conditions . . . the problem of African independence will come to be a demand of urgency to them and not a utopian dream, as it is regarded by many today, or again by many others as a practical impossibility'. H. Rathbone, 'The Problem of African Independence', in *The Labour Monthly* (April 1936) **18**, 4, 248.

35. Kettle, *An Introduction to the English Novel*, p. 193.

CHAPTER 10 – *Between cultures*

1. Conrad, *The Secret Agent* (London, 1961 ed.) p. 118.

2. E. M. Forster, 'The Art of Fiction', in *The Paris Review* (Paris, 1953) **1**, 1, 33.

3. Cary, 'Prefatory Essay', in *Aissa Saved*, p. 10; Joyce Cary, 'Prefatory Essay', in *An American Visitor* (London, 1961 ed.) pp. 9–10; Malcolm Foster, *Joyce Cary*, p. 227.

4. For example, Lawrence, letter to Catherine Carswell, 8 October 1924, in *The Letters of D. H. Lawrence*, ed. Aldous Huxley pp. 617–18.

5. Saul Bellow, 'Ideas and the Novel', in *Dialogue* (Washington, 1969)

2, 3, 60.

6. Compare 'Those who have read certain pages of mine will see at once what I mean when I say that Dominic, the padrone of the *Tremolino*, might under given circumstances have been a Nostromo', – Conrad, 'Author's Note', in *Nostromo*, p. 12.

7. E. M. Forster, 'Two Egypts', in *The Athenaeum*, 30 May 1919, p. 393.

8. T. S. Eliot, 'Rudyard Kipling', in *A Choice of Kipling's Verse*, ed. T. S. Eliot, p. 25.

9. It is likely that Kipling's father, John Lockwood Kipling, had a hand in this 'story'; see Carrington, *Rudyard Kipling*, pp. 158–9. But what matters is that Kipling accepts all its views of imperial realities as his own.

10. Leslie Stephen, *English Literature and Society in the 18th Century* (London, 1955 ed.) p. 22.

11. Rose Macaulay, *The Writings of E. M. Forster* (London, 1938) p. 188; K. Natwar-Singh, 'Only Connect . . .: Forster and India', in *Aspects of E. M. Forster*, ed. Oliver Stallybrass, p. 45. Malcolm Bradbury, 'Two Passages to India: Forster as Victorian and Modern', in *Aspects of E. M. Forster*, ed. Oliver Stallybrass, p. 135.

12. T. Walter Wallbank, *A Short History of India and Pakistan* (New York, 1958) pp. 119, 156.

Select bibliography

PRIMARY SOURCES – IMAGINATIVE LITERATURE

William Delafield Arnold:
  Oakfield or Fellowship in the East (London, 1853).
Joyce Cary:
  Aissa Saved (London, 1960 ed.).
  An American Visitor (London, 1961 ed.).
  The African Witch (London, 1961 ed.).
  Castle Corner (London, 1960 ed.).
  Mister Johnson (London, 1965 ed.).
Joseph Conrad:
  Almayer's Folly and Tales of Unrest (London, 1947 ed.).
  An Outcast of the Islands (London, 1951 ed.).
  The Nigger of the 'Narcissus', Typhoon and Other Stories (London, 1963 ed.).
  Lord Jim (London, 1963 ed.).
  Youth, Heart of Darkness, The End of the Tether (London, 1956 ed.).
  Nostromo (London, 1963 ed.).
  The Secret Agent (London, 1961 ed.).
  Under Western Eyes (London, 1957 ed.).
  'Twixt Land and Sea (London, 1947 ed.).
  Victory (London, 1954 ed.).
  The Shadow-Line and Within the Tides (London, 1950 ed.).
  The Rescue (London, 1949 ed.).
  Tales of Hearsay and Last Essays (London, 1955 ed.).
Daniel Defoe:
  The Life and Adventures of Robinson Crusoe (London, 1965 ed.).
E. M. Forster:
  Howards End (London, 1953 ed.).
  A Passage to India (London, 1959 ed.).
Rudyard Kipling:
  Plain Tales From the Hills (London, 1964 ed.).
  Wee Willie Winkie (London, 1964 ed.).
  Life's Handicap (London, 1964 ed.).
  Many Inventions (London, 1964 ed.).
  The Second Jungle Book (London, 1965 ed.).
  The Day's Work (London, 1964 ed.).

Stalky and Co (London, 1962 ed.).
Kim (London, 1962 ed.).
The Definitive Edition of Rudyard Kipling's Verse (London, 1960 ed.).
William Knighton:
Forest Life in Ceylon (London, 1854) Vols. I and II.
D. H. Lawrence:
Women in Love (London, 1957 ed.).
The Tales of D. H. Lawrence (London, 1948 ed.).
Kangaroo (London, 1954 ed.).
The Plumed Serpent (London, 1950 ed.).
Lady Chatterley's Lover (New York, 1959 ed.).
William R. Roff (ed.):
Stories by Sir Hugh Clifford (Kuala Lumpur, 1966).
Shakespeare:
The Merchant of Venice.
Othello.
The Tempest.
Sir Frank Swettenham:
Malay Sketches (London, 1895).
Leonard Woolf:
The Village in the Jungle (London, 1961 ed.).
Blackwood's Edinburgh Magazine (Edinburgh and London).

OTHER WORKS

Jerry Allen, *The Sea Years of Joseph Conrad* (New York, 1965).
Walter Allen, *The English Novel* (London, 1962 ed.).
Jocelyn Baines, *Joseph Conrad* (London, 1960 ed.).
James Baldwin, *The Fire Next Time* (London, 1967 ed.).
Michael Banton, *Race Relations* (London, 1967).
Michael Bell, *Primitivism* (London, 1972).
Ruth Benedict, *Race and Racism* (London, 1959 ed.).
William Blackburn (ed.), *Joseph Conrad: Letters to William Blackwood & David S. Meldrum* (North Carolina, 1958).
Robert Bloom, *The Indeterminate World: A Study of the Novels of Joyce Cary* (Philadelphia, 1962).
M. C. Bradbrook, *Joseph Conrad: Poland's English Genius* (New York, 1965 ed.).
Michael Barratt Brown, *After Imperialism* (London, 1963).

C. T. Buckland, *Sketches of Social Life in India* (London, 1884).

Charles Carrington, *Rudyard Kipling: His Life and Works* (London, 1955).

C. E. Carrington, *The British Overseas* (London, 1950).

Joyce Cary, *Power in Men* (Seattle, 1963 ed.). *The Case for African Freedom* (London 1941), (revised and enlarged edition, London, 1944). *Britain and West Africa* (London, 1946). 'The Way A Novel Gets Written', in *Adam International Review* (London, 1950) **18**, Nos. 212–13. 'A Novel is a Novel is a Novel', in *Adam International Review* (London, 1950) **18**, Nos. 212–13. 'The Novelist at Work' (discussion with Lord David Cecil), in *Adam International Review* (London, 1950) **18**, Nos. 212–13. 'My First Novel', in *The Listener*, 16 April 1953. 'A Novelist and his Public', in *The Listener*, 30 September 1954.

Joseph Chamberlain, *Foreign and Colonial Speeches* (London, 1897).

Nirad C. Chaudhuri, 'Passage to and from India', in *Encounter* (London, 1954) **2**, No. 6. 'On Understanding the Hindus', in *Encounter* (London, 1965) **24**, No. 6.

Gordon Childe, *Social Evolution* (London, 1963 ed.). *What Happened in History* (London, 1943 ed.).

Winston S. Churchill, *India: Speeches* (London, 1931 ed.).

James S. Coleman, *Nigeria, Background to Nationalism* (Los Angeles, 1963).

John Colmer, *E. M. Forster: A Passage to India* (London, 1967).

Joseph Conrad, *The Mirror of the Sea and A Personal Record* (London, 1960 ed.). *Notes on Life and Letters* (London, 1949 ed.).

David Craig, 'Idea and Imagination: A Study of Joyce Cary', in *Fox* (Aberdeen, 1954). *The Real Foundations: Literature and Social Change* (London, 1973).

Edward Crankshaw, *Joseph Conrad: Some Aspects of the Art of the Novel* (New York, 1963 ed.).

Frederick C. Crews, *E. M. Forster: The Perils of Humanism* (London, 1962).

W. R. Crocker, *Nigeria: A Critique of British Colonial Administration* (London, 1936).

Bonamy Dobrée, *Rudyard Kipling, Realist and Fabulist* (London, 1967).

R. P. Draper (ed.), *D. H. Lawrence: The Critical Heritage* (London, 1970).

Michael J. C. Echeruo, *Joyce Cary and the Novel of Africa* (London, 1973).

T. S. Eliot, *After Strange Gods* (New York, 1934). *Notes Towards the Definition of Culture* (London, 1959). 'Rudyard Kipling': T. S. Eliot (ed.), *A Choice of Kipling's Verse* (London, 1963). 'Shakespeare and the Stoicism of Seneca', in *Selected Essays* (London, 1963 ed.).

Frantz Fanon, *The Wretched of the Earth* (London, 1967 ed.).

D. K. Fieldhouse, ' "Imperialism": An Historiographical Revision', in *The Economic History Review* (Cambridge, 1961) Second Series, **14**, No. 2.

Boris Ford (ed.), *The Modern Age* (London, 1961).

Malcolm Foster, *Joyce Cary: A Biography* (London, 1969).

E. M. Forster, *The Hill of Devi* (London, 1953 ed.). *Goldsworthy Lowes Dickinson* (London, 1962 ed.). *Aspects of the Novel* (London, 1963 ed.). *Abinger Harvest* (London, 1967 ed.). *Two Cheers for Democracy* (London, 1965 ed.). *Egypt* (London, 1920). 'Reflections in India', in *The Nation & The Athenaeum*, 22 January 1922, 28 January 1922. 'The Art of Fiction', in *The Paris Review* (Paris, 1953) **1**, No. 1.

P. Singleton-Gates and Maurice Girodias (eds.), *Roger Casement: The Black Diaries* (London, n.d.).

Allen J. Greenberger, *The British Image of India* (London, 1969).

John Gross (ed.), *Rudyard Kipling: the man, his work and his world* (London, 1972).

A. J. Guerard, *Conrad the Novelist* (Massachusetts, 1966).

Lord Hailey, *An African Survey* (London, 1938).

A. J. Hanna, *European Rule in Africa* (London, 1961).

Melville J. Herskovits, *The Myth of the Negro Past* (New York, 1941).

Douglas Hewitt, *Conrad: A Reassessment* (Cambridge, 1952).

J. A. Hobson, *Imperialism, A Study* (London, 1938 ed.).

Charles G. Hoffmann, 'Joyce Cary's African Novels', in *The South Atlantic Quarterly* (North Carolina, 1963) **62**, No. 2.

Irving Howe, *Politics and the Novel* (Cleveland and New York, 1962 ed.).

Susan Howe, *Novels of Empire* (New York, 1949).

G. Jean-Aubry, *Joseph Conrad in the Congo* (Boston, 1926). *Joseph Conrad: Life and Letters* (London, 1927) Vols. I and II.

George McTurnan Kahin, *Nationalism and Revolution in Indonesia* (New York, 1963 ed.).

Arnold Kettle, *An Introduction to the English Novel* (London, 1962 ed.) Vol. 2.

Benjamin Kidd, *The Control of the Tropics* (New York and London, 1898).

V. G. Kiernan, *The Lords of Human Kind* (London, 1969).

Dennis Kincaid, *British Social Life in India, 1608–1937* (London, 1938).

Rudyard Kipling, *Something of Myself* (London, 1964 ed.).

Golden L. Larsen, *The Dark Descent: Social Change and Moral Responsibility in the Novels of Joyce Cary* (London, 1965).

D. H. Lawrence, *Mornings in Mexico and Etruscan Places* (London, 1956 ed.). *Psychoanalysis and the Unconscious* (London, 1961 ed.).

F. R. Leavis, *The Great Tradition* (London, 1962 ed.). *D. H. Lawrence: Novelist* (London, 1964 ed.). *The Common Pursuit* (London, 1962 ed.).

Robert F. Lee, *Conrad's Colonialism* (The Hague and Paris, 1969).

J. D. Legge, *Indonesia* (New Jersey, 1964).

V. I. Lenin, *Imperialism, The Highest Stage of Capitalism* (Moscow, 1966 ed.).

June Perry Levine, *Creation and Criticism: A Passage to India* (London, 1971).

Wyndham Lewis, *Paleface: The Philosophy of the 'Melting-Pot'* (London, 1929).

Arthur O. Lovejoy and George Boas, *Primitivism and Related Ideas in Antiquity* (Baltimore, 1935).

Lord Lugard, *The Dual Mandate in British Tropical Africa* (London, 1965 ed.).

Edward D. McDonald (ed.), *Phoenix: The Posthumous Papers of D. H. Lawrence* (London, 1961).

Fred McNair, *Perak and the Malays: 'Sarong' and 'Kris'* (London, 1878).

M. M. Mahood, *Joyce Cary's Africa* (London, 1964).

Frank S. Marryat, *Borneo and the Indian Archipelago* (London, 1848).

K. Marx and F. Engels, *On Colonialism* (Moscow, n.d.).

G. M. Matthews, 'Othello and the Dignity of Man', in Arnold Kettle (ed.), *Shakespeare in a Changing World* (London, 1964).

Jeffrey Meyers, *Fiction and the Colonial Experience* (Ipswich, 1973).

E. D. Morel, *Great Britain and the Congo* (London, 1909).

Julian Moynahan, *The Deed of Life: The Novels and Tales of D. H. Lawrence* (Princeton, 1966).

Marvin Mudrick (ed.), *Conrad: A Collection of Critical Essays* (New Jersey, 1966).

Zdzislaw Najder, *Conrad's Polish Background* (London, 1964).

C. W. Newbury, *The West African Commonwealth* (London, 1964).

Conor Cruise O'Brien, 'Author's Preface', in *Murderous Angels* (London, 1969).

William Van O'Connor, *Joyce Cary* (New York and London, 1966).

George Orwell, 'Shooting an Elephant' (1936), in *Collected Essays* (London, 1968 ed.).

Captain Sherard Osborn, *My Journal in Malayan Waters* (London, 1861 ed.).

K. M. Panikkar, *Asia and Western Dominance* (London, 1961 ed.).

Benita Parry, *Delusion and Discoveries: Studies on India in the British Imagination 1880–1930* (London, 1972).

Margery Perham, 'The British Problem in Africa', in *Foreign Affairs* (New York, 1951) Vol. 29, No. 4. *Colonial Sequence 1930–1949* (London, 1967).

V. S. Pritchett, 'A Pole in the Far East', in *The Living Novel* (London, 1960 ed.).

Robert Redfield, *The Primitive World and its Transformations* (New York, 1965 ed.).

I. A. Richards, *Science and Poetry* (London, 1935).

Andrew Rutherford (ed.), *Kipling's Mind and Art* (London, 1965 ed.).

Keith Sagar, *The Art of D. H. Lawrence* (Cambridge, 1966).

Alan Sandison, *The Wheel of Empire* (London, 1967).

Norman Sherry, *Conrad's Eastern World* (Cambridge, 1966). *Conrad's Western World* (Cambridge, 1971).

Percival Spear, *India, A Modern History* (Michigan, 1961).

Oliver Stallybrass (ed.), *Aspects of E. M. Forster* (London, 1969).

J. I. M. Stewart, *Joseph Conrad* (London, 1968). *Rudyard Kipling* (London, 1966).

Hugh Tinker, *South Asia* (London, 1966).

K. G. Tregonning, *Malaysia* (London, 1965 ed.).

Mark Twain, *King Leopold's Soliloquy* (London, 1907 ed.).

Alfred Russel Wallace, *The Malay Archipelago* (London and New York, 1890 ed.).

Robert Penn Warren, 'Nostromo', in *The Sewanee Review* (Tennessee, 1951) **59**, No. 3.

C. T. Watts (ed.), *Joseph Conrad's Letters to R. B. Cunninghame Graham* (Cambridge, 1969).

Michael Wilding, 'The Politics of *Nostromo*', in *Essays in Criticism* (Oxford, 1966) **16**, No. 4.

Robin W. Winks (ed.), *British Imperialism* (New York, 1966).

Leonard Woolf, *Imperialism and Civilisation* (London, 1928). *Growing: An Autobiography of the Years 1904–1911* (London, 1964 ed.).

Virginia Woolf, 'Joseph Conrad' (London, 1924), in *Collected Essays* (London, 1966) Vol. 1.

Andrew Wright, *Joyce Cary: A Preface to his Novels* (London, 1958).

Index

Academy, 94
Achebe, Chinua, 32, 196
Adams, W. H., 201
Addison, Joseph, 22; *The Spectator*, 21
African Witch, The, 53, 75, 163, 199, 212–21, 222, 223, 224, 233, 234, 235, 237, 238, 242, 243
Aissa Saved, 24, 163, 199, 200–8, 210, 212, 215, 223, 224, 233, 234, 235, 238, 242, 245, 248
Allen, Jerry, 51, 120
Allen, Walter, 103, 121
Almayer's Folly, 34, 52, 53–8, 61, 63, 69, 74, 77–8, 79, 80, 81, 84–5, 86, 87, 91, 92, 93, 94–5, 119, 136, 153, 245, 246, 249
American Visitor, An, 199, 208–12, 221, 222, 233, 234, 235, 237, 238, 242, 248
Anand, Mulk Raj, 32, 196
Arnold, Matthew, 30
Arnold, William, 25, 31, 32; *Oakfield*, 25–30, 168
'At the End of the Passage', 149, 237
Austen, Jane, 33, 153
Azikwe, Nnamdi, 243

Baden-Powell, Lord, 201–2
Baines, Jocelyn, 63, 114, 132
Baldwin, James, 196–7; *The Fire Next Time*, 139, 179, 197–8
'Ballad of East and West, The', 143
Banton, Michael, 219
Beckett, Samuel; *Waiting for Godet*, 142
Behn, Mrs Aphra, 22, 24–5; *Oroonoko*, 24–5, 90
Bellow, Saul, 249
Bendz, Dr Ernst, 120, 256
Benedict, Ruth, 10
Besant, Annie, 167–8
'Beyond the Pale', 147
Blackwood's Edinburgh Magazine, 27, 101, 228–9
Blackwood, William, 93
Bloom, Robert, 233–4

Boas, F., 3
Boas, George, 174, 184
Bobrowska, Eva, 51
Bradbrook, M. C., 83, 92, 116
Bradbury, Malcolm, 251
'Bridge-Builders, The' 236
Brooke, James, 62, 63, 65
Brooke, Rajah, *see* Brooke, James
Brown, Michael Barratt, 8
Burroughs, Edgar Rice, 13–14

Carlyle, Thomas, 126, 194
Carrington, Charles, 144, 268, 270
Cary, Joyce, 1, 2, 3, 4, 5, 32, 33, 45, 75, 114, 199–200, 207–8, 232–44, 246, 247, 248, 249–50, 252; *African Witch, The*, 53, 75, 163, 199, 212–21, 222, 223, 224, 233, 234, 235, 237, 238, 242, 243; *Aissa Saved*, 24, 163, 199, 200–8, 210, 212, 215, 223, 224, 233, 234, 235, 238, 242, 245, 248; *American Visitor, An*, 199, 208–12, 221, 222, 233, 234, 235, 237, 238, 242, 248; *Britain and West Africa*, 199, 235–6; *Case for African Freedom, The*, 240, 241, 268; *Castle Corner*, 199, 222–3, 233, 245; *Mister Johnson*, 136, 199, 222, 223–32, 233, 234, 235, 238, 242, 245, 247, 248, 250; *Power in Men*, 223
Casement, Roger, 1, 108, 114–15
Castle Corner, 199, 222–3, 233, 245
Césaire, Aimé, 196
Chamberlain, Joseph, 1, 10, 22, 143
Charteris, Leslie, 83
Chaudhuri, Nirad C., 163–4, 165
Cheyney, Peter, 83
Childe, Gordon, 11
Churchill, Winston S., 32, 164, 165–6, 167
Civil and Military Gazette, 147
Clifford, Sir Hugh, 1, 63, 75–6, 77, 91, 93–5, 115, 222, 240, 246, 248, 249, 260; *East Coast, The*, 78; *Fate of Leh, The* 75; *Freelance of Today, A*, 60–1;

Quest of the Golden Fleece, The, 75;
Studies in Brown Humanity, 94; *Umat*,
75; *Wan Beh, The Princess of the
Blood*, 75, 85; *Weeding of the Tares,
The*, 75
Cobbett, William, 126
Coleridge, Samuel Taylor; *Ancient
Mariner*, 101
Colmer, John, 150
Conrad, Joseph, 1, 2, 3, 4, 31–2, 33–5,
    50–3, 60–1, 74–6, 77, 92–8, 99, 119,
    134, 135, 150, 151, 205, 233, 243, 244,
    246, 247, 248, 249, 250, 252;
    Almayer's Folly, 34, 52, 53–8, 61, 63,
    69, 74, 77–8, 79, 80, 81, 84–5, 86, 87,
    91, 92, 93, 94–5, 119, 136, 153, 245,
    246, 249; 'Congo Diary', 109,
    114; *End of the Tether, The*, 34; *Heart
    of Darkness*, 34, 45, 99, 100, 101–18,
    119, 132, 151, 196, 234, 245, 248, 249,
    250; *Karain*, 34, 52, 53, 74, 101;
    Lagoon, The, 34, 52, 53; *Lord Jim*,
    25, 34, 52, 53, 61–8, 74, 75, 78–9, 80,
    81–2, 86–91, 93, 95, 96, 98, 101, 103,
    110, 153, 163; *Nigger of the
    'Narcissus', The*, 34, 40–6, 51, 52, 74,
    258; *Nostromo*, 4, 34, 68, 119–33,
    238–9, 244, 246, 247, 249, 250;
    Outcast of the Islands, An, 10, 34,
    52, 53, 57, 58–61, 63, 69, 74, 80, 81,
    86, 87, 91, 92, 93, 95, 119, 136, 153,
    245, 246, 249; *Outpost of Progress,
    An*, 34, 45, 99–101, 106, 109, 114,
    245, 247; 'Prince Roman', 97–8;
    Rescue, The, 34, 52, 53, 57, 63, 68,
    71–3, 74, 80, 81, 86, 87, 88, 89, 90–1,
    92, 95, 96–7, 98, 249; *Secret Agent,
    The*, 43, 51, 56, 71, 79, 81, 245–6;
    Secret Sharer, The, 34, 35, 36–8, 40,
    42, 101; *Shadow-Line, The*, 34, 35,
    36, 38–40, 101; *Typhoon*, 34, 40,
    46–51, 74, 119, 129; *Under Western
    Eyes*, 34, 43, 56, 57; *Victory*, 18, 34,
    47, 52, 53, 57, 68–71, 74, 75, 79, 80,
    81, 82–4, 88, 95, 98, 249, 257; *Youth*,
    34, 35–6, 101
Cornell, Louis L., 134, 135, 149
Craig, David, 30, 126, 223
Crankshaw, Edward, 57

Crews, Frederick C., 150
Crocker, W. B., 240–1
Cunliffe, Marcus, 197
Curle, Richard, 91, 114
Currie, James, 22, 23

Davies, H. O., 243
Defoe, Daniel, 22, 23, 232; *Robinson
    Crusoe*, 23–4
Dickens, Charles, 126, 194, 232
Dickinson, Goldsworthy Lowes, 151
'Dream of Duncan Parrenness, The'
    135–6, 137
Dryden, John; *Annus Mirabilis*, 21
Dufferin, Lord, 250
Dunman, Jack, 143
Dutt, R. Palme, 166

Edwardes, Michael, 145, 265
'Elephant', 245, 246
Eliot, George, 26, 33; *Felix Holt*, 26, 30;
    Middlemarch, 127
Eliot, T. S., 1, 19, 105, 115, 194–5, 250,
    264; *Waste Land, The*, 175, 196
Elizabeth I, 13, 18
Elliot, J. A. G., 201
Ellison, Ralph, 196
End of the Tether, The, 34
'Enlightenments of Pagett, M.P., The',
    250
Everyman, 83

Fanon, Frantz, 5, 27
Fieldhouse, D. K., 6–8
Fielding, Henry, 22, 232
'Flag of their Country, The' 145
Flaubert, Gustave, 33, 92
Forest Life in Ceylon, 25, 30–1, 32,
    104–5
Forster, E. M., 1, 2, 3, 4, 27, 32, 33, 96,
    134, 141–2, 150–2, 153, 170, 196, 243,
    244, 246, 247, 248, 249, 250, 251, 252;
    Abinger Harvest, 96, 152, 158, 259;
    'Art of Fiction, The', 247, 265, 266;
    Egypt, 152; *Goldsworthy Lowes
    Dickinson*, 151; *Hill of Devi, The*,
    152, 158, 163, 166, 265–6; *Howards
    End*, 142, 151–2, 154, 162, 214, 251–2;
    Longest Journey, The, 153, 154, 251;

Passage to India, A, 1, 28, 53, 110, 134, 139–42, 150–69, 210, 216, 217, 219, 244, 245, 246–7, 248–9, 250, 251, 252; 'Reflections in India', 150, 168; *Room with a View, A,* 153, 154, 158, 251, 265; *Two Cheers for Democracy,* 27, 29, 153; 'Two Egypts', 249; *Where Angels Fear to Tread,* 153, 154, 158, 245, 251, 265
Foster, Malcolm, 236, 269
Frazer, Sir James George, 2, 114

Gandhi, 1
Garnett, Edward, 34, 99, 119
'Gate of the Hundred Sorrows, The' 135–7
Gaugin, Paul, 196
'Georgie Porgie', 147–8, 149
Gladstone, William Ewart, 8
Graham, R. B. Cunninghame, 114
Greene, Graham, 5, 32, 75, 92, 252; *Quiet American, The,* 75
Guerard, A. J., 42, 45, 99, 110
'Gunga Din', 143–4, 150

Haddon, A. C., 3, 257
Hailey, Lord, 241
Hall, Stuart, 253
Hardy, Thomas, 141, 149
'Head of the District, The', 236–7
Heart of Darkness, 34, 45, 99, 100, 101–18, 119, 132, 151, 196, 234, 245, 248, 249, 250
Herskovits, Melville J., 12
Hewitt, Douglas, 110, 121
Hirst, F. W., 151
Hitchcock, Alfred, 81
Hobson, J. A., 6, 7, 68–9
Hodister, Arthur Eugene Constant, 114
Hoffman, Charles G., 227
Hogarth William, 22
Holloway, John, 3
Howards End, 142, 151–2, 154, 162, 214, 251–2
Howe, Irving, 125

Independent Review, The, 151, 167

James, Henry; *Europeans, The,* 179
Jenks, Edward, 151

Johnson, Dr Samuel, 22
Jones, Eldred, 18
Joyce, James, 233
Jungle Book, The, 145

Kahin, George McTurnan, 89
Kangaroo, 171, 185–6, 193
Karain, 34, 52, 53, 74, 101
Kettle, Arnold, 86, 87, 89, 91, 104, 121, 229, 242, 263
Kidd, Benjamin, 22, 61, 63, 91, 100, 113, 222
Kiernan, V. G., 48
Kim, 148, 152, 246
Kingsley, Charles, 63, 91
Kipling, Rudyard, 1, 2, 3, 4, 22, 27, 32, 33, 134–5, 140, 142–3, 149–50, 151, 236–7, 243, 244, 246, 247, 248, 249, 250, 252; 'At the End of the Passage', 149, 237; 'Ballad of East and West, The', 143; 'Beyond the Pale', 147; 'Bridge-Builders, The' 236; 'Dream of Duncan Parrenness, The', 135–6, 137; 'Enlightenments of Pagett, M.P., The', 250; 'Flag of their Country, The', 145; 'Gate of the Hundred Sorrows, The' 135–7; 'Georgie Porgie; 147–8, 149; 'Gunga Din', 143–4, 150; 'Head of the District, The' 236–7; *Jungle Book, The,* 145; *Kim,* 148, 152, 246; 'Lispeth', 146–7, 148, 149; 'Phantom Rickshaw, The', 135–6, 137, 263; 'Recessional', 145–6; *Something of Myself,* 135, 153; 'Song of the White Man, A', 144; 'Story of Muhammad Din, The', 149; 'Strange Ride of Morrowbie Jukes, The', 135–6, 137–9, 140; 'Tods' Amendment', 236; 'William the Conqueror', 236; 'Without Benefit of Clergy', 148–9; 'Yoked with an Unbeliever', 147
Klein, Georges Antoine, 114
Knighton, William, 25, 31, 32; *Forest Life in Ceylon,* 25, 30–1, 32, 104–5
Knox, Robert, 23
Korzeniowski, Apollo, 51

Lady Chatterley's Lover, 171, 194–5
Lagoon, The, 34, 52, 53
Lanzmann, Claude, 17
Larsen, Golden L., 207
Lawrence, D. H., 1, 2, 3, 33, 103, 170–1,
    177, 193–8, 199, 233, 243, 246, 247–8,
    250, 252; 'Elephant', 245, 246;
    Kangaroo, 171, 185–6, 193; *Lady
    Chatterley's Lover*, 171, 194–5;
    Mornings in Mexico, 185, 195;
    Plumed Serpent, The, 4, 171, 184–93,
    250; *Princess, The*, 171, 179–81, 186,
    193, 246; *Psychoanalysis and the
    Unconscious*, 171, 173; *Rainbow, The*
    193; *St. Mawr*, 171, 174–9, 180, 181,
    186, 193, 246; *Sun*, 173; *Twilight in
    Italy*, 173; *Woman Who Rode Away,
    The*, 171, 181–4, 187, 193; *Women in
    Love*, 39–40, 171–3, 176, 193
Leavis, F. R., 1, 196; on Conrad, 33, 77,
    78, 82–3, 116; on Forster, 153; on
    Lawrence, 175, 182; on *Othello*, 19,
    20–1
Leavis, Q. D., 265
Legge, J. D., 88
Lenin, V. I., 6, 7
Lessing, Doris, 252
Lewis, Wyndham, 195–7
Lingard, Jim, 63
'Lispeth, 146–7, 148, 149
Longest Journey, The, 153, 154, 251
Lord Jim, 25, 34, 52, 53, 61–8, 74, 75,
    78–9, 80, 81–2, 86–91, 93, 95, 96,
    98, 101, 103, 110, 153, 163
Lovejoy, Arthur, 174, 184
Ludlow, J. M., 63
Lugard, Frederick (later Lord), 239, 240

Macaulay, Rose, 251
MacDonald, Ramsay, 167
Mahood, M. M., 238
Marlowe, Christopher; *Jew of Malta*,
    16–17; *Tragedy of Dido*, 13
Marryat, Frank, 91, 259
Marx, Karl, 5, 9
Masterman, C. F. G., 151
Matthews, G. M., 21
Maupassant, Guy de, 33, 92
McNair, Fred, 92

Merchant of Venice, The, 17–18
Mister Johnson, 136, 199, 222, 223–32,
    233, 234, 235, 238, 242, 245, 247,
    248, 250
Moore, Henry, 196
Morel, E. D., 1
Morris, William, 126, 194
Moynahan, Julian, 182
Mudrick, Marvin, 263
Myers, L. H., 252

Naipaul, V. S., 32
Najder, Zdzislaw, 51, 87–8
Narayan, R. K., 32, 196
Natwar-Singh, K., 251, 265
Nehru, Jawaharlal, 1
Nehru, Motilal, 1
Newby, P. H., 253
Ngugi, James, 32
Nietzsche, Friedrich Wilhelm, 141–2
Nigger of the 'Narcissus', The, 34, 40–6,
    51, 52, 74, 258
Nostromo, 4, 34, 68, 119–33, 238–9, 244,
    246, 247, 249, 250

Oakfield or Fellowship in the East,
    25–30, 168
O'Brien, Conor Cruise, 8; *Murderous
    Angels*, 2
O'Connor, William Van, 238
Orwell, George, 105, 145, 164
Osborn, Sherard, 85, 90, 92
Othello, 18–21
Outcast of the Islands, An, 10, 34, 52,
    53, 57, 58–61, 63, 69, 74, 80, 81, 86,
    87, 91, 92, 93, 95, 119, 136, 153,
    245, 246, 249
Outpost of Progress, An, 34, 45, 99–101,
    106, 109, 114, 245, 247

Park, Mungo, 32
Passage to India, A, 1, 28, 53, 110,
    134, 139–42, 150–69, 210, 216, 217,
    219, 244, 245, 246–7, 248–9, 250,
    251, 252
Perham, Margery, 134, 135, 239, 241,
    242, 268
'Phantom Rickshaw, The', 135–6, 137,
    263

Phaulkon, Constant, 63
Picasso, Pablo, 196
Plumed Serpent, The, 4, 171, 184–93, 250
Pope, Alexander, 22; *Rape of the Lock, The*, 21–2
Powell, Enoch, 10, 22
'Prince Roman', 97–8
Princess, The, 171, 179–81, 186, 193, 246
Pritchett, V. S., 34, 86, 98

Rainbow, The, 193
Rathbone, H., 242, 269
'Recessional', 145–6
Reid, Stephen A., 114
Rescue, The, 34, 52, 53, 57, 63, 68, 71–3, 74, 80, 81, 86, 87, 88, 89, 90–1, 92, 95, 96–7, 98, 249
Rhodes, Cecil, 1, 10, 22, 103, 143
Richards, I. A., 194
Richardson, Samuel, 22
Ripon, Lord, 143, 250
Rivers, W. H., 3
Robinson Crusoe, 23–4
Robson, W. W., 135
Rodway, A. E., 145, 146
Room with a View, A, 153, 154, 158, 251, 265
Roscoe, William, 22–3; *The Wrongs of Africa*, 22–3
Ross, Angus, 23
Rushton, Edward, 23
Ruskin, John, 126, 194

Sandison, Alan, 149
'Sapper', 83
Sartre, Jean-Paul, 5, 140
Scrimgeour, Cecil, 42, 45
Secret Agent, The, 43, 51, 56, 71, 79, 81, 245–6, 259
Secret Sharer, The, 34, 35, 36–8, 40, 42, 101
Seeley, Professor, 6
Selkirk, Alexander, 23
Shadow-Line, The, 34, 35, 36, 38–40, 101
Shakespeare, William, 8, 13, 21, 24, 32; *Macbeth*, 83, 139; *Merchant of Venice, The*, 17–18; *Othello*, 18–21; *Tempest, The*, 14–16, 21
Sherry, Norman, 63, 77, 93, 114, 116
'Song of the White Man, A', 144

Soyinka, Wole, 196
Spear, Percival, 32
Spengler, Oswald, 1, 196
Sprat, Thomas, 103
Stanley, Colonel Oliver, 1, 241
Stephen, Leslie, 250
Stewart, J. I. M., 79–80, 99, 115, 116
St. Mawr, 171, 174–9, 180, 181, 186, 193, 246
'Story of Muhammad Din, The', 149
'Strange Ride of Morrowbie Jukes, The' 135–6, 137–9, 140
Sun, 173
Swettenham, Sir Frank, 1, 91, 248, 249
Swift, Jonathan, 22

Tarinayya, M., 143
Tempest, The, 14–16, 21
Tennyson, Alfred, Lord, 144
Thackeray, William Makepeace, 41, 205
Times, The, 144, 145
'Tods' Amendment', 236
Trevelyan, G. M., 151
Twain, Mark, 1
Tylor, Sir Edward Burnett, 2, 114
Typhoon, 34, 40, 46–51, 74, 119, 129

Under Western Eyes, 34, 43, 56, 57
Unwin, T. Fisher, 258

Victory, 18, 34, 47, 52, 53, 57, 68–71, 74, 75, 79, 80, 81, 82–4, 88, 95, 98, 249, 257

Wallace, Alfred Russel, 65, 90, 91
Warren, Robert Penn, 121
Wedd, N., 151
Where Angels Fear to Tread, 153, 154, 158, 245, 251, 265
White, Samuel, 63
Whitman, Walt, 142
Wilding, Michael, 121, 127, 129, 131
'William the Conquerer', 236
'Without Benefit of Clergy', 148–9
Woman Who Rode Away, The, 171, 181–4, 187, 193
Women in Love, 39–40, 171–3, 176, 193
Wood, Charles; '*H*', 2
Woolf, Leonard, 9, 153, 239, 242; *Village in the Jungle, The*, 155

Woolf, Virginia, 110, 153, 233
Wordsworth, William, 5
Wyndham, Mr, 63

Yeats, W. B., 1, 196
'Yoked with an Unbeliever', 147
Youth, 34, 35–6, 101